A Woman of Quality:
Sarah Vinke, 'The Divine Sarah', and the Quest for the Origin of Robert Pirsig's Metaphysics of Quality, in his Book *Zen and the Art of Motorcycle Maintenance*

by James Essinger and Henry Gurr

© **Copyright 2018 by Henry S. Gurr. All rights reserved.**

The material and information presented in this book *A Woman of Quality: Sarah Vinke, 'The Divine Sarah', and the Quest for the Origin of Robert Pirsig's Metaphysics of Quality, in his Book "Zen and the Art of Motorcycle Maintenance"*, is for your OWN PERSONAL USE ONLY. Any form of copying and re-dissemination to other people or electronic media, including posting to news groups and Internet Web Pages is EXPRESSLY FORBIDDEN without the prior written consent of Henry S. Gurr. In the case of individual authors (other than Henry Gurr), whose written articles (or other material), appears in this book, prior written consent of EACH author is ALSO required.

NOTE: Copyright has been applied for, and was approved on October 3, 2018. It was assigned registration number TX 008659055. If additional information is available, it will be placed on our special supplementary Internet Web Pages =>"*Sarah Vinke Biography Resource Page*", which Google will quickly find.

Contributors To This *Sarah Vinke Biography.*

James Essinger is the author of very many successful books, the two most recent being: 1) *Ada's Algorithm.* (also titled A *Female Genius* or *A Woman of Intelligence.*), which is a biography of Lord Byron's daughter Ada Lovelace, a Computer Pioneer, and 2) *Machines of the Mind*, a biography of the nineteenth-century computer pioneer Charles Babbage. ... Reading this above mentioned Ada Lovelace Biography, it is quite striking how Mr. Essinger goes out of his way to defend a Victorian era woman (back when women were regarded small brained second-class citizens), and goes on to present Ada as *A Woman of Intelligence* AND also as a caring person ... a person, in effect, of Quality.

[NOTE: To find more information, please Google ... *James Essinger Writer, Editor, Publisher. Canterbury England.*]

Karyn Sealy Bland, cover artist for this *Sarah Vinke Biography*, and website creator, is a graduate of the Clemson University, School of Architecture.

Henry S. Gurr has for 16 years now, researched the history of Robert Pirsig's book *Zen and the Art of Motorcycle Maintenance* (ZMM). In 2002 he in addition, photo documented the physical road trip sites, mentioned in ZMM. From this large body of Research Findings, Henry has assembled considerable ZMM Resource Information, which is presented in an extensive series of Internet ZMM Research Information Pages and Internet ZMM Research Photo Galleries, available on the Internet.
Also Henry Gurr's Sarah Jennings Vinke Field Research Findings, are available on a Special Supplementary Internet

Web Page, which is titled *"Sarah Vinke Biography Resource Pages"*, which Google will quickly bring up. This Resource Page has considerable biography information greatly exceeding what could be in this Sarah Vinke Biography *A Woman of Quality*.

From this body of work, the idea of a *"Sarah Vinke Biography"* (SVB), grew in Henry Gurr's mind and wouldn't go away, until, now you have it in your hand!

[NOTE: Google will also quickly find more about SVB, such as A Facebook Page, and How to purchase eBook Digital Version), by search for .... *A Woman of Quality Sarah Vinke Divine* **Amazon** ....   ]

Henry Gurr's long interested in the process of Human Discovery, Flash of Insight **AHA**, has developed *A Theory of How Our Mind Works*. This theory explains Sarah's notion of *"Quality"*, AND Robert Pirsig's *"We instantly know what is best"*. (For more on this topic, see Chapter 10.) ... Henry's "real job" was in Experimental Nuclear & Neutrino Physics, as well as a University Professor & Physics Teacher.

[NOTE: To find more information, please Google
   ... *Henry S Gurr Professor of Physics USCA Home Page.*
   ... **OR**
   ...*Henry S Gurr Proto Theory of Mind Thesis Panorama*
   ....   ]

**Please Re-Cycle Your Book
To the Archives of Your Local Library!**

For the Sake of History & Sarah Vinke.

We hope our readers understand the extreme importance of the ZMM book itself, one of the most remarkable and most thought-provoking books ever written, and surely an immortal one. Also we hope the reader will realize *the absolutely vital role Sarah Vinke played in it, and the key inspiration she gave its author Robert Pirsig to focus on Quality.*

Therefore:

When You Are Finished:

Please Ask Your Local Library To Place Your Copy of Sarah Vinke Biography In Their Archives, For The Above Reasons, & Preserve for Posterity.

Thank You.

Forward

'He had asked Sarah, who long before had come by with her watering pot and put the idea of Quality in his head, where in English literature quality, as a subject, was taught.'

'Good heavens, I don't know, I'm not an English scholar,' she had said. 'I'm a classics scholar. My field is Greek.'

'Is quality a part of Greek thought?' he had asked.

'Quality is <u>EVERY</u> part of Greek thought,' she had said, and he had thought about this. Sometimes under her old-ladyish way of speaking he thought he detected a secret canniness, as though like a Delphic oracle she said things with hidden meanings, but he could never be sure.'

    Robert Pirsig, *Zen and the Art of Motorcycle Maintenance.* Chapter 28.

"And SHE had a sense of Quality. A brilliant teacher. They [her students] *called her 'The Divine Sarah.'*"

    Robert Pirsig, *On the Road with Pirsig,* a film produced and edited by Dr. Anthony McWatt, 2009.

'You must shake your fist at fate. You mustn't let the gods think they are getting the better of you.'

Sarah Vinke to her students (quoted by Dennis Gary)

-o00O00o-

The authors extend their warmest thanks to Dennis Gary for the enormously useful assistance he has given us, and to Dr. Anthony McWatt for his work on this project and his information on Robert Pirsig.

o00O00o

Henry Gurr wishes to dedicate this book, *A Woman of Quality,* to the memory of his grandparents, George Alexander Smart and his wife Edna Foreman Niswanger Smart. Without Edna's good thrift and George's good investments, the financial resources for writing this book would not have been available.

o00O00o

Grateful acknowledgement is made to HarperCollins Publishers for permission to quote from *Zen and the Art of Motorcycle Maintenance*. Copyright © 1974, 1999 by Robert M. Pirsig. All rights reserved.

Table of Contents

Preface by Henry Gurr 10

Chapter 1: Sarah Vinke and Quality: An Introduction 23

Chapter 2: Sarah Vinke: A Heroine Amidst A Nation In Crisis 38

Chapter 3: Zen and the Art of Motorcycle Maintenance 45

Chapter 4: Sarah Makes Her Entrance 64

Chapter 5: Echoes of Sarah, In Memories And Historical Documents 78

Chapter 6: Between the Lines: A View of Sarah As Seen In Her Two Works: 112

Chapter 7: Influences On Sarah, Gleaned From 1914 and 1915 Bulletins of Grinnell College. And The University of Wisconsin Graduate School, For Sarah's School Years, Fall 1919 Thru, Spring 1923. 159

Chapter 8' You're Quality, Mr. Gary!' Sarah As Teacher And Inspiration Of Montana State University Student Dennis Gary 193

Chapter 9: The Dennis Gary Interview With David Swingle 222

Chapter 10: Quality: A Dialog Between The Authors 233

Conclusion: Summing It All Up: Sarah's Legacy 326

Please note:

In quoted passages, our explanatory comments are enclosed in square brackets as [...] Also please be aware that this book uses UK Spell Check, and thus British UK spelling.

We abbreviate the title of Pirsig's book *Zen and the Art of Motorcycle Maintenance* (1974), to *ZMM*, except when the book is first mentioned in each chapter or when the title is referred to in full in source material.

In this book, we give an initial capital letter to the word 'Quality' only when we are using the word in the sense in which Sarah Vinke used it.

For this biography, we have tried to find all that is known of Sarah Winnifred Jennings Vinke. However, our research findings include much material that, while interesting, is too detailed to belong in this biography book, a format that is aimed at the general reader. ....This *"detailed"* biographical research material (greatly exceeding what is currently in this book), is now available in a Special Supplementary Internet Web Pages, titled *"Sarah Vinke Biography Resource Page"*, which Google will quickly find.

To Readers Desiring Back-Of -Book INDEX

Please consider the considerable virtues of electronic digital word search (plus copy & paste ability), that are available in the eBook Version of this Sarah Vinke Biography (SVB). This "Edit > Find" is simple and easily use on The Amazon Kindle Reader, **free with Amazon purchase, and easy to install on most Cell Phones & Computers** You may read installation instructions and purchase an eBook SVB for 99 cents here https://www.amazon.com/dp/B07KDG7F59

Preface by Henry Gurr

'I am a mystic,' Sarah J. Vinke once said to me [Robert Pirsig] *at a faculty party when there wasn't much to talk about. 'You can't be a mystic,' I said, 'a mystic doesn't define himself as anything.' She thought about this and said, 'You're right. I am not a mystic.' She smiled a little, and that was the last thing she ever said on the subject.'*

    Robert Pirsig in a letter to the authors of *Guidebook to Zen and the Art of Motorcycle Maintenance,* May 3, 1987

The Mystery ... The Mystique ... The Enigma ... of Sarah Vinke has only increased with time, ever since Henry Gurr first began to wonder why and how it came to pass that Sarah asked Robert Pirsig in ZMM three times *"Are you teaching Quality?"* This is especially intriguing, because as of now, there is no clear pattern from Sarah's life as to why she would do this!! So, along with my research and collecting information about Mr. Pirsig and his ZMM, I began to ask everyone, including Mr. Pirsig, about Sarah and her use of that word *'Quality'*.

Sarah Vinke (1894-1978), born Sarah Winifred Jennings, plays an enormously important role in the world famous and hugely influential 1974 book *Zen and the Art of Motorcycle Maintenance (ZMM)* by Robert Pirsig.

Sarah and Pirsig were colleagues when he worked at Montana State University from 1959 to 1961. He was a Professor of English Rhetoric. Sarah had been the head of the English department, and was about thirty-four years older than Pirsig. But in 1945 she had given up on administration, which she did not enjoy, to devote her full energy to her teaching career. Rather than Sarah being Pirsig's boss, a more accurate description of their professional relationship was that Sarah was Pirsig's mentor, although he doesn't mention that point explicitly in *ZMM*. The mentor relationship came about, most likely, because despite their age difference they were to some extent kindred souls in their great and intelligent sensitivity to culture and to experience, and because there was also a sense in which they were both largely misfits in any prosaic and formal organizational structure.

In any event, Robert Pirsig wrote me a letter, quoted below, that momentously gave much more detail about the nature of Pirsig's working relationship with Sarah. At the very least, he seems to have seen Sarah as providing him with enormous, indeed vital, inspiration, as well as support and encouragement, in a job which he did not find especially congenial.

Overall, the mystery, mystique and enigma of Sarah Vinke has only increased with time. Surely a biography about her is long overdue?

According to Pirsig in *ZMM*, on three separate occasions Sarah asked him – we might even say prodded him with – the elemental, even primal, query *'Are you teaching Quality?'* Pirsig was disturbed, provoked and above all intrigued by this thrice-repeated question. *ZMM* details, among other things, Pirsig's reaction to being asked this question. In effect, Sarah provoked him into a writing an entire book about her proddings.

Pirsig did not ask Sarah what she meant by the word 'Quality', and she apparently did not venture an explanation. It seems very likely, in fact, that her reason for not elucidating to Pirsig what she meant by the word 'Quality' was that she wanted him to go away and figure out what she meant. That is precisely how a mentor might inspire a person they're mentoring. As for Pirsig, perhaps he felt that asking Sarah for a precise explanation of what she did mean by 'Quality' might have been undignified, or perhaps he felt it would have been pushing his luck to have asked that question. Or even – which, if *ZMM* is anything to go by, may in fact be the most likely explanation – the moment Sarah said to Pirsig what she said, he was so fascinated by her remark that he plunged into a fever of deep, introspective musing on it, and wasn't interested in anything as mundane as asking Sarah to clarify what she meant.

It's important to emphasize right away that the word 'Quality' in Sarah's terminology is not 'quality' in the consumer marketing sense, but rather is a precious, splendid and eternally resonant way of thinking, acting, and being about life, and living a life truly worth living. One of the most troubling points about Quality is, as we shall see, that it can't be easily defined, and indeed probably can't be defined at all. Over the past forty years, I've been ever more deeply curious about Sarah, and especially about her use of the word Quality and why the word had such a powerful effect on Pirsig. This book arises out of those years of curiosity.

In 1976, two years after *ZMM* was published, I accepted a position on the physics faculty of the University of South Carolina at Aiken, where I taught Sophomore physics until my retirement in 2002. As well as teaching the factual details of physics, much of my work was devoted to finding better, more satisfying ways for my students to learn about science, reasoning, and about themselves.

As Pirsig himself says in an introduction to *ZMM*:

> *The real cycle you're working on is a cycle called yourself.*

Then Pirsig, in effect, confirms that, at least at one level, his *ZMM* is a book about physics.

> *A motorcycle functions entirely in accordance with the laws of reason, and a study of the art of motorcycle maintenance is really a miniature study of the art of rationality itself. The motorcycle is primarily a mental phenomenon.*

I first read *ZMM* in 1985. After my first reading, I didn't understand its main messages, nor perceive that this was a really important book. That realization took me some time. Gradually, with repeated readings, I came to realize that *ZMM* is a highly original book, perhaps one of the most original books ever written. It seems to me beyond question that it's the sort of book you tend to think about a great deal after you've read it. It is certainly, in my view, a work of genius. Gradually I started to appreciate the applications of the book to writing, human psychology, philosophy of mind, problem solving and so on, and also to internalize the vital importance of living in the present: a lesson powerfully expressed in *ZMM*.

As Pirsig says in his book:

The past exists only in our memories, the future only in our plans. The present is our only reality.

For me personally, due to temperament and inclination, the lesson of living in the present, was one I found difficult to learn. To take just one example, back at the time when I was first reading *ZMM*, my wife and I had a boisterous Spitz puppy called Suki, who loved getting attention, and especially enjoyed being petted. For example, as I was heading for the front door of our home, Suki would get in my way and want to be petted. I did this quickly and begrudgingly. But she would still want to be petted, and I tended to get grouchy with her and shoo her out of the way.

With my reading of *ZMM*, I finally realized that by behaving in the way I was, I was depriving myself of the enormous pleasure of living in the present. Influenced by the book, I managed to change. When Suki got in my way, I forced myself to stop, and not-only enjoy petting Suki, but I would consciously look around and enjoy the trees, the wind, the sunshine.... *to be in the moment ... right now!*

Eventually, I found I didn't need to force myself any more. I became much more patient with Suki and much more tolerant. I realized Suki was not, in fact, bringing me a demand, she was bringing me an *opportunity*.

Well, so what was the opportunity she was offering? Basically to stop my hurry, pause, enjoy the act of petting her, and ... *to be!* ...*To be in the now! ... To be alive*! As Pirsig says: *The present is our only reality.*

This was for me only one example of many attitude changes I gleaned and absorbed from *ZMM*.

I've never indeed really understood why there hasn't been a full biography of Sarah Vinke, or at the very least why more is not known about her life. In the absence of being able to find a biography I could read and enjoy, I decided to try to find out all I could about Sarah.

Over the years, I've been fortunate to find many people who've shared my enthusiasm for Sarah and her utterances to Pirsig about 'Quality'.

One of the persons who was most helpful in my quest to find information about *ZMM*, and in my quest, to find out more about Sarah was Robert Pirsig himself. I've been privileged to have had some eighteen letters of correspondence from him, which are among my most prized possessions.

Here is how our first correspondence came about. Starting in 1993, I decided to ask my Physics 'A' Students to read *ZMM*. I felt there were many important and valid reasons for this requirement. But I worried that other teachers or administrators might become critical and stir up a lot of trouble. So I sought additional support for this teaching practice, especially since this *ZMM* requirement was quite unusual. Thus, late in June 1994, I ventured to write to Robert Pirsig to ask him if he knew of other schools that also required *ZMM* in their classes. As an afterthought I also asked him about the total circulation of *ZMM*. I was delighted to receive a full and detailed reply from Robert Pirsig himself. His response was as follows:

Dear Dr. Gurr,

It's good to see that you are taking up *Zen and the Art of Motorcycle Maintenance* with your students. Many just read it and say, 'Isn't that interesting,' and then go on with other things. To keep you interested, I'm enclosing two other books that you may not have read yet. Your question 'a)' is answered in Section 2 of *Guidebook to Zen and the Art of Motorcycle Maintenance.*

In answer to question 'b)' I would estimate that somewhere between 10 and 60 per cent of colleges and high schools use *Zen and the Art of*

Motorcycle Maintenance in one or more courses. Usually these are literature or philosophy courses, sometimes psychology and sociology— rarely science. U.S. sales have been running at about 100,000 per year for the last 20 years, a really unusual figure. It has been stated in the London *Daily Telegraph* and by the BBC that *Zen and the Art of Motorcycle Maintenance* is the 'most widely read philosophy book - ever.' I give credit to the academic system for this, but I don't have any accurate information on who is using it or where it is being used.

    I didn't pay for the two enclosed books, so you shouldn't either. But please pay attention to the assertion by the Metaphysics of Quality in *Lila* that *quality* is an empirical phenomenon. It is traditional for scientific thinkers to deny this but I don't think it is rational for scientific thinkers to deny this. This is the central assertion of *Zen and the Art of Motorcycle Maintenance*, but the Metaphysics of Quality shows how, once this assertion is accepted, it is possible to construct an overall view of things that integrates such things as physics and morals without doing damage to either.

                                      Best regards,
                                        Robert Pirsig

Many fellow *ZMM* enthusiasts have accompanied me on my journey to find out more about Sarah and to better understand what she meant by that resonating word, Quality. What follows, in this biography, is the result of, among other things, years of research into Sarah and my numerous readings of *ZMM*, along with thinking about that life-changing book, as well as my discussions and collaborations with many *ZMM* enthusiasts, most especially Dennis Gary and my co-author James Essinger. James is the author of, among many other books, *Ada's Algorithm* (also titled *A Female Genius*), a biography of Lord Byron's daughter Ada Lovelace, the computer pioneer, and *Machines of the Mind*, a biography of the nineteenth-century computer pioneer Charles Babbage. This book is now entitled *Charles and Ada* and is scheduled for publication in the UK in August 2019 by The History Press.

I have long been interested in the process of human discovery and the development of new ideas. Once I finally thought I understood Pirsig's notion of Quality and how vital and revolutionary it was, I naturally began to wonder about the origins of Quality, and wondered if it might be possible to ponder this and go even deeper into the matter than *ZMM* does.

This question came to a focus in a September 2008 letter to Pirsig, in which I asked if he knew just why Sarah said to him repeatedly: 'Are you teaching Quality these days?' I was privileged to receive from Robert Pirsig – he wrote the letter on September 15, 2008 – a remarkable reply, which reads as follows. This letter expands very considerably on what Pirsig says about Quality, and Sarah, in *ZMM*.

Dear Prof. Gurr,

In *Zen and the Art of Motorcycle Maintenance* I wrote that there were two main groups who responded to the word, quality': those who thought it was a subjective and relatively meaningless term, and those who thought it was so obvious it didn't need to be discussed. The DeWeeses were in the latter group. I don't recall them ever using the term except in reference to my use of it. Bob DeWeese was a little cynical about intellectualizing anything. The quality *Zen and the Art of Motorcycle Maintenance* talks about is just something they did without intellectual analysis. I remember Bob used the term 'nice' for something he really liked, but beyond that, nothing. The artist who influenced me the most was Phyllis Downs, a next door neighbor in Minneapolis. When people discussed art, her usual comment was 'They haven't got a clue.' In MOQ [Metaphysics of Quality] terms, what the serious artist seeks is indefinable Dynamic Quality.

Sarah's maiden name was Jennings. I believe she said she studied at Bryn Mawr and was part of the Daisy Chain. I'm not sure if this referred to the Seven Sisters colleges generally or to a Bryn Mawr ceremony at the turn of the 20th century. This is all I know of her background.

When Sarah asked if I was teaching Quality, I think she was teasing, just to see how I would answer. I answered with the same kind of suppressed smile, saying I was making a special effort at it. She knew that was a lie and she knew that I knew it was a lie and this sort of tickled her, so she kept up the teasing.

Later one of the teachers asked where I got all these ideas about quality. I said I got them from Sarah. The teacher's expression brightened, and he said,

'That's why she has always supported you!' This was the first time I realized others were *not* supporting me. Much later Sarah came out of one such discussion and said to me furiously, *'Don't pay any attention to them! It's over their head!'* Her opinion and her angry expression of it has come back to me many times, consolingly, since then.

Best regards,
Robert Pirsig

The idea of whether it might be possible to write a biography of Sarah Vinke grew in my mind and wouldn't go away until I found myself asking just about every professional writer I knew or found on the Internet, whether they were willing to take on the project. I was looking for writers who were truly energized by the idea.

Finally, on an Internet tech news page, I discovered a very favorable book review of James Essinger's biography of Ada Lovelace.

Reading this biography, it struck me that James was presenting Ada Lovelace not only as a genius, but also as a caring person and a person, in effect, of Quality. This was very much how Pirsig had presented Sarah Vinke, who was in turn Pirsig's great inspiration in his world famous book *ZMM*. Also, I was very much impressed that James went out of his way to support and actively defend Ada Lovelace's abilities, even though she was a woman living at a time - the nineteenth century - when women were regarded very much as second-class citizens. They didn't even have a vote. Many men liked to believe that women's brains, being on average smaller than men's (which is true) were inherently less intelligent than men (which is nonsense). Maybe many men believe this even today. I contacted James. He was initially -- reasonably enough, I think -- concerned that there was not sufficient material about Sarah to make a biography, but after undertaking his own research into her life, he became convinced that there was very likely sufficient material, and gradually we embarked on a collaboration that became this book.

As will become clear, James and I don't agree about everything to do with Sarah and how we present her or her notion of Quality. But I'm sure it wouldn't be good for our book if we did agree about everything. In particular, I feel strongly that Sarah's notion of Quality absolutely can't usefully be defined, or even much discussed in words. By contrast, James, although accepting this notion in principle, frequently finds himself trying to define Quality anyway, even trying endlessly, relentlessly, to discuss it in words. From this dynamic creative tension between us -- and, more importantly, from the dynamic creative tension between our heroine Sarah Vinke, and Robert Pirsig -- springs this book, *A Woman of Quality: Sarah Vinke 'The Divine Sarah', and the Quest for the Origin of Robert Pirsig's Metaphysics of Quality, in his Book Zen and the Art of Motorcycle Maintenance.*

Henry Gurr   Nov 2018, Rev's July 2019.

citizens. They didn't even have a vote. Many men liked to believe that women's brains, being on average smaller than men's (which is true) were inherently less intelligent than men (which is nonsense). Maybe many men believe this even today. I contacted James. He was initially -- reasonably enough, I think -- concerned that there was not sufficient material about Sarah to make a biography, but after undertaking his own research into her life, he became convinced that there was very likely sufficient material, and gradually we embarked on a collaboration that became this book.

As will become clear, James and I don't agree about everything to do with Sarah and how we present her or her notion of Quality. But I'm sure it wouldn't be good for our book if we did agree about everything. In particular, I feel strongly that Sarah's notion of Quality absolutely can't usefully be defined, or even much discussed in words. By contrast, James, although accepting this notion in principle, frequently finds himself trying to define Quality anyway, even trying endlessly, relentlessly, to discuss it in words. From this dynamic creative tension between us -- and, more importantly, from the dynamic creative tension between our heroine Sarah Vinke, and Robert Pirsig -- springs this book, *A Woman of Quality: Sarah Vinke 'The Divine Sarah', and the Quest for the Origin of Robert Pirsig's Metaphysics of Quality, in his Book Zen and the Art of Motorcycle Maintenance.*

Henry Gurr   Nov 2018, Rev's July 2019.

Chapter 1: Sarah Vinke and Quality: An Introduction

Our book, *A Woman of Quality,* is indeed about an idea —the notion of Quality as Sarah saw it. But it's also a book about a person, Sarah herself, and in that respect, it is a detective story as much as a biography.

Of course, there is a sense in which all biographies are detective stories. The duty of the biographer is to investigate all the disparate elements of the subject's life and to piece these together into a coherent and compelling story.

That story aspires to be the solution to what is, in effect, the mystery represented by the unexplored life of the subject, just as a detective aims to furnish an accurate explanation of a crime.

In Sarah's case, not only is our subject no longer alive but information available about her is sparse – surprisingly sparse, really, considering her charismatic personality and the dramatic impact of her personality on so many people, including of course Pirsig.

The enormity of Sarah's impact on Pirsig is unquestionable. Shortly after explaining, in *ZMM,* how Sarah first asked him her question about whether he was teaching Quality, he goes on to explain that Sarah asked this question

> *...in a la-de-da, singsong voice of a lady in her final year before retirement about to water her*

plants. That was the moment it all started. That was the seed crystal.

After Sarah's brief appearance in Chapter 15 of *ZMM*, the remainder of the book is essentially all about her idea of Quality, and so we are justified in regarding Sarah as a major character in *ZMM*; indeed arguably the major character after Pirsig himself.

It might very reasonably be asked. why there is so little already known about Sarah, whose apparently (and perhaps intentionally) offhand remark about 'Quality' to Pirsig inspired some of the most exciting and influential thinking of the twentieth century? Why has there never been a biography of her before? Why is she not a better known figure?

Certainly, despite the huge importance of Sarah's laconic, epigrammatic, yet momentous role in *ZMM,* very few people would recognise the name Sarah Vinke.

One of the fundamental reasons why her full name isn't well-known, despite millions of people having read about her, is because the book that mentions her, and which catapulted her to fame, doesn't in fact mention her surname. Perhaps also, the very fact of the prodigious success of *ZMM* in the United States and beyond its shores, plus the deep and powerful personality of its author, Pirsig, has too often tended to drown out Sarah's enormously important, but gentler, less insistent and more feminine voice.

As with Ada Lovelace, whose momentous importance in the history of the computer, has too often been drowned out by the reputation and status of her friend Charles Babbage, we also see that Sarah has herself had something of a raw deal from history. In the case of Ada, that raw deal is now being rectified and her own status and reputation around the world are nowadays higher than they have ever been. If, here, we can go some way towards rectifying the same problem in the case of Sarah Vinke, the job of researching and writing this biography of Sarah will have been more than worthwhile.

Here are the basic biographical facts of our heroine's life.

Sarah Winifred Jennings was born on April 28, 1894 at Dallas Center in Iowa. Her background was rural; she was born on a farm, and it says much about her determination to make something of her life, that she emerged from her life on the farm, and humble small town beginnings, to go to college at a time when very few women from the United States, or indeed from any other country, did.

Sarah was the daughter of Sarah Elizabeth Adams Jennings and Jacob Jennings. Sarah earned her BA degree at Grinnell College in 1914 and gained her MA and PhD at the University of Wisconsin in 1921 and 1923 respectively. The attainment of these three degrees are confirmed in the commencement records of Grinnell College and University of Wisconsin respectively.

Sarah taught Latin and History in High Schools in Iowa between 1916 and 1920. From Fall 1920 to 1923, Sarah was an assistant in Classics while she completed her education at the University of Wisconsin. She was an instructor in English at Montana State College (MSC) from 1923 to 1926. Between 1926 and 1927 she attended university in London and travelled in Europe. Upon her return to the United States, she became Assistant Professor at MSC from 1927 to 1932, when she left teaching to marry Dr. Louis Vinke, Professor of Animal Husbandry at MSC.

After the death of her husband in 1935, Sarah returned to teaching and became Associate Professor of English at Colorado State College. She returned to MSC in 1945 as Head of the English Department, but soon gave up administration, which she did not enjoy as much as she enjoyed teaching, to devote her full energy to her teaching career. In 1962, she retired due to failing health, loss of sight, and difficulty walking, even with a cane. The latter problem appears to have been due to Parkinson's Disease.

Sarah was widely regarded at MSC as having been a vital force in extending the intellectual frontiers of students in the Humanities area. She was considered an inspired teacher, capable of developing within her students a passion for literature, and for Greek mythology, especially in students who had limited educational backgrounds because of having been raised in isolated Montana communities. Her influence was widely known at the time, and she became famous after Pirsig mentioned her influence in his courageous heroic legendary epic: *Zen and the Art of Motorcycle Maintenance.*

Here is how Robert Pirsig, in Chapter 15 of *Zen and the Art of Motorcycle Maintenance*, has Sarah introduce her version of the word Quality to him:

> *She* [Sarah Vinke] *came trotting by with her watering pot between those two doors, going from the corridor to her office, and she said, 'I hope you are teaching Quality to your students.'*

That is the modest yet also stupendous first mention of the word Quality used in this particular way in literature. As well as this, the passage makes clear that Sarah had a reputation for leaving indelible impressions on people who met her.

Ms. Jean Bartos remembers Sarah as "one of the finest teachers on the MSC Campus" From Ms. Bartos's long reminisce, high impact excerpts are these:

> I had her for Oral and Written Communication. The first day of class, she came in with an armload of books, dropped them on her desk, and surveyed the class. Then she said, "Will someone please open a window? ---Preferably male!" The whole class was stunned for a moment and the one of the guys opened a window. My 4th course with Dr. Vinke was Shakespeare. We were to write a one page

discussion … It was to have footnotes. …. but I couldn't see the value of a footnote in a one-page paper. I couldn't believe it when my paper came back with a D! … I had NEVER had a D in my college career. …. I asked Dr. Vinke about it. …. She said that if I could prove to her that I was right, she'd raise by grade to a C. … I presented my findings at the next class. She changed my grade and wrote on the board two sayings:
"To err is human, to forgive divine!"
"He who has not erred has not lived."

Sarah also had a major impact on her other students, especially Dennis Gary, who in the late 1950s, was marked for life!

> I remember pondering her statements, that I had character and Quality, during the next few weeks. This is difficult to express, but it really is how I feel: I felt as if I'd been given an enormous charge or responsibility or indeed the authority to do something significant with my life.

This book, *A Woman of Quality,* is as much the story of the idea of Quality in the special sense in which Sarah Vinke used the word, as the story of Sarah herself.

Sarah, for her part, profoundly believed in the notion of 'Quality' as the basis for a well-lived, meaningful life.

Many people today believe Sarah's Quality to be a new foundation for Western Philosophy and indeed for understanding the universe. But what exactly does Quality in the Sarah sense actually mean?

Before discussing this we need to say that sometimes in this book, we need to separate from our dual author persona and state what we feel as individuals.

So here, Henry believes that instead of futilely scratching around for a definition of Quality, it's much better to identify real-world manifestations of Quality, when it actually happens, and working out what we think it is about those manifestations that makes them Quality. In any case, Henry believes that dictionaries don't offer any help with understanding what this Quality means in terms of how Sarah used it.

> **James says in response:** I agree to some extent with Henry's position on defining Quality, but not completely. It strikes me that a language doesn't use a word at all unless the word has some useful meaning, and this surely applies to the word Quality in the sense of how Sarah used it, as much as any other word. Of course, abstract words like 'Quality', 'love' and 'God' clearly have different *kinds* of meanings compared with words like 'table', 'spoon' and 'airplane'. Rather than saying that Sarah's version of Quality can't be described at all, it would perhaps be more true to say that Sarah's version of Quality can't be defined other than

in general, and perhaps not very useful, terms. This may itself not be a very helpful statement but nonetheless it's at least a starting-point.

After all, many other concepts that matter to us greatly as human beings, also can't be defined other than in very general terms. One of these, for example, is indeed 'love'. Yes, the dictionary makes a stab at defining it, but no definition of love tells us more than a very little about it. The manifestations of love that we see, experience and feel in our lives are not only infinitely greater than any dictionary definition of the word 'love', but in a very real sense make the dictionary definition seem just prosaic and in fact put it to shame. Still, at least the dictionary gives some approximate idea of what the word means. After all, if you looked up the word 'love' in a dictionary and the dictionary said, 'this word cannot be defined', you would feel, not unreasonably, that the people compiling the dictionary had not done their job properly.

What is true of 'love' is certainly even more true of the word Quality, in terms of how Pirsig quotes Sarah as referring to it in *ZMM*. Indeed, he addresses this precise point in *ZMM* when he remarks near the end of Chapter 18 of his book, during a mountain climb food break:

> *'That's all the Quality talk for today. I guess, thank goodness, I don't mind the Quality, it's just that all the classical talk about it isn't Quality.'*

This is an especially meaningful statement by Pirsig even by the extremely high standards of the thinking in *ZMM*. Surely Pirsig is saying here, in effect, that what makes him excited, inspired and energized about Quality <u>isn't</u> attempting to intellectualize its meaning but rather the feeling Quality gives him that it is the key to making sense of what life is and indeed what worthwhile living is all about. Through it all, we need to keep his remark, 'it's just that all the classical talk about it isn't Quality' in mind throughout *this biography*..

Trying to discuss or define Pirsig's Quality, is indeed like trying to talk about or define the concept of God. Arguably, as soon as you do so, you have already altered, misdirected and diminished what the concept of God might be. It's like admiring a rose and loving its scent, adoring the quintessence of its rosiness in its appearance and fragrance. But dissect it and it's no longer a rose.

So what we should perhaps do, and indeed, *all we can do*, is point to 'God in action', or 'Quality in action', in ourselves, in our lives, and in the lives of other people. We can't, as a matter of common sense, do this unless we have at least some idea of what God means to us, just as we can't point to love in action unless we have some idea what love means.

Of course, in popular usage, which a dictionary of course exists to record, Quality is defined. For example, to quote from the *Oxford English Dictionary*, as 'the degree of excellence possessed by a thing'. Certainly, the word Quality is used every day worldwide to mean, in particular, some manufactured product or some delivered service of a high level of excellence. But this definition of the word only remotely echoes the meaning which Sarah attaches to it.

Formerly, the word 'quality' was employed to describe people of excellence in social standing. For example, Sir George Downing (1632-1689), who built the row of townhouses in London on what is now called Downing Street that include the official residence of the British Prime Minister, decreed that those houses should be, as he put it, 'for persons of good quality to inhabit it.'

It's true that the word Quality as used in this book certainly embraces the word as used to mean an excellent manufactured product or an excellent delivered service or a person of excellence, but any everyday definitions of Quality really only skim the surface of what Sarah or Pirsig really means here.

Owen Barfield, in his book *History in English Words,* gives a historical insight into the meaning and origins of word quality:

> In the common words we use every day the souls of past races, the thoughts and feelings of individual men stand around us, not dead, but frozen into their attitudes like the courtiers in the

garden of the Sleeping Beauty. The more common a word is and the simpler its meaning, the bolder very likely is the original thought which it contains and the more intense the intellectual or poetic effort which went to its making. Thus, the word quality is used by most educated people every day of their lives, yet in order that we should have this simple word Plato had to make the tremendous effort (it is one of the most exhausting which man is called on to exert) of turning a vague feeling into a clear thought. He invented the new word *poiotes* ... 'what-ness'. as we might say, or 'of-what-kind-ness', and Cicero translated it by the Latin *qualitas*. Language becomes a different thing for us altogether if we can make ourselves realize, can even make ourselves feel how every time the word quality is used, say upon a label in a shop window, that creative effort made by Plato comes into play again. Nor is the acquisition of such a feeling a waste of time; for once we have made it our own, it circulates like blood through the whole of the literature and life about us. It is the kiss which brings the sleeping courtiers to life.

One way of initially thinking about what we are calling Quality (productive actions of persons in a society), has arisen because it represents our successful use as a species of our brains to solve life's problems and create both physical objects and systems of knowledge that make our lives better and that help us live better and feel better.

This idea is surely both congenial and believable. In setting down this view of Quality, though, it's important to add right away that the word, 'objects' in this context has the widest remit. It would include not only manufactured tools and machines and indeed manufactured products of all kinds, but also cultural artefacts such as books, movies, musical works, sculptures, drawings, paintings and so on. Our brains, <u>automatically</u> as it were, strive to produce good and effective answers to dilemmas: Answers that we can trust, rely on and in which we can put our faith. In fact, Pirsig adds considerably to his Quality by saying Quality is what happens in art:

> '*Art is* [any] *endeavor. Whether it's gonna come out right or not. It's still Art. It's what you do. It's who you are as a person that makes it Art or not Art.*'

Overall, Quality in terms of how Sarah used the word is a kind of overall, wide-reaching philosophy of excellence in all endeavours, life choices and outputs.

In *ZMM*, Pirsig is, in effect, proposing the goal of Quality as a kind of secular religious objective, a sort of accessible Zen for the world, and antidote to mental, cultural and economic confusion, despair and mediocrity.

Above all, the action of Quality make us feel comfortable, positive, happy, and that we are in control in some significant degree of our lives and that being human is a blessing rather than a curse. In *ZMM*, the idea that Quality leads to 'peace of mind', is an idea repeated twenty-seven times. As Pirsig writes:

> *'Peace of mind isn't at all superficial, really,' I expound. 'It's the whole thing. That which produces it is good maintenance; that which disturbs it is poor maintenance. ... What really counts in the end is their peace of mind, nothing else. The reason for this is that peace of mind is a prerequisite for a perception of that Quality which is beyond romantic Quality and classic Quality and which unites the two, and which must accompany the work as it proceeds. The way to see what looks good and understand the reasons it looks good, and to be at one with this goodness as the work proceeds, is to cultivate an inner quietness, a peace of mind so that goodness can shine through.'...*

Pirsig then generalizes this to all of life:

> *So the thing to do when working on a motorcycle, as in any other task, is to cultivate the peace of mind which does not separate one's self from one's surroundings. When that is done successfully then everything else follows naturally. Peace of mind produces right values, right values produce right thoughts. Right thoughts produce right actions and right actions produce work which will be a material reflection for others to see of the serenity at the center of it all. That was what it was about that wall in*

Korea. It was a material reflection of a spiritual reality.

There is a passage in Joseph Conrad's novella, *Heart of Darkness* (1899), which exemplifies much about what Quality means, by -- as always should be the case -- providing an example rather than attempting to devise a definition.

At the point in the novella when this scene occurs, the narrator, Marlow, who is in charge of a steamer travelling up the River Congo (though the river is never mentioned explicitly by name), is feeling utterly overwhelmed and disorientated by his sense of loneliness and isolation in an environment he finds malign, sinister, macabre, chaotic, indifferently cruel, and nightmarishly meaningless. What saves him is his accidental discovery of a dry old seamanship manual that Conrad brilliantly describes as offering the great consolation of technical excellence: This old dusty book becomes an unmistakably real, salvation from his daily nightmare of commanding a steamship up the Congo. into the wretched heart of colonial moral decay, that he dramatizes with fabulous vividness, as *The Heart Of Darkness*. As Conrad writes in the voice of his narrator Marlow:

> It was an extraordinary find. Its title was *An Inquiry into some Points of Seamanship*, by a man Towser, Towson - some such name - Master in his Majesty's Navy. The matter looked dreary reading enough, with illustrative diagrams and repulsive tables of figures, and the copy was sixty years old. I handled this amazing antiquity

with the greatest possible tenderness, lest it should dissolve in my hands. Within, Towson or Towser was inquiring earnestly into the breaking strain of ships' chains and tackle, and other such matters. Not a very enthralling book; but at the first glance you could see there a singleness of intention, an honest concern for the right way of going to work, which made these humble pages, thought out so many years ago, luminous with another than a professional light. The simple old sailor, with his talk of chains and purchases, made me forget the jungle and the pilgrims in a delicious sensation of having come upon something unmistakably real.

Marlow, if he had had access to Sarah Vinke's use of the word Quality, would perhaps have described Towson or Towser's seamanship guide, not only as *absolutely real,* but also a work of Quality, and indeed about Quality.

In fact, Quality doesn't *only* apply to objects such as books, manufactured items and works of art. It applies equally well to other, more abstract, but no less real (or indeed perhaps even more real), things such as advice, relationships, and other aspects of our interpersonal involvement with other people, and the physical world around us.

Chapter 2: Sarah Vinke: A Heroine Amidst A Nation In Crisis

Americans celebrating the New Year on Tuesday, January 1, 1974 might have been forgiven for wondering whether their nation was in freefall and heading for complete disaster.

Less than eleven years before, President John Fitzgerald Kennedy, who became president at the age of forty-three -- the youngest president elected to the office in the history of the United States and the first US president born in the twentieth century -- was struck down by rifle bullets while visiting Dallas in Texas. Even today, conspiracy theories abound. Barely five years later, on June 6, 1968, President Kennedy's younger brother, Robert, was himself assassinated while campaigning for the presidency. He had been widely expected to be elected President. A little more than two months before Robert Kennedy was assassinated, Martin Luther King Jr., the great leader of the Civil Rights movement, had tragically been the victim of an assassin's bullet.

In 1974, the emotional and psychological scars of these murderous events were still raw in the American psyche.

The years previous to 1974 had featured an almost continual political crisis in the world's richest nation. These laws allowing segregation in many states began with the great challenges of reassembling a nation of the late 19th century after the American Civil War, which lasted from 1861 to 1865. The nation had been torn apart socially based on the polarizing factions in the Northern and Southern states. The 13th amendment formally abolished slavery in the United States. While some African Americans remained in Southern states, great numbers eventually migrated North for work and opportunities.

By the mid-20th century, a strong grass-roots movement called for desegregation and an end to racial discrimination in the United States. Internally, American culture was already greatly altered in the aftermath of World War II. Entering the War had caused division across the country on the basis of whether or not the U.S. should intervene in the largely European conflict. By the end of the war the U.S. had suffered casualties, women and minorities entered the workforce and the military in great numbers, and urban living and the automotive industry grew dramatically. The patriotic fervor during the war shifted the population and forced Americans to face intimate legal problems involving discrimination and racial segregation. In 1954 the Supreme court ruled that segregation in public schools was illegal. The Civil Rights Act of 1964 ended segregation and outlawed discrimination in the workplace, schools and public places. This movement challenged the nation and set a precedent for human rights for the world.

In 1965, President Johnson sent the first United States soldiers to Vietnam. The US had become embroiled in a war that had long been regarded, even by its most enthusiastic advocates, as being probably unwinnable, a war that had already cost around 50,000 American lives. By 1967, there were more than 389,000 US troops in South Vietnam, which the US was supporting in its bid to prevent the communists of North Vietnam from uniting South Vietnam with North Vietnam under their leadership.

By early 1968, US public opinion, which initially had been moderately in favor of the war, had begun to be inclined towards 'de-escalation' of the conflict. University sit-ins and general public anti-war protests, draftee resistance, drafted troops in Vietnam evading and even disobeying their superiors' military orders: these factors and more were all part of the burgeoning movement that was soon not so much an anti-war movement, but rather a movement about utter hatred of the war. Added to this were the all too graphic daily television depictions of the awfulness and futile violence of the war, streaming into everyone's living room. Even today, the scars of those images linger even in the minds of non-combatants.

On March 31, 1968, Johnson announced in a television address that bombing north of the 20th parallel would be stopped and that he would not seek re-election to the presidency in the fall.

Talks began between the US and Hanoi, the name of the North Vietnamese capital that became synonymous with the Communist leadership (Viet-Cong), which was the name for communist insurgents in South Vietnam, not for the proper,

North Vietnamese government. US involvement in the war started slowly to reduce, though even in the summer of 1969 there were more than 540,000 military personnel in South Vietnam. Peace talks continued sporadically, and US commanders in the field were instructed to keep US casualties 'to an absolute minimum.'

By late in 1970, US personnel in South Vietnam had been reduced to less than 335,000, and throughout the ensuing year the gradual withdrawal of American troops proceeded, yet peace talks remained stalemated. In 1972, US bombing of Hanoi and other North Vietnamese cities resumed. 1973 saw peace talks starting again in Paris, and by the end of 1973 there were few US military personnel left in South Vietnam. But the war between the two Vietnams continued.

The United States was spiritually and emotionally shattered by its involvement in the Vietnam War. The war had created major fault lines and emotional divisions in US society, especially between the young and the older, which made millions of people question the values by which they lived and by which they had been urged to live. The US was also physically bereft of the 58,307 people killed in action or in other incidents during the war.

Coinciding with the Vietnam defeat and peace talks, the year 1974 had also seen the United States embroiled in the fall-out of what became known as the Watergate scandal. In June 1972, five men had been arrested for breaking into the Democratic Party's national headquarters at the Watergate office and apartment building in Washington, DC. It was subsequently learned that the burglars had been hired by the Committee to Re-Elect the President (CRP), chaired by John Mitchell, a former US Attorney General. He subsequently resigned as director of CRP.

As things turned out, these events had no substantial outcome on the elected government leadership or on the election that fall. The Democrats retained majorities in both the Senate and the House. Republican candidate Richard Nixon won a landslide victory over Democratic nominee Senator George McGovern.

But in 1973 it was revealed that an attempt to suppress knowledge of the connection between the Watergate affair and the CRP involved highly placed members of the White House staff. Subsequently, the Watergate affair was complicated by the revelation of other irregularities. In particular, it became known that a security unit of the White House had engaged in illegal activities, and worse, this purely political party action, was under the cloak of official government national security.

Nixon's personal finances were being questioned, and Vice President Spiro T. Agnew resigned after pleading no contest to charges of income tax evasion. On December 6, 1973, Nixon's nominee, Gerald Ford, was approved by Congress as the new vice president. As 1973 came to an end, there was the very real possibility that Nixon himself would at some point in 1974 be impeached.

So, as 1974 got underway, the United States was deeply enmeshed in a spiritual, emotional and psychological crisis. It was a crisis not only of faith but also of values. The American Dream, and, it seemed, much of America's moral fibre, had alike been blasted away, just as surely, as bullets and bombs had done so much damage to the peoples of Vietnam. In the late 1960s and 1970s there was a huge shift in culture where masses of people were leaving their factory jobs, their daytime jobs and going to India and discovering themselves. People were running from a culture that was full of conformity, and the restriction of the individual. They found they were, in a culture that didn't seem to work, unless that individual was wealthy, famous, and influential.

Who would have thought that, four months into the New Year, in April 1974, a highly unusual and spectacularly original book would be published that would cause an almost immediate and immense stir in the United States and subsequently around the world and would go a long way towards restoring, for millions of people, a sense that there were, after all, values in which they could truly believe?

Moreover, who would have suspected that the book would have had, as its real-life heroine, a lady who by 1974 was already elderly and infirm, but who had given the author of the book a wonderful sense of inspiration, and a key-word that was at the core of the new value system he had embraced: a new value system at the core of the book?

The book was *Zen and the Art of Motorcycle Maintenance,* by Robert Pirsig.

The lady who gave him his inspiration was Sarah and the key-word was *Quality*! This was Sarah's own translation to English of the Ancient Greek word: *Arête.*

Chapter 3: Zen and the Art of Motorcycle Maintenance.

The nature of Pirsig's specific intention for *Zen and the Art of Motorcycle Maintenance* is expressed in his subtitle, *An Inquiry into Values.*

By contrast, anyone setting out to read the book might be forgiven for thinking that it is just one more road novel. While at one level at least, *ZMM is* indeed a road novel: it is far more than that. Yet the very first paragraph does indeed suggest that the journey in the book is going to be a literal one:

> *'I can see by my watch, without taking my hand from the left grip of the cycle, that it is eight-thirty in the morning. The wind, even at sixty miles an hour, is warm and humid. When it's this hot and muggy at eight-thirty, I'm wondering what it's going to be like in the afternoon.'*

We are taken at once, and urgently and dramatically, into the core of the journey. Also on the face of it, the book is a novel in the sense that it is a first person narrative, which tells a story. That the story comes across as reading like a memoir doesn't necessarily mean that the book shouldn't be categorised as a novel. After all, a novel may be written so convincingly in the first person that it seems to be a memoir even though we might have reason to think that it isn't.

Ultimately, whether you decide to regard the book as a novel or a personal memoir is largely a matter of taste. Nowhere in the book does Pirsig suggest directly that the narrator is, in fact, himself, although it's very reasonable for us to assume that he is.

In fact, there is extensive anecdotal evidence, exterior to the book, that *ZMM* is based on a true account of much of Pirsig's real life, including of the journey which Pirsig made with his son Chris and some friends through America. And most certainly one of the many addictive elements about the book is the seemingly fully felt conviction (and the sheer interest generated by the fact that) it seems at heart, a novel about being on the road. But it isn't, for example, anything like a road novel such as is Jack Kerouac's novel *On The Road* (1957).

Certainly, Pirsig writes beautifully and evocatively about life on the road. But beyond this, the real road provides the setting, for him to report remembered experiences that have happened to him, and then, showing the Quality (and Value), he derived from these experiences.

We discover, in due course, that what *ZMM* is really about, is Sarah's use of the word Quality, and the meaning that she -- and Pirsig -- attach to this word. This is another way of saying that this remarkable book is an investigation into modern humankind's search for purpose and meaning. After all, Pirsig's book is subtitled *An Inquiry Into Values.*

ZMM doesn't bring all aspects of life into its investigation. To take one example of what it leaves out: the book has very little to say about emotional life. Moreover, we soon realize that it is as much a work of philosophy as a novel. What is clear almost from the outset, though, is that the book is original, and unique, in a way that few books are. *ZMM* has, in fact, created a genre of its own.

Given that *ZMM* seemed bizarre to most book buyers in the mid-1970s, the eventual huge success of the book was impossible to predict at the time. However, this is more understandable in retrospect, given, as we've seen, the moral and ethical crisis in which the United States found itself in the middle of that decade.

ZMM arrived in bookshops at a time when America was questioning its values with great intensity. Even more to the point, *ZMM* offered real, timely, thoughtful answers. Above all, in *ZMM*, Pirsig continually and highly effectively oscillates between setting down factual statements of events that have happened to him in his life, and then, in effect, pointedly showing us, by way of example, the Quality (and Value) he derived from those life experiences. The oscillation is visible to some extent in most paragraphs in the book, through which Pirsig tends to gently suggest the answers from his derived Quality. He makes gentle suggestions, rather than force the answers down the reader's throat, which makes his approach all the more compelling, readable, and inspiring. Yet it is only mid-book that Pirsig actually introduces the concept of Quality explicitly by name. This is when we first meet Sarah, and in Pirsig's narrative, it is she who explicitly introduces him to Quality.

Robert Pirsig was born on September 6, 1928 and brought up in Minneapolis Minnesota from a family that was of German and Swedish descent. His father was a law graduate of the University of Minnesota Law School (UMLS) and began teaching at the school in 1934. Pirsig's father became the Dean of the UMLS from 1948 to 1955. Pirsig himself was a highly intelligent child whose IQ was measured at the age of nine at 170.

Because of Pirsig's intelligence and fascination by knowledge and thought of all kinds, he was allowed to skip several grades at school. He won his High School Diploma in May 1943 when he was only fourteen years old and he entered the University of Minnesota in the summer of 1944 to study biochemistry. In *ZMM,* Pirsig names the main character in the book Phaedrus, who clearly is based on Pirsig's own earlier life: We are told, with emphasis, that Phaedrus, being not at all a typical student, was studying science not as a way of establishing a career but rather as an idealistic goal in itself.

It was while Pirsig (as Phaedrus) was carrying out his laboratory work in biochemistry that he became greatly troubled by realising that there was often more than one workable hypothesis to provide an explanation of any given phenomenon, and indeed that frequently, with increased research, the number of possible hypotheses appeared unlimited or close to it. He couldn't find, even with increased research, any obvious way of minimising the number of hypotheses and so he became bothered by the way that hypotheses were generated within scientific practice. The fact that this was an extremely abstruse area of thought did not placate his frustration and even the feeling of distress at these realizations. The question of this multiplicity of hypotheses distracted him to such an extent that he lost interest in his studies and didn't maintain good grades. Eventually, he was actually expelled from the university.

In 1946, four years before the onset of the Korean War, the young Pirsig decided to enlist voluntarily in the United States Army. He was sent to South Korea where he remained until 1948. After an honorable discharge from the army, he returned to the United States and lived in Seattle, Washington State, for some months, at which point he made the decision to continue his education. He earned a Bachelor of Art in Eastern Philosophy in May 1950 at University of Minnesota Twin Cities.

Pirsig then made the decision to go study in India. He attended the Banaras Hindu University where he studied Eastern Philosophy and Culture. Pirsig didn't obtain a degree there but, nineteen years later, did go on to perform important graduate-level work in philosophy at the University of Chicago. The difficulties he had as a student in a course at the University of Chicago, were later described, most likely with some minor changes for artistic purposes, in *ZMM*.

In the early 1950s, Pirsig travelled to Minnesota, Mexico and Nevada, while simultaneously working as a freelance journalist and technical writer. At this time, he also focused his energies on writing short stories.

From September to December 1953, along with Nancy Ann James, he was engaged in co-editing *The Ivory Tower* edition of the *Minnesota Daily*, the literary magazine of the University of Minnesota.

In 1955, Pirsig became involved in summer humanitarian work for the United Press Service in Minneapolis. In that same year, he was also employed to write educational booklets for students in the seventh and eighth grade of school. Next, in 1956, he was employed on production of marketing educational film for the *Minneapolis Grain Exchange*. The same year, he penned articles on Research and Development for the General Mills Research Labs. In April 1958, he left his work at General Mills and received his MA in Journalism, which in 1959, enabled him to become Professor of English Rhetoric at Montana State College (since renamed Montana State University). Here he taught for the next two years Oral and Written Communication and English Composition.

While the importance of Sarah and of Montana State College (MSC) in *ZMM* is in-contestable and un-arguable, it is also true that Pirsig did not have a high opinion of MSC. Here is what he says about it in *ZMM*, Chapter 13:

> [MSC] *was what could euphemistically be called a 'teaching college'. At a teaching college you teach and you teach and you teach with no time for participation in outside affairs. Just teach*

> *and teach and teach until your mind grows dull and your creativity vanishes and you become an automaton saying the same dull things over and over to endless waves of innocent students who cannot understand why you are so dull, lose respect and fan this disrespect out into the community. The reason you teach and you teach and you teach is that this is a very clever way of running a college on the cheap while giving a false appearance of genuine education.*

While it's clear that Pirsig didn't have a high opinion of MSC, the college was not certain what to make of him, either.

"In the People's Interest, A Centennial History of Montana State University." => Includes this passage about Pirsig:

> The end of the 1950s and early 1960s, the period of Pirsig's tenure at MSC, was a period when English department faculty were moving in and out with some regularity. Pirsig was one of these transients, a 'real eccentric' as one colleague remembered him, who came to Bozeman as an instructor following ten years in India in the study of oriental philosophy. Colleagues also remember him as being consumed with a quest for 'quality.' He was an exceedingly intense person who approached everything with a certain fanaticism. ... On May 10, 1954, Pirsig got married. He and his wife Nancy subsequently had two children: Chris who was born in 1956 - and who features extensively in *ZMM* -- and Theodore who was born in 1958. Pirsig was divorced

from Nancy in 1978, and on December 31, 1978, he married Wendy Kimball. Tragically, on the evening of Saturday, November 17, 1979, Chris Pirsig was murdered in San Francisco by street muggers in a senseless and motiveless attack.

In retrospect, many of the problems young Pirsig suffered as a student, due to the nature of his thinking, can be traced to the fact that he was a creative genius and like many – though not all – creative geniuses naturally found the somewhat hidebound nature of academic study restricting and demoralizing. Unfortunately, he suffered some psychological problems in the early 1960s and had some stays in psychiatric hospitals between 1961 and 1963. He was diagnosed with paranoid schizophrenia and clinical depression and on numerous occasions suffered treatment by electro-convulsive therapy, which was fashionable in those days for many psychiatric problems including severe depression.

The great originality and brilliance of Pirsig's thinking are the real reasons for the success of his magnificent book. His philosophy is highly personal, but Pirsig, in effect, implies in *ZMM*, that in the modern world the only way to develop a workable philosophy *is* to make it a personal philosophy. *ZMM* is replete with an energetic and almost always clearly expressed holistic, value-centered philosophy, with the word 'philosophy' meaning here worthwhile and profound musings and thoughts about life and the human condition and the nature of the world and indeed what value we should consider living our lives by. This philosophy is slowly revealed in the book to be based around the idea of seeking Quality and finding Quality meanings and meaningfulness in life, as a specific personal life goal, of course for Pirsig himself, but by implication for the *ZMM* reader as well.

Perhaps what is most remarkable of all about *ZMM* -- the novel, or the philosophical memoir, or whatever it is -- *ZMM* manages to be deeply philosophical and deeply fascinating, while actually remaining extremely readable and compelling, partly because the road trip is in itself interesting. Moreover, the road trip narrative itself, does such a good job of framing and emphasizing, the philosophy-laden content of the non-road portions of the chapters.

In addition to being, at least at one level, a kind of example of a road trip story, *ZMM* follows in another tradition of American literature in that the author's childhood experience is very often part of the story and gives the book an extra depth. Early in the book, when the Narrator points out to his son Chris that he's just seen a red-winged blackbird (one of his just mentioned childhood memories), as they were driving along, with Chris riding pillion behind the Narrator. Chris isn't impressed by him saying that he'd seen this particular blackbird and shouts back, '*I've seen lots of those, Dad.*'

The Narrator remarks:

> *At age 11 you don't get very impressed with red-winged blackbirds. .. You have to get older for*

> *that. For me it is all mixed with memories that he doesn't have. Cold mornings long ago when the marsh grass had turned brown and cat tails were waving in the northwest wind. The pungent smell then was from muck stirred up by hip-boots while we were getting in position for the sun to come up and the duck season to open.*

This lovely lyrical and evocative style, using memory to bring the author's past completely into the present, is one of the many wonderful features of *ZMM*. As we've seen, this narrative combines memories of real-life events while emphasizing either immediate experience or the qualitative of it. This continues into the second half of *ZMM,* but with the word Quality being used as the major point of discussion.

The ideas in the book themselves are infused with a warm empathy for the need for human beings to make the most of life. One feels very often that Pirsig is deliberately, yet gently, trying to develop a philosophy for modern man, modern man living in a technological age who is confronting technological wonders and, indeed, wonders himself what to make of them.

In one of the most justly famous remarks Pirsig makes in his book, he directly relates notions of the Godhead from the distant past to the present day, when people such as the narrator of the book, are trying to get their motorcycles to work with maximum efficiency.

> *'The Buddha, the Godhead, resides quite as comfortably in a circuit of a digital computer or the gears of a cycle transmission as he does at the top of a mountain or in the petals of a flower. To think otherwise is to demean the Buddha – which is to demean oneself.'*

That passage is all Quality in the Sarah Vinke sense, and indeed is a kind of *leitmotif* for the entire book.

This philosophy for modern man is, we discover on reading the book, essentially the same as the investigation into the nature of Quality.

In much of the early part of the book, Pirsig uses the metaphor of keeping his motorcycle well-serviced by his own endeavors so that it will run efficiently, as a way of understanding life, too. The metaphor also works at a practical level; Pirsig writes with great insight and energy about how he thinks people should make the most of technology and derive maximum benefits from it. These thoughts are extended to his friend, John Sutherland, with whom he makes the journey – John's wife Sylvia is riding pillion on John's motorbike – has a more chancy, happy-go-lucky approach to motorbike maintenance, and is content to let his bike do what it wants to do and address problems, if and when they arise. The narrator has a more analytic and scientific approach and is continually looking at the state of the bike and deciding if anything needs to be done to make it run more smoothly, and prevent costly inconvenient future mechanical breakdown. John's approach, by contrast, is a more romantic don't-worry approach, trusting either that nothing will happen, or that needed technical help will automatically be just around the corner.

Ultimately, however, no summary or account of *ZMM* can replace the experience of reading it. Let's never forget, either, that reading *ZMM* is profoundly enjoyable; it's a passionately engaging and exciting book. Many books claim to change lives: *ZMM* really does. As well as writing a fascinating account of a journey through America with all the emotions, setbacks, joys, opportunities for exploration (and awareness of the potential for dullness) Pirsig also regularly and coaxingly brings his philosophical notions about life to the attention of the reader.

ZMM gains much of its interest from the fact that the philosophical disquisitions it contains are an integral part of the story of the road trip. In his book, Pirsig calls these disquisitions 'Chautauquas'– a name he attributes to what he calls the 'travelling tent show Chautauquas' (adult education movements, named after Chautauqua Lake where the first one was held) that used to travel around the United States. Pirsig's Chautauquas are written in an attractive, entertaining, engaging style, which somehow always manages to stay user-friendly, rather than straying into the territory of lecture.

Pirsig, engaged on writing a book that was Quality in every sense, nevertheless had a struggle to find a publisher for his book. His query letter about it finally came to the attention of John C Willey, editor-in-chief at William Morrow and Company in New York. In fact, Willey was the only publisher out of more than a hundred Pirsig approached who took an interest in the book, passing it on to one of his editors, James Landis, whose comments to his colleagues about the book included:

> The book is brilliant beyond belief, it is probably a work of genius, and will, I wager, attain classic stature.

Landis's comments proved completely and wonderfully accurate, even visionary.

An introduction to *ZMM* (contained in some editions, and seemingly written by the publisher), is a useful guide to what the book offers its readers:

> *ZMM* is, essentially three books: An account of a motorcycle trip from Minnesota to California, a philosophical meditation on the concept of Quality and the story of a man pursued by the ghost of his former self. Within these three books we find allegory and psychological tension, a lesson in eastern and western schools of thought, a conundrum about the meaning of the self, a commentary on the American social and physical landscape, and some helpful tips on the care and maintenance of a motorcycle. In short, there is something for everyone in this sprawling, brilliant book that looks both inward and outward at

the prospect of achieving enlightenment in a complicated world.

For 'achieving enlightenment' we should think Zen Enlightenment, as well as 'achieving a life of Quality'.

Some readers of *ZMM* may think this reference to the care and maintenance of the motorcycle in the above paragraph is slightly tongue-in-cheek. Certainly, Pirsig himself, in his own Author's Note to the book, is witty on this subject. His Author's Note reads as follows:

What follows is based on actual occurrences. Although much has been changed for rhetorical purposes, it must be regarded in its essence as fact. However, it should in no way be associated with that great body of factual information relating to Orthodox Zen Buddhist practice. It's not very factual on motorcycles either.

After *ZMM's* astonishing, and unexpected success, Pirsig said, in an Afterword to a subsequent edition of his book, that there was

' ... *fan mail—week after week, month after month. The letters have been full of questions: Why? How did this happen? What is missing here? What was your motive? There's a sort of frustrated tone. They know there's more to this book than meets the eye. They want to hear all. There really hasn't been any 'all' to tell. There were no deep manipulative ulterior motives.*

Writing it seemed to have higher quality than not writing it, that was all.'

ZMM has sold more than five million copies to date and still sells, worldwide about 100,000 copies per year. It's taught as an assigned Literature or Philosophy Text at perhaps forty percent of colleges and high schools in the United States.

ZMM achieved near instant fame as 'one of the most unique and exciting books in the history of American letters' and soon became a bestseller at a time when the Vietnam War was tearing the heart out of America and making millions of Americans question the values presented to them by the government and by the *Zeitgeist*. It was a time when the idea of a slightly eccentric writer spinning beautifully expressed, strangely informal and frequently deeply profound and highly engaging wisdoms from the back of a motorcycle as he toured America with his son and a couple of friends, was immensely attractive. Today, the book still retains its appeal, attractiveness and sheer readability.

Reading Pirsig on Quality, one is reminded of what the poet W. B. Yeats observed towards the end of his own life: 'Man can embody truth, but not know it.'

In *ZMM,* Pirsig is, in effect, proposing the goal of Quality as a kind of secular religious objective, a sort of accessible Zen for the world, and a profound and even sweeping antidote to mental, cultural and economic confusion, despair and mediocrity.

ZMM also aspires to establish a foundation for western philosophy. This aspiration is partly confirmed by Pirsig's statement:

> '*If you are going to up-end all human understanding, you've got to go back to the beginning.*'

The correspondence between Pirsig and William Morrow and Company provides fascinating insights into Pirsig's aims and intentions for his book. His first contact with the organization that was to become his publisher was in one of Pirsig's many speculative query letters. He wrote this letter on June 6, 1968 to John C Willey, editor-in-chief at William Morrow and Company:

> Dear Mr. Willey:
>
> I am working on a book with a somewhat unusual title 'Zen and the Art of Motorcycle Maintenance' and am now looking for a publisher.
>
> The book is, as the title says, about Zen and about Motorcycle maintenance, but it is also about a communication of spiritual feeling and technological thought. Part of its thesis is that the division between these is a deep root of the discontent of our age, and it offers some heterodox solutions.
>
> Two sample pages are enclosed. If you're interested in seeing more, please let me know.

Four days later, on June 10, 1968 James Landis replied to Pirsig.

> Dear Mr. Pirsig:
> John Willey has passed along to me your letter of June 6 concerning your *Zen and the Art of Motorcycle Maintenance*. The book sounds fascinating and we would be pleased to consider it, either complete, or as much of it as you now have ready. You may direct it to my attention.

Over the next four years, as Pirsig finalised his book, he and Landis enjoyed a correspondence during which time the two exchanged updates, ideas and thinking about the book, and Landis provided encouragement where necessary.

The first draft of *ZMM* was finished by March 3, 1970. It was not, however, until two and a half years later, in November 1972 that the book was finally submitted to Landis, who gave an interim report on his feelings about the book on November 21, 1972 in which he said that he was enjoying it and that it was 'wise and fun and sad' and that it had 'taught me something.' However, he did have reservations about publishing it because of its length, which was at that time about 200,000 words. (The final published length of the book is around 143,000 words.)

Pirsig remained loyal to Landis throughout this entire process, although that was no doubt mainly because of the 122 publishers who received his initial query letter in 1968, William Morrow was the only one that made an offer (in 1973) for the completed manuscript. Landis presented the book to his colleagues in an editorial presentation that left no doubt as to his brilliant intuition and confidence that the book had the potential to become the classic it was, in fact, to become.

> EDITOR'S PRESENTATION (4/73)
> TITLE: ZEN AND THE ART OF
> MOTORCYCLE MAINTENANCE
> *KEYNOTE:*
> This is, in an ultimate sense, a book about living, about how to live and, at least by inference, about why. It's a book that can be read on several levels... To oversimplify: it is the autobiographical story of a man who takes a motorcycle trip with his son. The man, in his past, went mad. The man he is now is, he thinks, an entirely different man from the man he was before he became insane. On the motorcycle trip, this man, the narrator (never officially designated as Pirsig), confronts himself, his past and his son, Chris, who is eleven and has been diagnosed as having 'the beginning symptoms of mental illness.' ... The book is brilliant beyond belief; it is probably a work of genius and will, I'll wager, attain classic stature.

In an interview in 1974 with National Public Radio in the United States, Pirsig said that writing the book took him four years. During two of these years, Pirsig continued working at a job he then had, which involved writing computer manuals. He related how combining the two activities caused him to fall into a hectic and somewhat unusual schedule. He woke up very early every day and wrote the book from two in the morning to six in the morning, then had breakfast and went to his day job. He would sleep during his lunch break and then go to bed at about six o'clock in the evening. Pirsig subsequently joked that his colleagues at his workplace noticed that he was 'a lot less perky' than everyone else.

This creative routine evidently worked well for Pirsig. Posterity ought to be grateful for that routine, which allowed Pirsig to bring into being one of the most remarkable, and fundamentally, *useful* books written in the twentieth century.

Chapter 4: Sarah Makes Her Entrance

Pirsig's first mention of Sarah's
'I hope you are teaching Quality to your students'

… This statement in *Zen and the Art of Motorcycle Maintenance,* is a great epiphany and is arguably the book's most dramatic moment. Specifically, it is what Sarah said that sets the narrator off on a series of thoughts about the concept of Quality, which lasts from where Sarah introduces the concept to the end of the book.

The material that mentions Sarah comes at the end of Part Two of the book, in a chapter which describes how the narrator -- again we can reasonably regard this person as Pirsig himself, although Pirsig never explicitly says in the book that the narrator is definitely him -- revisits the town of Bozeman in Montana. As part of his visit there, on a quiet sunny afternoon, he returns to Montana State University where he used to teach. Unannounced, he pulls open the heavy door, and enters Montana Hall, the building where he taught for two years.

There is no sense in the narration at this point of the narrator worrying about being challenged by any security guard or finding any other people there, and the visit consequently has something of the quality of a dream about it. Especially as by now in the book the narrator has got into the habit of sometimes referring to himself mysteriously in the third person.

This third-person character, named Phaedrus, is a kind of half-deranged, implied insane, ever watching ghost, who is the alter ego of the narrator of *ZMM*, whom Pirsig sometimes uses particularly when he wants to describe an intense emotional experience and seems to prefer to do so by referring to himself in the third person.

In *ZMM*, Pirsig's visit to MSU is described in a way that invests the visit with a dream-like quality, but it seems highly likely that the visit took place in reality. The likelihood that Pirsig's visit to MSU happened is substantiated by the fact that Pirsig gave an almost identical version of these events in a conference presentation he made. This doesn't prove that the events happened, but it seems to make it likely that they did.

The visit, as related in the book, and irrespective of whether it happened in reality or was imagined, was creepy and frightening. This is emphasised, in effect, by Pirsig's frightened son Chris who, as the narrator and Chris enter the university whispers,

'Why are we here?' but gets no response from the narrator, who just shakes his head. Chris goes on to whisper, *'I don't like it here. It's scary in here,'* at which the narrator continues:

'Go outside then,' I said.
'You come too.'

'Later.'
'No, now.'
He looks at me and sees I'm staying. His look is so frightened I'm about to change my mind, but then suddenly his expression breaks and he turns and runs down the stairs and out the door before I can follow him.
The big heavy door closes down below, and I'm all alone here now. I listen for some sound... Of whom... Of him?... I listen for a long time.'

We might momentarily imagine that the 'him' to which the narrator refers is Chris, but it isn't. It's very soon clear that the narrator is, in fact, referring to himself in the third person as the imagined alter ego, deranged ghost, Phaedrus. The atmospheric quality of the writing at this point in the book is extremely powerful. There is a stark immediacy about the narrative, which takes us right into the classroom that the narrator visits and, in particular, the office where he used to work.

He then does finally meet someone at the college, a young woman in her late twenties, a woman he deliberately mentions as not being very pretty. He doesn't recognise her, but she recognises him and she knows about his mental illness. She says:

'We heard you were in hospital...'
'Yes,' I say.
There is more embarrassed silence. That she doesn't pursue it she probably knows why. She

hesitates some more, searches for something to say. This is getting hard to bear.
'Where are you teaching?' she finally asks.
'I'm not teaching any more,' I say. 'I've stopped.'

The conversation with the young woman ends awkwardly, but she doesn't seem to have any objection to him wandering around the part of the university he used to know.

He soon finds himself opening one more door 'compulsively' as he puts it. He goes into another room, where he sees a painting on the wall that he now suddenly realizes he ordered, although it is a print of a painting, rather than a painting as such. The moment he sees the print, he realizes that this is the office where he used to work and now the memory becomes more intense. And now this is the part of the book where he first mentions Sarah.

Pirsig makes clear in *ZMM* that the notion of Quality was emphatically not something he thought up himself, but rather that it was something imparted to him by 'Sarah', when he was teaching at an educational institute whose name he does not specify in the book but which was in fact Montana State University (MSU) located at Bozeman, Montana. It was there that he experienced an epiphany: to use James Joyce's useful and here particularly appropriate term.

Pirsig, imagining revisiting his office at MSU, recalls something he'd never forgotten: what Sarah said to him.

> *'All this comes back now. This was his office. A find. This is the room I am looking for.*
> *I step inside and an avalanche of memory, loosened by the jolt of the print, begins to come down. The light on the print comes from a miserable cramped window in the adjacent wall through which he looked out and across the valley onto the Madison Range and watched the storms come in and while watching this valley before me now through this window here, now... started the whole thing, the whole madness, right here. This is the exact spot.*
> *And that door leads to Sarah's office. Sarah. Now it comes down. She came trotting by with her watering pot between those two doors, going from the corridor to her office, and she said, 'I hope you are teaching Quality to your students.' This in a la-de-da, singsong voice of a lady in her final year before retirement about to water her plants. That was the moment it all started. That was the seed crystal.'*

In *ZMM*, Pirsig sometimes switches from the first to the third person, and describes himself as Phaedrus. Later in the book, again remembering Sarah speaking to him, Phaedrus recalls, when reminiscing about his own personal experiences:

> *'The one sentence 'I hope you are teaching Quality to your students' was said to him, and*

> *within a matter of a few months, growing so fast you could almost see it grow, came an enormous, intricate, highly structured mass of thought, formed as if by magic.'*

In the next paragraph, Pirsig elaborates on the slightly comic, beguiling, interaction he had with Sarah. Again, he refers to himself here, in the third person, as Phaedrus.

> *'I don't know what he replied to her when she said this. Probably nothing. She would be back and forth behind his chair many times each day to get to and from her office. Sometimes she stopped with a word or two of apology about the interruption, sometimes with a fragment of news, and he was accustomed to this as a part of office life. I know that she came back a second time and asked, 'Are you really teaching Quality this quarter?' and he nodded and looked back from his chair for a second and said 'Definitely.' and she trotted on.'*

Finally, and this is the third (and next to final), occasion when Sarah is referred to by name in *ZMM*, we get a rather quaint, almost epigrammatic reminiscence, which by focusing on how Sarah 'trotted' consummates Pirsig's affectionate reminiscences of his conversations with Sarah, who comes across as a rather whimsical, perhaps herself somewhat eccentric but warm-natured woman who, like the great philosophers, soothsayers and seers of the past, doesn't say much, but what she does say is full of meaning and resonance:

> 'A few days later when Sarah trotted by again she stopped and said, 'I'm so happy you're teaching Quality this quarter. Hardly anybody is these days.'
> 'Well, I am,' he said. 'I'm definitely making a point of it.' 'Good.' she said, and trotted on.'

Describing Sarah as 'trotting' suggests the affectionate regard in which Pirsig clearly held her, and this always seems to be how he has regarded her ever since. He gave more information about Sarah in a media interview seen in the short video by Dr. Anthony McWatt's DVD *The MOQ at Oxford* (*Metaphysics of Quality*). Pirsig explained how in 1959 to 1960, he was in the town of Bozeman, Montana, teaching English and how he found himself having to confront problems he was encountering in his teaching.

> 'I had a textbook in front of me that told me what to tell students, and I could see the students sitting back there bored and I was not connecting [to these students] in any way. I didn't know how you could teach English in such a way they would really learn it, other than to simply imitate what I was telling them. And this became a deeper and deeper problem as I went on. And I tried all sorts of experiments.

> *And then there was a really sweet old lady there named Sarah Vinke. And just to tease me a little she said, 'Well, I hope you are teaching Quality to your students, you know'. She knew very well, that I didn't know what she meant by that, but it was part of her wisdom to keep asking that question.'*

Pirsig continues to describe his friend Sarah:

> *'So she was gradually drawing me into this question. 'What is Quality?' And that got me into the situation where I wanted to teach something about English honestly, but I found that the way* [the teaching environment] *was set up, I wasn't teaching anything honestly. I was just teaching them rote things* [such as]*: Get your sentences straight. Don't dangle your modifiers. Organize your outlines and all this stuff. But it really, really, wasn't there. And then came this comment from this lady, a former Greek scholar, who said, 'I hope you are teaching Quality.' And that began this migration which has led us here.'*

Pirsig stated unequivocally that it was important to him that Sarah was a Greek scholar. As he explained:

> *'If you are going to up-end all human understanding, you've got to go back to the beginning. And our Western understanding does really start with the Ancient Greeks. God knows why.... God doesn't know how they got started on that particular questioning which led to their love of reason and their ability to organize*

things… it was lost… The Romans never really picked up on it. But I asked [Sarah] *the question: 'Did the Greeks, the Ancient Greeks, think that Quality was part of their thought?' And she* [Sarah] *said, 'It was <u>every</u> part of their thought.'*
'

Pirsig emphasized, "<u>every</u>" in his conclusion. (Above, we use underline, where Pirsig used a stronger voice.)

'And SHE had a sense of Quality. A brilliant teacher. They [her students] *called her 'The Divine Sarah.''*

Dennis Gary, a former student in many of Sarah's courses, one of which was Oral and Written Communication, is such an important source of information about Sarah, that he gets an entire chapter to himself here in our *Sarah Vinke biography*. However, for the moment, it's pertinent to note here that, at one particularly interesting moment in his reminiscences, Mr Gary recalls how Sarah once complimented him by saying, '*You've got character, Mr. Gary,*' and that she followed this by saying, '*You're Quality.*'

In his account of knowing Sarah, Dennis Gary adds:

In my bewilderment I told her that I associated the term quality with laundry detergents, coffee brands and Buicks. Then she went off on a discussion of Character and Quality, but I just remember being surprised and confused by her reaction. For weeks after that in my study room at the Phi Sigma Kappa house or in the dark of the fraternity dormitory, I pondered what she had said.

Dennis Gary continues:

Weeks later I was still pondering her statement that I 'had Character and Quality'. It was as if I had been given a charge to do something with my life... In fact the following year in the darkness of my attic room at Mrs. Elliott's boarding house in Klamath Falls, Oregon, with my lights out and waiting to doze off, I would wonder about it, after a day teaching high school English. What kind of charge had she given me? 'You've got Character, Mr. Gary... You're Quality.'

Dennis Gary, one of the few people alive today who knew Sarah quite well, is one of the most important witnesses for any biography of Sarah.

In the meantime, returning to Pirsig's *alter ego* of Phaedrus, it's important to note that Pirsig uses Phaedrus as, among other things, a vitally important seeker after truth. In one especially powerful and poignant moment in the *ZMM* (during the mountain climb with Chris near end of Chapter 20), Pirsig, as Phaedrus, seeks to relate the seeking for a better understanding of Quality with an ancient and revered Chinese text. The following excerpt from *ZMM* adds considerably to the scope and meaning of Pirsig's interpretation of Sarah's understanding of the notion of Quality:

> *It was the 2,400-year-old Tao Te Ching of LaoTzu. He [Phaedrus] began to read through the lines he had read many times before, but this time he studied it to see if a certain substitution would work. He began to read and interpret it at the same time.*
>
> *He read:*
>
> *The quality that can be defined*
> *... is not the Absolute Quality.*
>
> *That was what he had said.*
> *The names that can be given it*
> *... are not Absolute names.*
>
> *It is the origin of heaven and earth.*
> *When named it is the mother of all things . . .*
>
> *Exactly.*
>
> *Quality* [romantic Quality] *and its manifestations* [classic Quality] *are in their nature the same. It is given different names* [subjects and objects]
> *when it becomes classically manifest*
> *Romantic quality and classic quality together may be called the 'mystic.'*
>
> *Reaching from mystery into deeper mystery, it is the gate to the secret*
> *of all life.*

*Quality is all-pervading.
And its use is inexhaustible.
Fathomless.
Like the fountainhead of all things . . .*

*Yet crystal clear like water it seems to remain.
I do not know whose Son it is.
An image of what existed before God.*

*Continuously, continuously it seems to remain.
Draw upon it and it serves you with ease . . .
Looked at but cannot be seen . . .
listened to but cannot be heard . . .
grasped at but cannot be touched . . .
these three elude all our inquiries and hence blend
and become one.*

*Not by its rising is there light,
Not by its sinking is there darkness
Unceasing, continuous*

*It cannot be defined
And reverts again into the realm of nothingness
That is why it is called the form of the formless
The image of nothingness
That is why it is called elusive*

*Meet it and you do not see its face
Follow it and you do not see its back
He who holds fast to the quality of old
Is able to know the primeval beginnings
Which are the continuity of quality.*

Phaedrus read on through line after line, verse after verse of this, watched them match, fit, slip into place. Exactly. This was what he meant. This was what he'd been saying all along, only poorly, mechanistically. There was nothing vague or inexact about this book. It was as precise and definite as it could be. It was what he had been saying, only in a different language with different roots and origins. He was from another valley seeing what was in this valley, not now as a story told by strangers but as a part of the valley he was from. He was seeing it all.
He had broken the code.
He read on. Line after line. Page after page. Not a discrepancy. What he had been talking about all the time as Quality was here the Tao, the great central generating force of all religions, Oriental and Occidental, past and present, all knowledge, everything.'

o00O00o

Did Pirsig have other conversations about Quality with Sarah, conversations that he doesn't reveal in ZMM? This momentous question did get asked, and there is, in fact, something of an answer to it.

In September 8, 2008, Henry Gurr and Lee Glover asked Pirsig the following: 'Beyond the information given in ZMM, could you tell us more about the Sarah Vinke story and how she contributed to your thinking. Surely there is much more of interest to this story, than space allowed in ZMM?'

They also asked: 'In view of a general lack of information concerning Professor Vinke, could you tell us, for the sake of history, what you remember of Sarah Vinke, as a teacher and a person? And can you give us a mini-biography, which expands on the facts already given in ZMM? For example, do you have any information about what she studied in her formal education?'

We have already quoted above, in the Preface, Pirsig's extensive and fascinating reply in his letter of September 15, 2008. The reader may wish to read this again starting on page 17: We note that although Pirsig mentions that Bob and Gennie DeWeese did not use word Quality, Pirsig did not say anything about Sarah's use of Quality, despite his being directly asked this! ... Puzzling!!

Chapter 5: Echoes of Sarah, In Memories And Historical Documents.

So little is known about Sarah that information about her life has to be pieced together from isolated fragments of memories, scraps of documentary evidence, and hunches. We're calling this chapter 'Echoes of Sarah' because that's what these fragments basically are.

Eventually extensive research led Henry to a particularly fruitful source, Mrs. Shirley Luhrsen, a long-time Montana resident. Mrs. Luhrsen was familiar with MSU, and indeed had briefly met Pirsig when he was an instructor there. She had also been a student of, mentored by, and had worked closely with, our Sarah as Professor Sarah Vinke.

Henry writes: "Not only did I ask Mrs. Luhrsen's help finding information concerning events or persons in *ZMM*, I asked her to ask all her friends for the same help. Mrs. Luhrsen, being a long-time member of the Bozeman Chapter of the American Association of University Women (AAUW), asked for *ZMM*-related information at their monthly meetings.

This yielded an interesting letter by Sarah to Mrs. Stella Anacker. Both were like Shirley Luhrsen, long time members of AAUW. Written in Sarah's own characteristic handwriting, the handwriting was huge, *unlike* Sarah's handwriting when she was a professor. (Thanks to Dennis Gary for this observation.) Was Sarah in her later years, like Shirley Luhrsen, going blind?

Some notes are necessary: Hank Nixon is Sarah's reference to the then USA President Richard Nixon. ABM means Anti-Ballistic Missile. There is also a reference to the book *The American Challenge* by Jean-Jacques Servan Schreiber. Although Sarah in this letter uses the word *Quality* once, it is only in the sense of 'products and services. For the record, in *ZMM*, Pirsig uses *Quality* 471 times.

Sarah's reference above to the 'dusky brother' is something we would like to have edited out of this letter, as-well-as his unusual language style & spelling. But to have done so would not have been scholarly or true to the source. Sarah's attempt at wit, like that of any witty person, might sometimes backfire, as it does here. We apologise to anyone who is, not unreasonably, offended by this reference.

4/18/69

Dear Stella

To be writing 1968 Xmas letters at May-Day time make me think of the dusky brother who maintained that he 'didn't have no debts no mo',because the interest done et' up the principel' Today Hank Nixon has met the press with a message of restraint about the Korean downing of the U.S. Intelligence plane and message of the opposite about the ABM and an admission that he rejected a famous scientist because he disagreed on the ABM.

Of course you know when I sent my money (all I can now do is send money) last year: To Nora, Grnening of Alaska, M'Cartrhy, LePrvy Collins of Florida, Humphrey --- my stden [unclear, probably student] in the '40s in M.S.C. called my Apt, in the Evergreen by the old title of Oxford: Home of Lost Causes.

One can only hope for a resurrection of Common Sense, [this] it seems to be a Scarce Commodity. At least Nixon (whom Reinhold Niebuhr calls an acute politician) knows that the root of all this youth unrest is the Viet Nam [sic] War --- Were I of Draft age, I would not in the Vietnam War -- like Steve, your son, I'd face it (I hope) and take what the Draft Board has to offer (It is getting a Judicial treatment now) for this is not a war for justice nor anything moral and our Pride a nation that cannot admit a mistake cannot make the waste of human lives, ours and the Vietnamese, any thing but revolting. You should be humble in the presence of the Great Spirit of your Steve --- the Very Best that America has produced. Like you I feel that his influence will be sourly [sorely?] needed in the future. But my heart aches for you in your fearful anxieties.

It is wonderful I have a letter from you with an account of these young lives (your 'Hostages to the Future') and their interests. What demands on your Love and Intelligence and Restraint ---- and how blessed they are to be your children instead of the children of so many parents, as bewildered as their offspring,

One of the best analyses I've seen of the American dilemma was in a report by the President of Cornell Perkins. He said the older generation have two concerns :

1. To avoid another deflation [unclear; this word might be economic 'depression'.]
2. To avoid another World War
The college people have two concerns:
1. Justice for the Negro
2. The Quality of Life.

It is idle to tell you more that I had a Vicious Virus from Dec - 6 to March1. I feared for the future of the THING ---- that has me in its clutches ---- but I'm still ambulatory. [This word is a slightly clichéd expression, used in North America and meaning 'still alive']. And now for two books that friends have sent that have given me Some new perspectives. First: the American challenge by Servan Schreiber ---- hard common sense economics has won the respect of Europe and America. No doubt you've thrilled to it by now. The other is by Andrei Sakharov (father of the Russian H bomb) Progress, co-existence and intellectual freedom ---- a book which seems impossible from Russia --- so simple, so full of the great spirit of 'Riders of the – World' ------- so astonishing in its revelation of the similarity of Russian problems to our own ----- even the problem of pollution (it's Lake Baikal l and the Caspian Sea). Maybe there is yet fish to survive. And now I shall end on A note that will astound you. Somehow all these years, I have missed what I consider one of the Great Ideas of our times: Reinhold Niebuhr's belief that the Doctrine of Original Sin is only a symbol of the perpetual universal self interest in all human beings. My love to you

Sally Vinke

['Sally' was a nickname Sarah sometimes used for herself.]

o00O00o

One of the most interesting echoes of Sarah is a short but fascinating article, *'Books I've Enjoyed'* which she wrote for *The Montana Library Association Quarterly*, The Montana Library Association Quarterly. Vol 5, No. 3, Page 6 (April 1960) which she discourses whimsically on her affection for certain books. This article is especially valuable because, in our limited direct knowledge of Sarah's personality, we can *clearly see exactly this*, reflected in her writing about the admirable qualities and characteristics of the persons in the following stories. In Sarah's article below, we hope the reader will especially study the bolded words, which we as biographers feel express important characteristics of Sarah's personality and/or examples of topics and ideas, we known from other facts about her, that Sarah felt especially strong about:

Books I've Enjoyed
by Sarah Vinke

Herewith I declare my abiding love and loyalty to *Winnie the Pooh* and *The House at Pooh Corner*. Whimsy and philosophy mingle in the little stuffed animals who people these pages. The **'stubborn contrariety'** of human individuals is delightfully convincing. Piglet, terrified by the gale roaring among the tree top in the 100 Aker Wood appeals to Pooh: 'Supposing a tree fell down, Pooh, when we were underneath it?' 'Supposing it didn't, Piglet,' said Pooh. Or: 'Rabbit's clever?' said Pooh thoughtfully. 'Yes, said Piglet, Rabbit has brain.' There was a long silence. 'I suppose,' said Pooh, 'that that's why he never understands anything.' Kanga, the devoted mother of Baby Roo, Eeyore, the donkey, whose entire energy is devoted to feeling sorry for himself, and the dull, pompous Owl, who overawes the other animals because he can write his own name, WOL, have recognizable qualities of their human prototypes. These books never pall.

 Isak Dinesen has woven an enchanting web of mystery, psychology, urbanity in her *Seven Gothic Tales*. It has a highly civilized – perhaps even decadent – atmosphere, where the ghosts of past romantic writing (Gothic Tales are tall tales with the aura of tradition) are a burthen of which the reader is always subtly aware. These exquisite, gossamer tales could have no appeal for the practical mind. The mood of reverie which pervades them is luminous with mellow worldly-wisdom. 'The clouds parted, and a few of the constellations stood clear in the sky. The Great Bear preached its lesson. **'Keep your individuality in the crowd.'** '**Chivalrousness**, I think, **means this: to love, or cherish, the pride of your partner, or adversary, as highly or higher than your own.**' A vein of humor adds to the charm of these stories: 'Your side hurts you now where your rib was once taken out.' The old captain of the sailing vessel contemptuously likens the modern steamer to a self-supporting woman. The riches of the mind are offered with a grain of salt.

 On the serious side, there is *Creative Society,* John MacMurray herein furnishes a compass for use amid the philosophical and religious confusions of our day. Written soon after Communism became a force in the world, the avowed purpose of *Creative Society* is to point out the **fundamental difference between Christianity and Communism**. But the author finds it necessary to define what Christianity means. In showing that all religion is the expression of community; that Christianity, by its assertion that there is only one God, affirms that all mankind belong to one community, that a community by releasing its members from fear and replacing fear with love, unfolds human potentialities, MacMurray defines Christianity. He then contrasts the all-embracing love of the Christian ethic (however its followers may fall short of the goal,) with the purely material concept of Communism. His homely application of Christian principles I find wonderfully wholesome after the plethora of foggy analyses of world situations.

On the train, a year ago, I chanced upon a former student who held out the copy of *Quiet Yelled Mrs. Rabbit,* which she was reading, saying 'You ought to be reading this.' She was quite right. The sheer fun of being the mother of five demanding, persistent, energetic young individuals bubbles up in every line, despite the obstacle race which is her life. All the solemn instructions on family life fall before the vigor of this 'so story'. Spirits like Hilda Espy's can solve our problems of juvenile delinquency.

Currently (and climactically) there is the literary banquet of Fitzroy MacLean. No detective story could afford more excitement and suspense than the Dramatic accounts of real experience in *Disputed Barricade, Eastern Approaches* and *A Person from England.* One of the trusted representatives of

Churchill in World War II, he gives some of his turbulent adventures in the African desert behind Rommel's lines, in central Persia on a mission to kidnap General Zahidi, in Jugoslavia where he parachuted into Partisan headquarters. **Physical and mental courage, the zest for adventure, sensitive human understanding, urbanity, the quiet humor of understatement** – all are here combined in books of rare literary grace. That anyone who has helped to make recent history should have the breadth of vision and the detachment manifest in *Disputed Barrricade*, an interpretation of the life and times of Tito, and in *Eastern Approaches*, which embraces much of World War II, is a tribute to the sound health and self-confidence of the old Anglo-Saxon blood which relishes insecurity.

After having read Sarah's *Books I've Enjoyed,* Henry wrote this to Dennis Gary:

My original 'Mental Picture' of Professor Vinke based on *ZMM*, was that of an academic professor, completely immersed in Greek Classics. And this was what I was anticipating when I started my research into Sarah's published articles, teaching emphasis, etc. So I have to confess, that when I first saw Sarah's *'Books I've Enjoyed'* I was in a state of shock. Here I had expected her writing to confirm my *Zen and the Art of Motorcycle Maintenance*' image, of her: I expected it to show that she was a life-committed, deeply-oriented, academic, as well as a thoroughgoing, Greek Classicist. Her article, blew my image away. ... But upon reflection I'm becoming ever more convinced that Sarah is her most natural self in this article, where she is a chatty, populist and the mostly the very opposite of academic. An example of this is her philosophy of Winnie the Pooh. All said and done, perhaps there IS deep academics and philosophy in what Sarah finds in sayings of Winnie the Pooh, but I would have to read her '*Books I've Enjoyed*' a lot more closely, to see it.

Dennis Gary replied:

'Sarah's sentence structure and vocabulary seem pretty sophisticated, if not academic, to me: 'burthen'? Personally, I think she has a great sense of style and the subtleties of language. I speculate the Greek Classics facet of her persona, is an 'add-on' from education and not part of her youthful self, prior to external academic influences. I don't know whether Sarah's article shows that her interest in Greek was an add-on, more likely another facet of a multi-faceted [mature] personality. We tend to separate periods out, ignoring the common threads that run through all. It might show populist values in that she thrived at Montana State, Bozeman. ... other professors have said that country kids out of small towns deserved culture too. Our readers can tell us what they think.

oOOOOOo

Also revealing about Sarah, though in a less formal way, was the recollection of one of the male students at MSC who studied there when Sarah was teaching there, though it does not appear that Sarah actually taught him. This student calling himself a 'Montana Cowboy' preferred his name to be withheld. The interviewer here was Henry Gurr.

Henry: Do you recollect, Sarah Vinke, who was one of the professors there?
Student: Vinke, yes I remember the name.
Henry: She was head of the English Department.
Student: Yes.
Henry: And at that time she would, according to Robert Pirsig's book, would say [to him] 'Have you been teaching Quality to your students today? Are you bringing out their best writing and so forth? So do you remember anything he mentioned about Quality, or having to write about Quality in any way?
Student: Well, no. But the thing about Vinke is, the thing I do remember is, if you gave her a quart of watermelon pickles, you got an 'A' out of it.

Sarah's liking for watermelon pickles was well known at MSC at the time, and is corroborated by Dennis Gary.

o00O00o

Another echo of Sarah is this listing of books she once owned:

In this listing, the words in single quotation marks after the listing are what Sarah wrote inside the book to identify it as her own, where this is more significant than her just writing her name.

The books Sarah is definitely known to have owned are as follows:

Sophocles *The Oedipus Cycle*

Sophocles *Electra and Other Plays: Philoctetes, Women of Trachis, Electra, Ajax.* A new translation by E.F. Watling

Euripides Alcestis and Other Plays: Hippolytus, Iphigenia in Tauris, Alcestis. A new translation by Philip Vellacott.

The White Goddess: A Historical Grammar of Poetic Myth - Robert Graves
'Mrs Sarah Vinke, 521 West Arthur St, Bozeman Montana.'

The Dark Is Light Enough Christopher Fry

Shropshire Lad A. E. Houseman

Helen of Troy John Erskine

Euripides The Bacchae and Other Plays, Ion, The Woman of Troy, Helen, The Bacchae. A new translation by Philip Vellacott.
    On pages 9 through 12, in the introduction the following underlining's, presumably by Sarah, are found: *...integrity and intelligence combine in his search for the truth. ...the voice of the whole of that suffering, venturing, relentlessly thinking generation for whom Euripides wrote, ...sets it fairly in sight*

besides his orthodoxy for consideration. .....growing scepticism about mythical origins. .... almost certainly the son of some visitor to the Bacchic mysteries; .... He puts it to her that her seducer was not Apollo but a man ...... Creusa continues to believe in her divine lover ....she pursues belief like a duty. ....may look for guidance only to the honesty of his own heart.

The Montana Cree: A Study in Religious Persistence by Vern Dusenberry
[Hand written:] For Sarah Vinke with my deepest gratitude for her assistance both as a teacher and a colleague 'With dearest love to Sarah. Courage to go on.'-- Vern Dusenberry.'
[Also several pages later, is Mr. Dusenberry's printed acknowledgement of Sarah Vinke and Pirsig =>] 'Colleagues at Montana State College have encouraged and helped me. To Mr. Paul Grieder, Mrs. Sarah Vinke, Mr. George Douglas, and Mr. Pirsig of the college, go my special thanks .... '

o00O00o

An obviously especially fascinating echo of Sarah is her relationship with her husband Louis Vinke. As both Sarah and Louis were professors at

Montana State College, they may have met there. Sarah was one year older than Louis. In 1932, when they married, Sarah would have been thirty-eight and Louis thirty-seven. Perhaps Sarah, being from a farm background, found in Louis a soul mate, since he was a rancher and active agriculture and animal husbandry researcher and a fellow MSC professor. Sarah left teaching to marry Louis in 1932, and with him, moved from Bozeman to Billings – a distance of about 152 miles. Louis then unfortunately (as seen in newspaper obituaries below), contracted a 'prolonged illness', and dies in 1935. The precise nature of his illness is only mentioned in the Dallas Center Times: "Louis E Vinke dies at 40, following a long illness due to Addison's disease." So the portion of their married life that consists of good days was not, apparently, a whole lot more than two years.

With exception of newspaper articles and Google discoveries, very little unfortunately, is known about Sarah's relationship with her husband. However, *Louis Vinke: An Obituary* from *The Independent Record,* Helena MT. page 3, 1935, fills in some blank lines:

> Former State College Professor Passes
> BILLINGS, Aug. 30 (AP) --~-
> Louis Vinke. 40, former Stillwater County stockman and one-time professor of animal husbandry at Montana State College, died here today after an extended illness.
> He was on the State college staff

for 10 years and on leaving that institution moved to Billings in 1933. Here he was a broker for Dry Pulp products of The Great Western Sugar Company.

Mr. Vinke was born at South Holland, Ill., and came to Montana in 1916. He operated a ranch near Columbus until 1919.

His father, John N. Vinke of South Holland, was with him at The time of death. Survivors include his widow and several brothers and sisters living in Illinois.

Louis was born in 1895. Louis conducted extensive research on sugar beet pulp as a stock feed. This research, sponsored by the Western Sugar Company, was a progressive response to the Montana introduction of sugar beet agriculture, and manufacturing of sugar. The consequent availability of low cost dry beet pulp, and use as animal food, avoided costly disposal of an otherwise a noxious waste product. We can immediately appreciate why a sugar production company, would want Dr. Vinke as head of their sales. A newspaper report from 1932 says the following:

Vinke to Sugar Factory:
Louis Vinke, '21, is now with the Western

sugar factory at Billings. This factory recently
installed a pulp drying plant, and Mr. Vinke will have charge of the selling agency.

There are more details in the *Montana Butte Standard,* Butte, Montana, 11 June 1933.

Louis Vinke Resigns at College
Bozeman, June 10 --(Special) –

Louis Vinke, head of the livestock department of Montana State college, has resigned, effective Aug. 1 to go with the Great Western Sugar company at Billings.

Mr. Vinke first came to the college in 1925 after several years work in agricultural education in the Middle West. [at Wakefield Kansas High School] In Montana, first as assistant in the animal husbandry department at the college and in charge of livestock feeding experiments, and, since 1931, as head of the department, Mr. Vinke has become one of the outstanding livestock authorities in the West.

Shirley Luhrsen, in writing of her memories of Sarah from when she knew her in 1945, remarks:

Sarah was a romantic and recommended that I'd be a better teacher of Freshman English courses if I were married. She let me play her grand piano on her beautiful blue-bordered Oriental rug, browse her book cases and let me take a couple of them. ...

Sarah cared for the beauty of love ... She loved Louis so much ... She Cherished 'love'. --- Caring for beauty ... And truth --- Caring --- giving what she   Cared for [with] all her energy.

Shirley continues:

Sarah was a romantic. Her husband, Dr. Louis Vinke, had died after six [s/b 3] years; she never forgot the joys of matrimony. She was wise.

After Louis died, Sarah taught at Colorado College. Several photos of her there, seem to show extreme grief, as opposed to the other photos we have.

o00O00o

Mention of Sarah's own publications certainly belong in this chapter about echoes of Sarah. These publications, as far as is known, include: *The Philosophy of Horace,* Masters Thesis 1921, *Catullus, Stylistic Study,* PhD Thesis, University of Wisconsin-Madison 1923 (Published in the *University of Wisconsin Studies* in 1928), *Self-Criticism in Speech* in *Western Speech* 1949, and *Books I've Enjoyed.*
[See Chapt 6, for full discussion of Sarah's *Horace and Catullus Thesis.*]

As we might perhaps expect from what we know of her; Sarah was one of those teachers whose own education never really ended.

Sarah took post-doctoral studies at Cornell University in 1929 and at the University of Chicago in 1936. In 1948, during a spell at Anatolia College in Greece, she taught extension classes in English and in 1949 she fulfilled a lifetime ambition to visit Istanbul. She returned to Greece and Turkey in 1951 and in 1954 and 1956 she toured Europe.'

Here are two news stories from the *Bozeman Daily Chronicle* reporting on Sarah's travels at around this time.

> *Bozeman Daily Chronicle* 17 December 17, 1948
> **Dr. Sarah Vinke Leaving to Visit in Greece; Will Also Tour Turkey and Visit Friends in Paris, France**
> Dr. Sarah Vinke of the Montana State College faculty, will leave tonight for New Orleans, from where she will sail Dec. 21 for Greece. She has been granted a six-month leave of absence from her college duties.
> While in Greece, Mrs. Vinke will teach extension English classes at Anatolia College, where a long-time friend, Mary Ingle, is dean of girls.
> Miss Ingle visited Mrs. Vinke in Bozeman during the summer of 1947, during which time she interviewed Helen Talcot, an MSC student,

who later went to Anatolia College to teach home economics.

Before returning to Bozeman, Mrs. Vinke expects to spend some time in Istanbul, Turkey and in Paris, where she will visit Dr. Phil Eckert and his family.

Bozeman Daily Chronicle March 5, 1949.
MSC English Professor Is Guest Lecturer While on Tour of Europe
[This date seems to be the correct date but it is hard to read in the Xerox copy that is our only source here.]

First hand observation of current-day life in the countries of Greece, Turkey and France were included in the experiences of Dr. Sarah Jennings Vinke of the English Department at Montana State College, who returned last week from a six-month's tour of the continent.

Dr. Vinke, on leave of absence from the college, was visiting professor conducting classes and lecturing at a number of colleges in both Greece and Turkey.

At the invitation of organizations distributing relief in the military zones of Greece, Dr. Vinke reported that she had the unusual opportunity to see the conditions in the areas still under the control of the Greek Nationalist army.

With groups of both the agricultural and engineering staffs of the Economic Cooperative Administration, she made expeditions into the communities of Greece, Turkey and France.

Dr. Vinke was the guest of Mr. and Mrs. Phil Eckert in Paris for a week before she sailed from Cherbourg on her return trip to the United States.

o00O00o

Sarah is known to have been a devoted member of the branch of the American Association of University Women (AAUW) in the town of Bozeman in Montana. In 1927. she represented the Bozeman Branch at the International AAUW Meeting in Amsterdam. Later in her life, in 1954, she was a member of the National Committee for AAUW International Study Grants. In 1955, she went to Washington DC to help select foreign women students to receive grants, and in 1956, she was representative to the International Federation of University Women (IFUW) in Paris.

Sarah was the first fellowship chairman of the Bozeman Branch of the AAUW and was a compelling force in broadening the intellectual horizons of Bozeman women who worked with her. In 1961, she was honored by establishment in her name, a yearly $500 grant in aid, called 'AAUW fellowships ... awarded to help gifted women carry on advanced research.'

Bozeman Daily Chronicle Sunday November 12, 1961. Page 10
AAUW Meets and Establishes $500 Grant
Members of the Bozeman Branch of the American Association of University Women met Tuesday night in Herrick Hall to pay tribute to Dr. Sarah Vinke - first fellowship chairman of the Bozeman Branch, past state chairman of

international relations of AAUW, and a former national officer and member of the committee on international study grants.

Mrs. F. A. Boettcher, present fellowships chairman, while introducing Dr. Vinke, announced the realization of the Dream of the organization - to designate funds toward a named grant of $500 to honor Dr. Vinke. 'This amount,' she said, 'has been raised mainly through the courage, leadership, and persistence of the women who have kept the second-hand bookstore operating.'

Mrs. R. R. Renne first permitted the Branch to use the basement of The Book Shelf for used books donated for sale by interested persons. When she sold The Book Shelf, the project was moved to The McGill Museum where it continued to operate under the supervision of Mrs. Charles Bradley and Mrs. Sidney Whitt who have worked with the project from the ¬beginning.

Mrs. Whitt and Mrs. Bradley stressed the present need for books to stock the depleted shelves.

All money realized from the sale of used books goes toward supporting the fellowships program.

Dr. Vinke, in reviewing the Fellowships Program, paid special the tribute to Alice Oliver whose correspondence with National Headquarters of AAUW made possible Marie Burger's entering MSC as the first foreign student to come to Montana under AAUW's international and reconstruction aid program. Dr.

Burger, who came from Czechoslovakia, is now a research worker at Madison, Wis.

Dr. Vinke referred to Fellowships as 'the purple stripe on the toga' in that the fellowships program is that distinctive service of the organization which is indicative of the high purpose of AAUW, namely, to make it possible for women to have their part in spreading the boundaries of knowledge.

'For more than 60 years, AAUW fellowships have been awarded to help gifted women carry on advanced research,' Dr. Vinke said. 'Many agencies have looked for leadership throughout the world to these women who as recipients of AAUW Fellowships, have been able to fit themselves for positions of leadership in their fields of study.'

o00O00o

Soon after Sarah's retirement spring of 1962, she was offered an honorary doctorate by MSU, but she declined this honour because, unfortunately, she could not travel to attend the ceremony due to poor health.

Sarah maintained a lifelong interest in people and politics into her old age. In particular, she had a strong interest in the Mississippi Freedom Democratic Party, a political party that advocated civil rights and equality between African Americans and whites. This letter below shows that Sarah made a contribution to this party. The letter also confirms her address, in Florida, later in her life. The date of this letter is not known, but presumably, it was sent soon after October 23, 1968.

> Mississippi Freedom Democratic Party
> P.O. Box 147
> Sunflower, Miss. 38778
>
>
> Mrs. Sarah J. Vinke,
> Asbury Towers 1533 4th Avenue
> W. Bradenton, Fla. 33505
>
> Dear Mrs. Vinke:
> This will acknowledge with gratitude your check in the amount of $10.00 dated October 23, 1968. It came at a most needed time. It is gifts such as yours which make our work more effective.
> We appreciate your interest and concern, and hope that our relationship will be a continuous one.
>
> Many thanks.
> Sincerely,
> Joseph Harris
> Office Manager

Sarah died on January 24, 1978 at the Asbury Towers retirement home in Bradenton Florida, after suffering from poor health, including, very likely Parkinson's Disease, for some years.

Shirley Luhrsen said that Sarah, had moved there soon after retirement, to live in the same retirement community as her sister, Catherine B.

Jennings, who was already evidently there. Catherine died in 1979, probably also at the same retirement community as Sarah. There is no evidence of Sarah or Catherine having (or communicating with) any living relatives while they lived in Florida.

o00O00o

Dennis Gary has conducted some exemplary research directed at uncovering some details of Sarah's life from contemporary newspaper cuttings. These newspaper cuttings provide fascinating glimpses of Sarah's life. In chronological order, these cuttings contain the following paragraphs about Sarah:

The Independent Record (Helena, Montana) – Monday, July 11, 1949
English Teachers to Convene in Missoula Friday
    Features of the conference will include displays of material available for the teaching of English; a demonstration teaching class under Agnes Boner, visiting summer session lecturer at the university, and an all-university coffee hour at which Mrs. Sarah Vinke of Montana State College, Bozeman, will give an informal talk on 'Some Aspects if Education in Greece'. Mrs. Vinke returned recently after several months in Greece.

The Daily Inter Lake (Kalispell, Montana) – Sunday, May 2, 1954
MSC Students Plan Educational Trip

Bozeman – Twelve students and teachers have registered for the educational trip into seven European countries this summer through the cooperative plan sponsored by Montana State College and Circle M tours.

The group will sail through the St. Lawrence river from Montreal for Europe on the Ryndam and come back on the United States' speediest luxury liner. Scotland, England, Holland, Belgium, Germany, Switzerland and France will be visited during the 47-day period in Europe.

The tour will be directed by Dr. Harold Mcleave, 3409 Second Ave. North Great Falls. The assistant director will be Dr. Sarah Jennings Vinke, of the Montana State College English Department. Each student making the tour will earn six college credits through the MSC history department, headed by Dr. M G. Burlingame

The Independent Record (Helena, Montana) – Monday, October 24, 1955
Dr. Sarah Vinke Tells About United Nations
'The United Nations is a place where even those of antagonistic views can express their ideas and we can listen with poise to our worst enemy,' Dr. Sarah Vinke, English professor at Montana State college, told about 60 persons who attended the Soroptimist dinner observing the 10th anniversary of the founding of the UN at the Montana club Saturday night.

Dr. Vinke spent a full year in Greece, studying the effects of invasion on youth. Later she took a group of university students there on tour. She was graduated from Grinnell College,

Iowa, received her PH.D. degree from the University of Wisconsin and studied at the University of London.

'The idea of the UN is not new,' she said. 'As far back as the Roman Empire, people have been trying to find a way to talk over their troubles without inflicting physical punishment on others. The UN proves that an idea with real strength never dies. It is a clearing house for discussion and its success marks the first time actually hostile people have come together to express their ideas. They may walk out, as France did, but this very fact gives potency to the UN.'

She said the world is in the midst of three revolutions: The end of colonialism, the revolution of science and the revolution of the minority groups of the world. 'The UN is the hope of the world is solving these revolutions,' she said.

Dr. Vinke quoted from Lincoln Steffan, whose mother told him to 'always talk yourself clear.' The UN, she said, is the one place where all nations can 'talk themselves clear.'

She was introduced by Norman Weinstein, state chairman of the anniversary observance. UN flags decorated tables and pictures of the UN building were used on place mats.

The Independent Record (Helena, Montana) – Sunday May 8, 1955

Current Literature Study Group Has International Theme

Dr. Sarah Vinke of the English department at Montana State College was speaker for the general meeting at AAUW in February. Dr. Vinke is State AAUW Fellowship chairman and she very ably brought her rich background and experience into her review of Trygve Lie's recent book *In the Cause of Peace*. [In this book, Trygve Lie, who was the first Secretary-General of the United Nations and who served in this post from 1946 to 1952, chronicles this phase of his career.]

The Independent Record (Helena, Montana) – Tuesday October 18, 1955
Dinner Saturday Night Honors United Nations
All civic clubs have been invited to the no-host affair, which will begin at 6.30 o'clock and will feature an address. 'The United Nations Stands Fast' by Dr. Sarah Vinke, professor of English at Montana State College, Bozeman. She is state chairman of international relations for [the] American Association of University Women.

These references to Sarah's membership of societies help to demonstrate Sarah's extremely sociable nature. By all accounts, she was always good company and loved conversation and teasing and shocking people. Shirley Luhrsen remembers back to 1947: 'earlier she [Sarah] had been to Deer Creek with other faculty women for a day on the slopes.' In phone conversations, Shirley said that Sarah and several other Montana State College faculty, would regularly go summer time mountain climbing, and even winter athletic daring mountain snow skiing, on slopes near Bozeman. Most especially these were experienced at Shirley's Deer Creek mountain cabins and property that Shirley also loved so much.

o00O00o

Sarah was, unquestionably, a gregarious and remarkably charismatic woman who had an amazing and lifelong impact on the lives of at many of her colleagues and students, and very likely also on many more of her colleagues and very more of her students. Sarah inspired in Pirsig, just as in Dennis Gary, the notion of Quality as being something by which to live one's life: something which enriches life spiritually, intellectually and emotionally and which, at heart, constitutes an entire life philosophy in one word.

As is of course well known, Sarah was a colleague of Pirsig when he taught at Montana State University in the late 1950s.

Pirsig found Sarah a compelling, even mystical, teaching colleague. The following passage is not in *ZMM* but comes from a talk Pirsig gave at a conference held from July 29 to August 1, 1993 in San Diego, California. The title of the conference was *The heart of the matter: values for a world community*. The event was organised by the Association of Humanistic Psychology. Pirsig was talking on the subject '*Metaphysics of Quality: A New Paradigm for Values and Healing*'.

'Then there was a lady named Sarah, her name was Sarah Vinke, she was known as 'The Divine Sarah' and I think she actually attended the University of Wisconsin at the same time as Abraham Maslow. She was a real artist at teaching. She had been such an imaginative, creative person that she had run the whole department into a panic... when I came in she was in her last year of teaching and she had some trouble with attendance [In her last teaching years,] *Sarah was unfortunately often sick and disabled enough to reduce her in-class teaching attendance* [and other duties], *she had a little bit of a trot* [again, this was likely Parkinson's Disease] *as she came into the classroom and everybody was saying 'Oh well, this is her last year' and that she had taught too many students and she's really out of it.*

But she kept asking this question: 'Well, I hope you are teaching Quality', and I said: 'Oh, yeah'. Well, this was just my first year and I was snowed under with problems, I didn't know what I was doing and I said 'Oh yeah, I am teaching Quality' and she knew I was lying and so she didn't put on or led on, she just came back the next week saying 'Well, I'm so glad you're teaching Quality' and I said, 'Oh, yeah, I really am' and it's wonderful and I am enjoying it all the time and she knew I was lying and she kept at it over and over and over again and finally forced me to ask the question: 'What in the hell am I talking about here when I say that I am teaching Quality?'

Here we should contrast this with Pirsig's remark, in his letter to Henry Gurr:

> *'Later one of the teachers asked where I got all these ideas about quality. I said I got them from Sarah. The teacher's expression brightened, and he said, 'That's why she has always supported you.' This was the first I realized others were not supporting me. Much later Sarah came out of one such discussion and said to me furiously, 'Don't pay any attention to them. It's over their 'heads.' Her opinion and her angry expression of it has come back to me many times, consolingly, since then.'*

The above-mentioned presentation by Robert Pirsig at the San Diego conference continues with a quotation so important we previewed it as an introductory quotation of this book

> *'At a party once, that we were at, she* [Sarah] *said 'I'm a mystic.' and I said: 'No you can't be a mystic', and she said 'Why not?' and, I said, 'Mystics never identify themselves as anything' and she thought of that for a while and said 'You're right, I am not a mystic' thus proving I guess that she was a mystic.'* [At which Pirsig, giving his presentation, laughed:]

This above paragraph echoes Pirsig's May 3, 1987 letter to the authors of *Guidebook to Zen and the Art of Motorcycle Maintenance.*

> *'I am a mystic,' Sarah J. Vinke once said to me at a faculty party when there wasn't much to talk about. 'You can't be a mystic,' I said, 'a mystic doesn't define himself as anything.' She thought about this and said, 'You're right. I am not a mystic.' She smiled a little, and that was the last thing she ever said on the subject.'*

Dennis Gary corroborates this party and conversation. As Mr. Gary says:

> 'The faculty party I went to, mentioned in the first memories doc, is the one where the mystic conversation took place. What triggered this specific memory is the source letter sited above which turns up several places on the Internet. Coming from a rural Montana background, I did not know what a mystic was, and Sarah walked off before I could ask her. Being uncomfortable around Pirsig, I looked around for some other faculty member to ask and chose Dr. Oviatt of the History Department. His response, after a brief hesitation was to suggest I looked it up in a dictionary.'

Here by contrast, is what Pirsig writes about mystics in *ZMM*:

> *'Phœdrus doubted at the time, however, whether mystical Ones and metaphysical monisms were introconvertible since mystical Ones follow no rules and metaphysical monisms do. His Quality*

was a metaphysical entity, not a mystic one. Or was it? What was the difference?
He answered himself that the difference was one of definition. Metaphysical entities are defined. Mystical Ones are not. That made Quality mystical. No. It was really both. Although he'd thought of it purely in philosophical terms up to now as metaphysical, he had all along refused to define it. That made it mystic too. Its indefinability freed it from the rules of metaphysics.'

We now should pause to consider Pirsig's above words, especially

    1) "*she was such an imaginative, creative person*"…
    2) "*that she had run the whole department into a panic*".
    3) "<u>*She*</u>*' became a personal pronoun*"…
    4) "*said to me furiously, 'Don't pay any attention to them. It's over their 'heads.'* [ie the English faculty]… "
    5) '*Her opinion and her angry expression of it*"
    …

From the evidence we mention various places in this Biography, clearly Sarah had her own strong opinions, and was regularly quite forceful. And we can righty imagine with her English Department Chairman position of authority, could well push her Department Faculty, to excel, or at the very least change, as she did to Faculty Member Robert Pirsig. Her methods worked well with Pirsig, but backfired with the rest of the Faculty, creating evident violent resistance *"panic"*! Now just as clearly, we must take Mr. Pirsig's above short abbreviated statements as quite significant events in Sarah's life, and thus very important biographical facts & facets of her personality! (Please consult next Chapter (Ch 6), for additional understanding of Sarah's personality, where we look for 'intimations Sarah's personality' in her University of Wisconsin Masters and PhD Thesis writing.)

It will be clear by now, here in *this her biography,* that Sarah was a person who had her own strong opinions, and was a forceful, deeply intelligent, charismatic and energetically opinionated person. Furthermore, from her advantageous position of her chairmanship of the English Department, she could well encourage or indeed push her colleagues at the department, to excel, which in some cases, meant she wanted to effect a paradigm shift in their sensibility. As suggested earlier, her reason, we suppose, for not elucidating to Pirsig what she meant by the word 'Quality' was very likely that she wanted him to go away and figure out what she meant. As we've also said, that is precisely how a mentor might inspire a person they're mentoring.

This method worked successfully with Pirsig, but evidence suggests it backfired with the rest of the faculty, who were often resentful of Sarah and even on occasion felt humiliated by her. Perhaps other members of the faculty even felt jealous of Sarah's charismatic intellect.

Looking back on Sarah's life close to four decades after she died, it is clear that most of her life is indeed unhistoric, in the sense of not being recorded in history books. Yet, what is also clear is that Sarah's influence on those around her was often enormous. As for Sarah's own preaching, *that* is deep and illuminating too, and that is precisely why embarking on the detective story of writing her biography seems a worthwhile undertaking.

While most of Sarah's life was unhistorical, it is, of course, far from being the case that *all* of it was. As Andy Warhol famously remarked in the program for an exhibition of his work at the Moderne Museet in Stockholm, Sweden, 'in the future, everyone will be famous for fifteen minutes'. While this is not such a modern sentiment as might be imagined (the expression 'nine days' wonder' goes back at least to the sixteenth century), Warhol's comment has become regarded as a pertinent modern take on the nature of fame in the era of mass communications.

Sarah's fame today is due to what may, in retrospect, seem a bizarre accident: that she was in the right place at the right time and as a result was lucky enough to be given immortality by the pen of a remarkably gifted writer. But the truth, very likely, is that that gifted writer was even luckier to meet Sarah than she was to meet him. Thanks to her, the word 'Quality' has a resonance and meaning today that it never had before Sarah used the word to the writer, who subsequently featured her in his book.

As mentioned in previous chapters, in two public presentations, Pirsig in discussing Quality and Sarah, says similarly:

> *And SHE had a sense of Quality. A brilliant teacher. They* [her students] *called her 'The Divine Sarah".*

And although there is no reason to doubt Pirsig's important two public revelations, we are not aware of any independent confirmation. So indeed, it isn't known who originated this very revealing description of her.

People don't get called 'Divine' for no reason. It's a word used, of course, to describe a woman's beauty. Sarah was not, in fact, a great beauty, though she was by no means unattractive. But she was called divine for another reason: People who knew her most fondly, felt that her thinking, and her approach to life, affected them in an incandescent, profound, unforgettable way. Sarah was a woman for all time, a woman for our times, a woman, above all, of Quality.

Chapter 6: Between the Lines: A View of Sarah As Seen In Her Two Works:
The Philosophy of Horace (Masters 1921) and
Catullus: A Stylistic Study (PhD 1923).

In the famous 1931 murder trial *Rex vs A, A. Rouse*, in the United Kingdom, Norman Birkett a barrister of legendary reputation in Britain in the 1930's, was working on a murder case where there was no direct evidence of the accused's guilt but an abundance of

> ...circumstantial evidence may be of such texture, such strength, such potency as to be superior almost to direct evidence.

Norman Birkett's assertion here is, we believe, extremely relevant to this chapter.
  It's an unusual chapter, because it seeks to do precisely, albeit for different ends, what Norman Birkett sought to achieve when presenting a plethora of circumstantial evidence in the case of Alfred Arthur Rouse ... who was accused of having deliberately committed a gruesome murder, staged to appear as his death, so he could disappear and start a new life, leaving his numerous financial and personal problems behind.
  Here, our intention is precisely the opposite: we want someone to *appear*: in this case Sarah.
  We want to bring into relief more of her character and outlook on life, and because there is indeed relatively little direct evidence which does

this. We propose here to look at Sarah's two main publications and see what of her character can be extrapolated from them.

In view of the limited biographical information there is about Sarah, we as co-authors are naturally very keen to present as much of Sarah's personality in this book as we are able to identify, prove, or infer. However, in our enthusiasm, it is important we don't give the wrong impression about the true nature and purpose of either her two academic theses, nor 'over-do-it' when we infer Sarah's 'personality' from either of her ninety-five-year-old academic studies respectively of ancient Roman Poetry and Philosophy. So here is what we see in Sarah's *The Philosophy of Horace* and her *Catullus: A Stylistic Study*.

On the face of it, the material might seem somewhat unpromising. These, her first publications, were academic theses, which Sarah submitted for the University of Wisconsin degrees of respectively Master of Arts in 1921, and PhD in 1923, when Sarah was respectively twenty-seven and twenty-nine years old and still Sarah Winifred Jennings, and very much still the farm girl from Dallas Center, Iowa.

Sarah's original typed paper copies of both her thesis are held in the Library of the University of Wisconsin. We use as primary resource, reproductions of both Sarah's theses:

A) Our copy of *The Philosophy of Horace by Sarah Winifred Jennings* is a facsimile edition by Nabu Public Domain Reprints

Company. It is significant that Sarah's Horace is now in print, and done so as 'culturally important' in the estimation of Nabu Company.

B) Our copy of *Catullus: A Stylistic Study, by Sarah Winifred Jenning,* is a scanned digital-download version sent by email to us by The University of Wisconsin Library. A Google search for above *italic,* will find this full text thesis, and perhaps even a Google Books version.

Sarah's two theses consist of a total of double spaced typed pages of 36 and 147 pages respectively. Of these pages, about three-quarters consists of Latin Language quotations (or phrases) from the works of the historically prominent Roman Poet Horace, and a similar amount from the works of the great Roman poet Catullus. These Latin passages are always followed by an English translation. It is not entirely clear who undertook the translations, but it seems likely it is Sarah who did this.

We believe that in writing both these theses, Sarah – perhaps unwittingly – reveals quite a lot about her own personality, in two ways.

Firstly, she says things about either Horace, or Catullus, which clearly illuminate how she sees the world. Secondly, the very fact that she chooses certain aspects of the philosophy of these writers to focus on, in either of her two theses, is unquestionably evidence of how she sees Horace (or Catullus), and how she sees life generally.

Obviously, the things people select to talk about, such as activities and other people they bring into their lives, tell us a great deal about who that particular person is as a human being.

The conclusions we draw in this chapter should not be seen as dogmatic. Ultimately, this whole process of reading between the lines, which gives this chapter its title, is of course a kind of detective work which would be unlikely to be taken very seriously in a court of law, where either direct evidence or compelling circumstantial evidence is what is required.

We're not suggesting that our conclusions here in this chapter invariably amount to compelling circumstantial evidence, but certainly believe they amount to valid evidence as we seek to reveal to the reader as much as we can appropriately detect of the personality of Sarah.

So it seems perfectly legitimate, to see what can be revealed about her in these two theses. After all, it's commonplace for biographers to make observations about the persona or personae shown in their fiction writing, even though it is perfectly possible that a writer might not necessarily be being himself or herself in their fiction writing... Likewise in the case of Sarah's non-fiction narrative theses, we conclude that what she says about Horace and about Catullus are indeed reasonably likely to be self-revelatory about her own attitudes. And indeed, as we show below *Sarah <u>actually says</u> this is true in her <u>own</u> words,* as she quotes Catullus saying the same.

Of course, for the reader, the facts should speak for themselves.

Let's Start With Sarah Writing About Horace.

He is, of course, one of the most important Roman writers. His full name was Quintus Horatius Flaccus. He was born on December 8, 65 BCE and died on November 27, 8 BCE. Known in the English-speaking world as Horace, he was the leading Roman lyric poet during the time of Augustus. The Roman rhetorician Quintillian once observed that he regarded Horace's *odes* as just about the only Latin lyrics worth reading.

As Quintillian says of Horace: 'He can be lofty sometimes, yet he is also full of charm and grace, versatile in his figures, and felicitously daring in his choice of words.'

Horace is generally known as a poet, but showing her own focus, Sarah entitles her thesis *The Philosophy of Horace*. And this is indeed what we see. Sarah is primarily interested in him, not as a poet, but as a philosopher, which involves her extrapolating from his work what she sees, or chooses to see, as his philosophy. We present here our selection from her written observations on Horace which we are suggesting in our view, illuminates Sarah's *own* attitude towards life, right living, virtue, value, and similar. Throughout, these comments by Sarah reveal a worldly, highly intelligent, urbane, pragmatic lady who is fascinated with life and with the experiences of life, and devotes full energy at enjoying life and gusto: Such revelations harmonise rather nicely with how living witnesses, such as Dennis Garry, remember Sarah. Beyond her writing, in a very high quality of English prose, we see her appreciation of the Roman Empire, of literature, and of the sensuous delights of life. Sarah writes this:

'Horace was thoroughly Roman, and the Romans, except only a few lofty souls such as Lucretius, Cicero, and Virgil, were of a practical, mundane nature. They cared little for abstractions or speculation. They were born to rule and the philosophy that appealed to them was that which would give them mastery over self, and hence over the world.

But everywhere around him Horace saw the tremendous waste of human energy, struggling man, feverishly pursuing the bubbles that do not satisfy, frittering away their manhood, consuming time and not achieving the mastery of life to which their heritage entitled them.

For such an audience, then, in which the will to live was the dominant characteristic, Horace, the sane, tolerant, and sympathetic man of the world, with the insight which comes from contemplation and the inspiration which comes from the realization of the dignity of his task, formulated his philosophy of living, a simple, practicable code of ethics, to help man to saner, worthier, happier lives: a code which furnished the solution to the problems of life. It is not an explanation of life, but a way of life, something tangible, a touchstone by which men may test their own worth and contentment. ….. '

Later, on pages 9 and 10, we see similar emphasis by Sarah, in her own words:

'His [Horace's] fresh beginning in Rome in a most humble position, gave him the first taste of the real struggle for the great mass of men for the mere means of existence. From this position he could see the weaknesses of the poor, their unrest, and idle craving for the wealth which they failed to see was not conducive to happiness. It is perhaps from this phase of his existence that Horace gained an appreciation of the simple joys of life which are attainable for all – sunshine, the shade of trees, the river, wine etc.

Lastly, his friendship with Maecenas [Maecenas was Octavian's right-hand man in civil affairs] coming after the bitterness of life, afforded him the leisure to devote himself to poetry. He [Horace] had learned too well the instability of position to value it over-highly, but from this relationship he Draws the principles which he lays down as guides for patron and client.

The burthen [that is, main emphasis] of Horace's philosophy of life is the attainment of happiness. Since he has tasted the sweetness and the bitterness of life, and now by virtue of his devotion to poetry is somewhat removed from the toil and moil of the world, he thinks that he has a better perspective, a better judge of the eternal values of the great majority of men,

> blinded to the larger view by the details, and hence first undertakes an explanation of the nature of happiness.
>
> Ultimately [Horace argues] happiness is the product of a definite attitude toward life. It is not a mere matter of chance. It is within the reach of all who care enough for it to pursue it in the right way. An idle, aimless, drifting existence would never obtain the goal. The thoughtless, short-sighted Roman world must be brought to realize this, must be aroused to a contemplation of the issues of life, for he who neglects them will suffer for his neglect.
>
> If a man really desires happiness he must have an aggressive attitude toward it, for what is worth achieving can be won only at the expense of vigorous effort.'

Sarah shows how Horace examines wealth, ambition, food and wine, and mirth as potential sources of happiness, declaring that Horace finds them all wanting. In particular, she demonstrates how Horace comes down hard in rejecting the common assumption that wealth is a potential source of happiness: But note that Sarah does not say that this assumption tends to be something that only wealthy people do. And Horace appears to have led a fairly comfortable life financially, for at least some of his life after he became friends with Maecenas.

She goes on to show that Horace deeply believed that seeking happiness from external factors and outward pleasures was never going to be very successful. As she says of external pleasures:

> 'It is not that within themselves these things are wrong – only that they *are* externals and one must not attach too much significance to them. It is because men have overestimated them that the three greatest curses of the age have come upon the world – superficiality, restlessness and greed.'
>
> 'Since men are always looking for something tangible as the secret of happiness they have become shallow, have grown to care too much for outward appearance, and far too little for inward appearance, and far too little for inward worth.'

Although we believe what Sarah says of Horace, is also likely her own view, we again must emphasise that this is Sarah talking about Horace's point of view, rather than explicitly giving her own point of view about life. This process of *talking through the author's point of view* (*as if this was one's own view*), is of course common when people write. Here is Sarah again looking at happiness through Horace's eyes:

> 'And this same belief that happiness lies in externals makes men restless – a feverishness that manifests itself in the form of travelling, forever pursuing the happiness -- which forever escapes them. How foolish it is to try to escape the things which baffle one by seeking another clime. [People who devote themselves to travel] are merely consuming time, not living, who are forever on the march. They exhaust their

energies and gain nothing but discontent. And these curses of looking to externals for happiness, perhaps the worst is the curse of avarice. Why seek for much in the world when one can use so little and more cannot delight? 'Let him to whose lot falls a competency, desire nothing more' The grasping continually for more only breeds dissatisfaction. --- 'He who is all too much delighted by prosperity will be shattered by a reverse. If you dot on aught, you will be loath to forgo it.'

One is reminded of Rosalind's comment to Jacques in Shakespeare's *As You Like It*: written about sixteen hundred years after Horace was writing but conveying much of the same sentiment.

> JACQUES
> I have neither the scholar's melancholy, which is emulation, nor the musician's, which is fantastical, nor the courtier's, which is proud, nor the soldier's, which is ambitious, nor the lawyer's, which is politic, nor the lady's, which is nice, nor the lover's, which is all these: but it is a melancholy of mine own, compounded of many simples, extracted from many objects, and indeed the sundry contemplation of my travels, in which my often rumination wraps me in a most humorous sadness.
>
> ROSALIND
> A traveller. By my faith, you have great reason to be sad: I fear you have sold your own lands to see other men's; then, to have seen much and to have nothing, is to have rich eyes and poor hands.
>
> JACQUES

Yes, I have gained my experience.

ROSALIND
And your experience makes you sad: I had rather have a fool to make me merry than experience to make me sad; and to travel for it too.

Sarah also quotes Horace as saying that of all the curses of looking to externals for happiness, perhaps the worst is the curse of avarice.

> 'Why seek for much in the world when one can use so little and more cannot delight?'

Sarah says, then continues, summarising much of Horace's philosophy as she sees it:

> 'If the secret of happiness lies not in wealth, ambition, mirth or any of these external things, which in a limited measure may contribute to the richness of life, but beyond the golden mean, pursued as an end in themselves, are the cause of so much misery, discarding all such incidentals men much look for the real source of happiness within themselves. When men are dissatisfied, it is not the world which is wrong, but their own attitude towards the world.'

Sarah goes on to say of Horace's philosophy that he believes this:

> 'For if we are dissatisfied with our fortunes, our bitterness will taint every relationship in life, but if we are sane, life will look back at us with the same calm expression.'

Horace repeatedly, in Sarah's thesis, is quoted as having an aversion to the belief that *riches bring happiness*. As she says through his voice:

> 'Once the love of riches has fastened himself upon a man he cannot escape it. If he only realized what a hard master it was, he would free from it as the fox did from the lion in the old fable.'
>
> 'When men do yield once to the domination of avarice, envy, anger, public opinion, they have lost their freedom just as did the horse which summoned man to help him drive out the stag, and then could not shake the rider from his back. '
>
> 'And of no less importance is self-confidence. And man will accomplish only so much as he feels himself capable of. Let him therefore trust his own ability and others will have faith in him.'

She goes on to quote something from Horace, which will surely strike a chord in most modern readers. After all, we live in a time when many people do not believe in the afterlife, which was not necessarily so, back in 1921 when Sarah wrote this thesis. As she says of Horace in his viewpoint:

> 'The surest way to get all the possible joy out of life is to live every day as though it were the last.'

And here she quotes directly from Horace, the translation being:

> 'Amid hope and care, amid fears and passions, believe that every day has dawned for you the last; so, welcome shall arrive the hour you will not hope for.'

Sarah then interprets this passage:

> 'If men keep this thought ever in mind, they will fill each moment so full of the richness of living that there will be no regrets, no joys postponed to a future day which will never be theirs, when the summons of death does come.'

Reading this quotation, and Sarah's interpretation, one is glad of having her clarification, because Horace, like most classical writers, sometimes seems slightly obscure, although this is doubtless partly due to the fact that Latin can never be translated perfectly well into modern English.
She goes on:

> 'For there is much to enjoy in the world – and most of the really worthwhile sources of pleasure are within the reach of all.'

She quotes Horace that as regards health,

> 'There is outdoor life, simple food which nourishes without stressing'

Then as Sarah puts it,

> 'There is sunshine free to all, of which Horace is so fond', and social intercourse, which Horace praises.'

And which Sarah obviously praises too. From what we already know of her, this won't surprise us.

> 'The life of a recluse cannot be the richest one, contact with other people is both necessary and valuable'

Sarah also quotes Epicurius as saying:

> 'friendship enhances the charm of life; it helps to lighten sorrows and heightens the joys of fellowship.'

In addition to Sarah's focus on Horace's philosophy of happiness, we also see her nearly equal focus on his philosophy of living in the right way.

Because our biography is in search for the origins of Quality (*Arête*), we can't help but notice how many of her own words (and quoting those of Horace), which are *Quality related*, such as => Virtue (17), wisdom/wise (6), worth (5), value (5), right-living (6), best (2), *summum bonum* (the highest good) (3), and peace of mind (2).

As for most of Sarah's Horace Thesis, she first discusses her understanding of Horace, then quotes Horace. We see several times, where Sarah emphasizes how an arduous and disciplined effort is required, for real-world achievement of these above mention life Qualities. Here are some clear examples, where Sarah's thinking is, so to speak, on-the-cusp of Quality, but hasn't quite yet formed, so to speak, the Q word itself.

A) Sarah's summarizes, then quotes Horace: When once men do come to acknowledge that happiness is not an accident, but the logical outcome of a well-considered and constantly pursued course of life, they should give prompt attention to these matters of vital moment, and Horace indicates the first step toward the new life. 'The beginnings of virtue is to avoid vice, and of wisdom to get quit of folly.' ... 'He who begins has got the half of the work; dare to be wise; make a beginning.')

B) Sarah's summary continues, then quotes Horace: If a man really desires happiness he must have an aggressive attitude toward, it, for what is worth achieving can be won only at the expense of vigorous effort. 'He who has been afraid of failure, has remained obscure.'

C) On the next thesis page, following a pointed Horace quote, Sarah's concludes: With this awakened interest, Horace thinks it well for each man to test to the full each of the things which men from time immemorial have deemed the summum bonum, with a view to adopting as his own, which one seems to have the most real value, to bring the calm and contentment, that are significant of a live well lived. The decision is a momentous one: 'He who has not skill to know how to distinguish from the purple of Sidon, fleeces steeped in the dye of Aquinum, will not sustain a more certain loss of one nearer his heart than he who will not be able to discriminate the false from the true:

D) Sarah then, almost using word Quality, as she emphasizes, Try virtue first of all! Then quotes Horace: 'If virtue alone can bestow this, manfully give up pleasures, and make your aim.'

E) Then one page later, again, almost using word Quality, she emphasizes, and then quotes Horace: Then having advised each man to try for himself, for each must be the best judge of his own life. 'It is right for each one to measure himself by his own foot-rule.'

D) In the course of her thesis, similar to the manner above, Sarah brings out other facets of Horace, with which no doubt she agrees:

1) The need to control anger, avarice, greed, loose tongue, drunkenness.

2) Mixed in are achievement of good in: Self-confidence, friendship, social intercourse, patronage, leadership, government, ...

We believe that such statements and general focus, A) through G) above, are clear precursors (fore-runners) of not only Sarah's Quality (*Arête*), but also the focus and life behaviour of the MSU Professor, that Sarah was to become.

Arguably, Sarah, in her late twenties, was already a life and blood incarnation of:

E) Virtue, Value (ie Quality) in the making, as well as,
F) Right-living, and 'the logical outcome of a well-considered and constantly pursued course of life excellence' (ie Quality *Arête*),

In other words, as Sarah wrote her two theses, she was indeed, A*n Incarnation of Quality!*

Sarah finishes this well-written, enjoyable, and illuminating thesis – which is readily available as a facsimile edition and which we recommend to any particularly avid student of Sarah's life – by quoting Horace's prayer which she describes as *'the best possible summary of Horace's own summary.'*

And in thinking back over all of her *Philosophy of Horace,* we realize this following *Horace Prayer*, is the nearest she comes to her own statement of, *A Manifesto of a life of Quality.*

'May I have what now I have or even less, provided I may live for myself the remainder of my days, if only the Gods will any to remain for me. May I have a good stock of books and of provisions for each year, and may I not waver, trembling on the hopes of the uncertain hour [of my eventual demise and death]. But it is enough to beseech Jove for what he gives and takes away, to give life, to give means; a contented spirit I will myself provide.''

o00O00o

Moving On Now To Sarah's Thesis About Catullus, We Come To A Very Different Work Which Offers Correspondingly Different But Discernible, Insights Into Sarah's Personality.

Gaius Valerius Catullus, who lived approximately from 84 BCE to 54 BCE, and so was only thirty years old when he died, was a Latin poet of the late Roman Republic who wrote poetry which is still much enjoyed today even by people whose knowledge of Latin is slim or zero.

The simplicity and vigour of the poetry by Catullus makes it comparatively easy to translate into modern languages. And because the language he uses tends to be fairly straight-forward, his poetry is particularly attractive to people who have a relatively small knowledge of Latin, and want (in English), to feel what the heartbeat felt like of a Roman. In his day, the poetry of Catullus was widely appreciated by Roman citizens, by members of the Roman Empire, and by other Roman poets. He is recognised as having greatly influenced poets such as Ovid, Horace and Virgil. His work was relatively forgotten after the collapse of the Roman Empire, but was rediscovered in the late Middle Ages. His explicit writing style has shocked many readers. He was not pornographic, but he was indeed explicit, and his love poems are often both bawdy and highly emotional.

French and Latin Professor Stanley F. Levine, an expert on European literatures, an aficionado of Catullus, and reads fluently in Latin, says:

> 'I like Catullus because he seems to me the most modern of classical poets. His focus on the complexity and ambiguity of the author / implied author / narrator, and how that establishes a multi-layered relationship with the reader, and his delight in, and play with language, are among the elements that underlay his appeal to a contemporary Post-Modern sensibility.'

(NOTE: Dr. Levine prior to retirement, was Professor of Latin & French, at the University of South Carolina Aiken.)

It's not particularly surprising that Sarah enjoyed the energy and sensuousness of Catullus' poetry. But as in the case of Horace, Sarah is primarily interested in Catullus as a philosopher, which involves her extracting and extrapolating from his work, what she sees, or chooses to see, as his philosophy.

Sarah's thesis about Catullus is approximately 24,000 words long. The scanned source text we used, apparently the only source text available of this obscure publication has numerous places where the scan does not show the original document clearly enough. All the same, most of the document is quite clear, as to Sarah's passion for Catullus' work, and her commitment to the subject she's writing about.

What immediately strikes the reader about Sarah's Catullus thesis is that it consists mostly of lists of Latin words and phrases contained in Catullus' work. These lists are mainly typed as run-on listings of Latin phrases, each having a reference code number indicating poem name and line. These are collected into Sarah's organizational categories of: *Epithets, Intensity, Simplicity, Descriptive Power.*

We believe that Sarah derived her skill, facility and power with Latin, from a) her high school, college, and university classics training, b) the four years Grinnell training required for Latin Teaching Certification, c) her four years teaching High School Latin and Ancient Roman History full time, plus d) her approximately three years graduate school Latin teaching assignments. This extensive teaching experience reminds Henry of two well-founded truisms: *The one who teaches, learns best and the most!. ... AND ... They who dare to teach, must and will, never cease to learn!*

Thus Sarah's skill, zest, passion, and thrill with Catullus' Latin Poetry words had its gestation in her eleven years of Latin teaching or preparation for teaching.

In each of her categories and sub-categories of her Stylistic Study, her emphasis is seeking out each and every shade and variation of Latin word phrase that Catullus works into his poems.

Nowhere does Sarah attempt to explain or justify the 'analysis' system chosen. Sarah's <u>only</u> explanation <u>anywhere</u> in her thesis, is this:

> As will be noted from the above list of categories, this study is exclusive of the lyrical and luminous qualities of Catullus Poetry.

So, on purpose we are <u>not</u> offered a study of these poems <u>real purpose</u>, but just categorized lists of phrases in Latin.

Clearly, Sarah - or probably more likely her thesis advisor, Professor Moses Stephen Slaughter - somehow thought that all these lists of individual words (with no comparative statistical analysis, intercultural, developmental, or other interweaved study) would somehow be of value or interest to those interested in Catullus.

In field research at Grinnell College Archives, we discovered a copy of Slaughter's *own* Johns

Hopkins University PhD Thesis (1891), *'The Substantives of* [Roman Poet] *Terence'*: Here Professor Slaughter partly supplies the needed answer, where on page 1, we read:

> 'No excuse is necessary at the present time, for a new venture in this line [over those of less ambitious investigators], since scholars are agreed that all satisfactory criticism must, at least in part, based on carefully prepared and exhaustive statistics. From such statistical, it is possible to judge with satisfactory certainty, rather than trust to impressions necessarily unsafe, however nearly a subtle appreciation of language may have suggested right conclusions.'

Approximately half of Slaughter's thesis is structured (as is Sarah's) with voluminous lists of Latin words, categorised (as also does Sarah), under Slaughter's thesis sections titled *'Proper Names'*, *'Words First Found In Terence'*, *'Greek Words'*, *'Compounds'*, *'Diminutives'*, etc.

Thus Professor Slaughter's *'exhaustive statistics'* is indeed what is seen in both his and Sarah's thesis! Apparently this is an early use of the branch of Literary Criticism, which came to be called 'Formalism', which in-turn seeks 'to place the study of literature on a scientific & statistical basis.' But for Henry, being "scientific" must go well beyond => A mere listing, unadorned counting, or dumb a̲c̲counting of piles of words!

What isn't explained is the intriguing: Why Sarah's PhD Catullus thesis should be, in so many ways so different, in approach and style of analysis, contrasted with her earlier Master's thesis on Horace.

As regards the actual logistics of producing the thesis, the mixture of Latin words and discursive English comment, along with English translations of some of the Latin words and phrases must have made this task a formidable typing job. Unfortunately, as is the case for her Horace thesis, we don't know for certain whether Sarah typed the thesis out herself, and it is unwise to assume she did, in the absence of any definite evidence either way. But we both believe that most likely it was Sarah who typed the thesis because the cost of getting it typed would be high at any time, and would seem particularly expensive for a student who, due to her farm background appears to have been fairly frugal and sensible with money. Life on farms in Ohio and Iowa earlier in the twentieth century was financially often difficult and the habit of frugality and making-do with her own efforts, would have most likely have been ingrained into Sarah from her childhood.

There is an another convincing reason why Sarah most likely did this typing: If she had been using some other person to do it, that other person would have had to have been an expert in Latin, or they would have found unbearably onerous, the task of typing accurately the seeming endless lists of Latin words. Moreover, if Sarah had used the third-party to type the thesis, the extra cost of someone who was able to type Latin seems it would have been very high indeed, and very likely beyond her financial means.

As this chapter deals with circumstantial evidence, we both think it is reasonable to conclude that Sarah most likely did type this thesis. If this is so, then she had accomplished an unquestionably great feat of high typing accuracy, since there are relatively few typing inaccuracies in the text attributable to the typist.

As we already stated, 'What Sarah says about Horace and about Catullus is reasonably likely to be, and can't help but be, self-revelatory about her own attitudes: And we also already showed how this applied to Sarah's writing in her *'Books I've Enjoyed'* and her Master's thesis, *'The Philosophy of Horace.'*

This is how Sarah *starts* her thesis about Catullus: We are immediately struck, with how this very necessity of a writer's 'self-revelation', is very much on the mind of Catullus, and even more so on the mind of our Sarah.

> 'La style c'est l'homme meme. [*'The style is of the same man,* 'meaning the man's readily recognizable manner and habits.] A poet's habits of expression are inexplicably interwoven with his habits of feeling and thinking. What the poet says and how he says it are fundamentally inseparable. His style is not a thing apart from himself, as the older rhetoricians would have us believe; composition follows the lines of the poet's own nature. It is precisely because he is such a man that he expresses himself in such a way. As Saint-Beuve has said, 'literature is the expression of personality.'

> It is in this broad sense of style – the man and his expression, one and inseparable, that I have prepared this study of Catullus. '

After her introduction, and at the very start of her Chapter 1, entitled *Epithets*, Sarah further brings out a writer's necessarily revealed, self-revelation:

> 'The essence of his style is in his epithets, for they reveal the man and the poet, his reactions to life, and his ability to express his reactions aptly.
> '

In the above two passages, *we see Sarah's own clear statement*, that a writer's own personality can't help but be in their words, which is of course, our position in this chapter. Perhaps this was on her mind as she was writing, and she deliberately 'wrote-herself-into' her theses, or at least did not seek to keep her personality at a distance. Here is an example, which is at the very start of her Chapter II on Catullus' Intensity:

> 'INTENSITY: *Odii et amo "I hate and I love"* is the burden of Catullus's song, proclaiming the depth of feeling that informs every line. Moderation is no virtue in his sight. The extravagance of youth is the dominant note in his nature. He gives free rein to his emotions, and reacts with passionate intensity to every situation in life. He is on the heights or in the depths, never at the calm level which self-control maintains. This intensity finds expression in

Contrast, Parallelism, Repetition, Fullness of Expression, Indefinites, Comparatives, Superlatives, and Diminutives.

These above nine divisions of intensity appear as sub-titles, in subsequent sections of Sarah's Chapter II.

She adds this explanation:

> 'Catullus faithfully follows the laws of emphasis by placing the important words in stressed positions, i.e. at the beginning and end of the line. In the following pages on contrast, repetition, etc., the words at the beginning of the line are capitalized, those at the end underscored.'

Much of this thesis is seemingly only for Latin specialists because much of it is in Latin, with Sarah quoting these endless lists Latin words, phrases and sometimes sentences from Catullus' work. She also (in Latin) makes reference to epithets used by other Latin poets. Although, fortunately the non-specialist, these Latin portions are everywhere followed by a translation to English.

Throughout the Latin material, Sarah offers very useful insights and observations about Catullus himself, especially a view into Catullus' philosophic generalisations about life. As was the extrapolated from the Horace thesis, we again suggest that Sarah most likely focussed on those aspects of Catullus' philosophy, with which she felt attuned as a human being. Yet although Sarah's material about Catullus is more formal, there is still the sense that, indeed between the lines, Sarah is responding to Catullus' verse in a very direct and human way. For example when she says:

> 'Catullus has a spontaneity and vigour of Homer without his physical exuberance. He [Catullus] has no idealistic visions about the great Roman world, as has Virgil. Living among men, seeing them with eyes that are often disillusioned he is yet _far_ from attaining the aloofness and gentle tolerance of life characteristic of Horace.'

Sarah then adds:
> Catullus is a fervid friend, a violent enemy, a passionate lover. He is too close to life to speculate upon it. Whatever his sensations may be they are to him worthy of communication.

It's important to bear in mind when Sarah wrote this thesis in 1923, the word 'man' in English meant something a little different from what it does today. In those days, the word 'man' very literally embraced women and meant something like 'humankind.' In our day, when very reasonably women resent being lumped together under the word for a male human being, 'man' means precisely that.

Some insights into Sarah's personality can be gleaned from how she seems particularly drawn to words and phrases in Catullus' work, which evoke bright colors and attractive and stirring sights. One feels that Sarah was very much alive to her senses. And indeed we can extrapolate this also, from some of the comments which people who knew her have made about her, such as Shirley Luhrsen's discussion of Sarah's apartment. Thus, Sarah seems to have been, we might say, a very alive sort of person. She liked bright colors, she liked radiance, she liked fine quality household furnishings, as well as the gleam of gold, silver, and other bright shiny metallic colors. She was a woman, one feels, who was visually very aware and found the visual and experiential right-now aspects of life extremely exciting. At one point in the thesis, commenting on Catullus' work, she observes:

'Sometimes there is a riot of color … '

And this indeed could be a fitting description of Sarah's own personality. She dwells for some time on the sensory aspects of epithets used by Catullus and offers us some very fine writing about the senses. For example:

'The most realistic of the sensory epithets [in Catullus' work] are those of touch. Sometimes in these physical sense is stronger than the metaphysical and they are lifted from the realm of sense only by the fine veil of imagination which association sheds upon them.'

Sarah goes on to observe:

> 'Because of this sensuous fondling of lovely things, in human and in animate, Catullus has been given the title of *'caresser of life.''*

Later in the same chapter, Sarah observes of Catullus:

> 'He writes frequently of banquets, but his anticipations and reminiscences of them are of the laughter and repartee, the brilliant interchange of ideas, almost never of the viandes.'

Reading this, one is reminded, perhaps, of the great Victorian novelist Charles Dickens, who himself of course wrote abundantly about meals but was anything but a foodie and tends always to focus on the conviviality of the event rather than the food itself, even what is perhaps the most famous food scene in Dickens, the scene in *David Copperfield* where Mr. Micawber comes to the rescue when David is trying to organise a dinner party but the joint of lamb that he's ordered to be cooked by his servant is inadequately cooked and pink in the middle. Mr. Micawber attends to this by making the lamb into a devilled grill which Dickens describes with such sensuous pleasurable, effectiveness that it is hard to read it (if one is not a vegetarian, at least) without wanting to immediately go away and have a devilled grill of lamb right that very moment. But all the same, and even in this scene, Dickens focuses on the conviviality rather than the food.

Concerning Sarah's above word *viandes*: Sarah seems to naturally use, the Latin word *viandes*. Wiktionary.org defines: 'Noun viande (feminine, plural viandes): 1) Meat, 2) (obsolete) food, 3) Sexuality an object of sexual desire; Literally a piece of meat.'

This explanation 3), above may be significant, if we think that from an 'earthy' farm upbringing, young-adult Sarah became this worldly? Is this connected with what Dennis Gary observes elsewhere in this book, *A Woman of Quality*: ?

> 'In our Shakespeare class she [Sarah] told us that all great Drama consisted of blood, guts, and sex.'

Sarah's comments on Catullus do sometimes include phrases and philosophies that are clearly also hers: At one point she remarks

> ' ... youth is often cruel to age ... '

Here it is clear that this is Sarah talking rather than Catullus. ... And yet she is never far from returning to her main subject: the sensuous and emotional energy of Catullus' work and the brightness and even incandescence of his language and his images. As she observes, for example:

> 'One of the chief sources of Catullus' power is found in the combination of sensory and emotional appeal... '

Sometimes, in reading both the Horace thesis and the Catullus thesis, one wonders whether Sarah actually chose these two immortal writers because there were aspects of their own philosophy and approach to life, which clearly to us, must have made a big impression on her. Is it at least possible, that what she often says about these writers, also applies to her? Conceivably, she may not have consciously been aware of this, but it certainly seems to have been something that needs raising here, as she might be projecting herself and her own personality into these theses. After all, people often choose to admire certain great writers because aspects of the great writers appeal to their own personalities. She even says of Catullus:

> 'Although Catullus does not prize wealth for its own sake, as we shall show later, a certain aristocratic refinement and elegance are necessary to him. Such refinement, with its freedom from self-consciousness, and from interest in material interests ... is the product of contact with others... and of a certain amount of leisure... In his judgment of people, [Catullus rates] physical attractiveness, conformity to the rules of social usage, and good taste ... very highly.'

In the above, we insert the ellipses ... where Sarah quotes Latin words from Catullus' work and the square brackets contain reasonable assumptions about what she meant when this is not clear. Sarah also comments on Catullus' own attitude towards the family:

> 'He has a strong sense of the dignity of family life, but the warmth of affection with which he invests family ties has a passionate intensity that few Romans manifested.'

Here, as elsewhere, one feels that Sarah did indeed see Horace and Catullus as kindred spirits: finding a philosophy of life congenial to her and to her intellectual interests and emotional preoccupation as a human being. This, we believe, was clearly of enormous importance to her. It is perhaps not going too far to say that seeking this philosophy of life was very likely a major reason for Sarah to have chosen to deeply study and write at all about Horace and Catullus. (This is a topic we closely examine in our next chapter, focusing on Sarah's Undergraduate School Grinnell College and Graduate School University of Wisconsin. We also include in our considerable research discoveries as to just who was her University of Wisconsin thesis advisor, Prof. M. S. Slaughter, PhD.)

Not surprisingly, given that Catullus is probably the greatest of the Roman love-poets, and one of the greatest love-poets of all time, Sarah gives careful consideration to what Catullus said about love.

> 'In Catullus' estimate the greatest human experience is love...that power which subdues the will of the mighty...sometimes it is a

soothing balm…sometimes it is at once a delight and a torture…sometimes it is suffering more acute than any physical.'

Sarah goes on to add:

'The ecstasy of love is the phrase which is most familiar to Catullus' turbulent nature it is like a destructive fire…it is a ruinous passion…and [it is] fatal to the peace of mortal minds…to Catullus, stolidity is one of the most irritating characteristics. The yearning for human love and companionship makes loneliness intolerable.'

We have mentioned Sarah's seeming endless lists of Catullus' Latin words, totalling about 3400 line entries. The following excerpt (on Love topic), will serve as an example of these entries. We choose this entry, since these are one of the easier for a speaker of English to penetrate her choice of Catullus' Latin. Where Sarah typed these as un-spaced, full lines of run-on-strings, we for reading clarity, separate into 14 successive 'paragraph groupings'. [We have below used Courier New, Size 12, since this duplicates Sarah's thesis typing. Due to above mentioned OCR errors, there are likely residual wrong spellings in a few of Sarah's Latin words, in this chapter. If an accurate version is needed, please consult Catullus' original poems.]

```
In Catullus' estimate the greatest human
experience is love, altus amor 68.117,
meae vitae 104,1,
```

that power which subdues the will of the mighty: flexanimo amore 64.330,

Sometimes it is a soothing balm, dulcis amor 66.1, 68.4, 68.96, dulces amores 78.3, iucundum amorem 109.1,

sometimes it is at once a delight and a torture,
duplex Amathusia 68.51, dulcem amaritiem 68.18,

sometimes it is suffering more acute than any physical pain: infesto amore 99.11, taetrum moribund 76.25,

The ecstasy of love is the phrase which is most familiar to Catullus' turbulent nature. It is like a destructive fire, Crudelior ignis 62.20, gravis ardor 2.8, impensius uror 72.5, vilior uror 72.6, levior uror 72.6, tenuis flamma 51.9, misellae ignes 35.14, incensua (Catullus) 50.8, flagrantia lumina 64.91, flagraes Laodamia 68.73, ardente corde 64.124, ardens (Ariadne) 64.197, ardenti iuveni 62.23,

or like madness: vesano Catullo 7.10, sana (Lesbia) 83.4

Once, in a powerful figure, he pictures love as the combination of these deadly forces: vesana flamma 100.7It

is a ruinous passion, perdito amore 91.2, impotente amore 35.12, misero amore 91.2, (though once he makes bold to jest about it [misery love] misero amore 99.15),

and fatal to the peace of mortal minds: impotens (Catullus) 8.9, ebrioa ocellos 46.11, indomitua

[Note that in following various forms of cupid ~= love]

(Catullus)50.11 , dominam cupidum 61.32, anxilo amautibua 61.47, cupido aure 61.549 cupido lumina 64.86, cupidae mentis 64.147, cupido marito 64.374, cupida mente 64.398, (cui) cupido 107.1, mihi cupido 107.4, 107.6, caeca (Ariadne) 64.197

Above we said 'one wonders whether Sarah actually chose these two immortal writers because there were aspects of their own philosophy and approach to life.' ... Does this really apply to her?'

To be really sure such was true in Sarah's two thesis, Henry went looking both for this, and specific examples of Sarah's personality. As he studied Sarah's thesis for the fifth time, and had just finished identifying, some 130 passages that he felt reflected aspects of her personality, he suddenly had a series of successive realizations:

A) Sarah's own poetical-metaphorical, writing style is readily revealed here, perhaps better than any of her other written works that we have.

B) Not only in her own English words of explanation, but also to the discerning eye hidden within those awesome long strung-on-multiple-series of Catullus' Latin Words.

Sarah was running on her pure love of the effect of Catullus' poetry.

C) Also, in typing these passages, she is feeling its power, she is resonating inside with her love of the sound of Catullus' Latin.

D) In other words, we can see in how she has 'flowed' Catullus' rhetorical gestures' into her typing, made them manifest, and has become strongly poetically moved herself.

E) Sarah, in setting down the words that she finds exciting, moving and emotional in her listing of Catullus' Latin words, is either accidentally, or subconsciously, or very likely deliberately, creating a new kind of poetic rhetoric: Let's call this "Sarah's Alternate Elevated Poetic Dimension", where she is resounding for the love of the sound of Catullus' Latin! In her typing, There we can see how she, in turn, was stimulated into excited poetical effect, that spoke in images, scenes, emotions, and inspirations.

F) Thus the Hidden Becomes Manifest! And the reader must read into Sarah's lines the same!

G) At first both James and Henry thought Sarah's typed run-on-strings, were mere listing of words:

H) And for this reason, Sarah's Alternate Elevated Poetic Dimension was hidden and almost entirely missed!

Clearly, Sarah wants us to 'get-into' the experiences and inspiration she sees, and then, join her to caress and love what she, with great effort, has so lovingly typed. Of course, in the process, we see how involved Sarah is in that Ancient Classical World, and thus just who Sarah is. She was, after all, as she said to Robert Pirsig "I'm a classical scholar".

Let's also remember that Dennis Gary recalled '[in class] Dr. Vinke reading short passages of Homer's Iliad aloud in Greek. It is also clear that Sarah was deeply interested in trying to communicate to the reader her fierce love of the effect of Catullus' poetry. In typing these passages, she is feeling its power. She is resounding for the love of the sound of Catullus' Latin. She is in 'a felt change of conscious', in the words of Owen Barfield. This love and excitement is what we see emerging.

Given that Sarah chose this Catullus thesis topic in the first place, it is highly likely that Sarah, like countless generations before, was fascinated and greatly inspired by Catullus. And then, as her thesis work progresses, she necessarily becomes deeply involved in the active searching and reading of Catullus's Poems: From this she is surely, all over again, inspired, prompted by, guided by the 'music of Catullus'. We must keep in mind that Sarah, as a thesis researcher, must comb repeatedly through the massive volumes of his poetry, looking for specific 'poetic characteristics', called for in various hierarchical parts of her thesis, such as in the love *(amor)* excerpt as we have given above.

As we said above: It is easy to <u>miss</u> what we describe here as Sarah's *Alternate Elevated Poetic Dimension*. This lack of "seeing" brings to mind Pirsig's Rule:

> *'The typical situation is that the motorcycle doesn't work. The facts are there but you don't see them. You're looking right at them, but they don't yet have enough value.'*

In honor of the Pirsig Rule, we offer the following *second* illustrative example of Sarah's many *elevated poetic passages*. This is to emphasize, and help you see the nature of Sarah's effect here: that she creates this new kind of poetic rhetoric out of what might at first appear to be, an apparent, mere listing of words.

In Sarah's *Brightness* category of Catullus' Latin below, we have again separated into successive 'paragraph groupings' what Sarah had originally typed into completely run-on-strings. Each grouping starts with her English word explanation of what she 'sees' in her chosen Catullus' Latin words.

As you read these, you will be stunned by how Sarah's examples of Catullus' '*Brightness*' just seem endless. This, by itself, will serve to illustrate just how Sarah is in love with these Latin words. She is resonating with her love of the sound of Catullus' Latin. Just grasp how she can get this excited over the string of words. Then just think how more thrilled she would have been by the total effect of Catullus' poems.

In the next paragraph below we present Sarah's *Epithets of Brightness* category of *Catullus' Latin,* just as Sarah typed into her thesis: You will see there is enough English sense in Sarah's Latin words, that you should start see how they do indeed "fit" the Poetic Effect that Sarah was trying to show you:

Epithets of Brightness.
Catullus habitually responds to the brightness of sight effects. These are his most striking

epithets. ... Like rays of light, they flash and gleam over his pages, expressing his delight in the dazzle of sunlight on water, in the soft radiance of the human body, in the delicate sheen of leaves and flowering trees.

First in importance is the blinding brilliance of sunlight, flammeus nitor 66.3, aurei oris 63.39, sole ardenti 64.354, radiantibum, oculis 63.39

that floods the world with its splendour, claram diem 61.89, oriente luce 64.376, claro lumine 64.408,

and symbolizes the acme of a lovers' happiness: candidi scles = 8.3, candidi soles 8.7,

Even the air is luminous, album aethera 63.40,

and the night is lovely with the shimmering light of the stars, micantium siderum 61.207, nicantia sidera 64.206, oaesariem fulgentiem 66.9,

some twinkling brightly, some dim in the distance, vario lumine 66.59,

or the glow of candlelight, like golden tresses: splendidas comas 61.78, aureas comas 61.95,

The gleam of quiet waters, which seem to laugh in the sunshine, linpidum lacum 4.2, liquontibus stagnis 31.2, liquidas undas 64.2, liquidie lymphis 64.162, the stormy seas, lashed to foam, albicantis litoris 63.87, candent 1. gurgite 64.14, cano gurgite 64.18, canae Tethyi 66.70,

the delicate sheen of leaves and bright flowers, flor idis ramulis 61.21 , nitens myrtus. 6122, alba parthenjoe 61.89, floridis corollis 63.66,

the glare of harvest fields, flaventia arva 64.364,

the dazzling brightness of the snow-capped mountain, nivei montis 64.240,

the flashing wings of white birds, albulus columbus 298, niveo columbo 68.125,

the shining fleece, eandentis lanae 64.31B, fulgenti auro 66.44,

the gleam of gold, and ivory, niveia sedibus 64.303, candido pede 61.115,

and precious stones, perlucidi lapidis 69.4,

and days of happiness are marked by a little white stone candidiore lapide 68.1481 candidiora nota 107,6,

all these are nature•a contributions ·to the great sum of brightness in the universe.

And there is a radiance where human hands have added, rasilem forem 61.168, politum pulvinar 64.48, splendida domus 64.46, fulgente templo 64.387, aurea corona 6660, inaurata status 81.4, which sometimes takes the form of shining raiment: candida vela 64.325, vestis candida 64.308, vestis pura 68.15, crocina tunica 68.134, aureoles pedes 61.163, luteum papauer 61.10.

Even the well-worn door sill has a polish: trito limine 68.71,

Yellow hair impresses Catullus: flavo vertice 64.63, flavo hospite 64.98, flaui vertiois 66.62, flavo viro 68.130,

Nor does he fail to note the flash of white teeth: candidos dentes 39.1, expolitior dens 39.20,

The old myths have their colorcolor too: aureolum malum 2.12, aureolum pellem 64.5,

and the brightness of white sails on the dark sea: candid vela 64235,

But the most delightful and imaginative of those epithets of brightness convey the subtle charm of youthful beauty, which appeals to Catullus as a kind of radiance, emanating from mortals as from gods.

His fancy arrays in such robes of light not only the gods, Cupido candidus 64.28,

and his cherished Lesbia, nitenti desiderio 2.5, candida diva 68.70, lux mea 68.132, lux nea 68.160,

but other lovely women as well: candida puella 13.4, candida puella 35.8, laceolae puellae 25.17, mitens uxor 61.193, candida Quintia 107.6,

The radiant bloom of youth is like the brightness of flowers: floridam puelam 61.57, viridissimo flora 17.14: florens lacohus 64.251, florida aetas 68.16.

Even the time-worn pulcher [poacher in Englsh?] is no longer vapid, but quickens into light under his touch: Thetis pulcherrima 64.28, femina pulchrior 6188,pulcherrima Laodamia 68.105, pulcher marrtua 61.198, Lesbius pulcher 79.1, pulcherrima (Lesbia) 86.5,

The soft glow of the human body fascinates Catullus, as it has the artists of every age: nudato corpore 64.17, nudatae surae 64.129, niveo pede 61.9, candida vestigia 64.162, niveos artua, 64.364, fulgentem plantam, arguta soles 68.72.

in flowers and the rosy flush of dawn: purpurea luce 64.275,

As you read Sarah's above *Epithets of Brightness*, we hope you were able to read Sarah's English words, and <u>combine with</u> each of Catullus' Latin words, and thus make use of any connections you see, that remind you of English words. This helps to bring alive what indeed might be termed the *Alternate Elevated Poetic Dimension* of Sarah's scholarly work about Catullus. We hope you saw how ... so ardently and lovingly ... Sarah wants us to become involved in Catullus' poetry.

French and Latin Professor Stanley F. Levine, an expert on European literatures, an aficionado of Catullus, and reads fluently in Latin (mentioned above), continues his thoughts, about the Sarah Catullus Thesis excerpts that appear in this chapter. Here is his response:

> Sarah's methodology in the excerpts you sent me is consistent with standard literary criticism, but she has done it exceedingly well. Sarah makes 'blindingly' evident Catullus' cascade of 'light' images. I had never realized this so clearly before, but reading her made me experience the interplay and texture of these images which she isolates and aligns within several pages. You are hit with wave after wave of brightness. It makes for very powerful reading. In order to get the same impact from reading Catullus' Poems, you would have to go through his entire volume of poems one after the other, and even then you might miss it. It is a fact, I really liked it. I did not expect this, and was so impressed at how well she does this. I find it a pity that this has never been published. PS: I really enjoyed the excerpt; its brightness left me dazzled! Before reading I should have donned a pair of sunglasses!!

Sarah's own poetical, metaphorical writing style is deeply revealed in the above: ... It is made manifest. Most of her 147-page thesis is like this. ... To our knowledge, this aspect of Sarah is illustrated nowhere else in any other of her written works. We see, and indeed experience, her thrilled enjoyment of Catullus' rhetorical gestures. We also see that she is wonderfully sensitive to Catullus' Latin and to the images and scenes in the poetry and to the emotions they inspire in her.

It is clear how thrilled she is by Catullus. And just as clearly wants us to be effected by all this poetic rhetorical effect. Of course, in the process, we see just who Sarah is.

ZMM enthusiasts who want to really see just who Sarah was, should have a good look at both her theses. Even readers who don't know Latin, will have a partial comprehension of the Latin, because so many English words (or parts, or variations), come from Latin. The more you try to find that 'sense' and 'poetic-ring', the more you will started to look for more of it, until the pattern became evident and powerful in total effect!

Dennis Gary recalls '*Dr. Vinke reading short passages of Homer's Iliad aloud in Greek,*'... even though Dennis and his fellow pupils couldn't understand it. Considering Sarah's experience and love of Latin, it would seem likely that she also read various classical works, such as in Latin, to her students, at University of Wisconsin Graduate School, at MSC, and her four years teaching High School Latin.

However, Sarah at some point must have had a considerable change of mind (discussed in our last

French and Latin Professor Stanley F. Levine, an expert on European literatures, an aficionado of Catullus, and reads fluently in Latin (mentioned above), continues his thoughts, about the Sarah Catullus Thesis excerpts that appear in this chapter. Here is his response:

> Sarah's methodology in the excerpts you sent me is consistent with standard literary criticism, but she has done it exceedingly well. Sarah makes 'blindingly' evident Catullus' cascade of 'light' images. I had never realized this so clearly before, but reading her made me experience the interplay and texture of these images which she isolates and aligns within several pages. You are hit with wave after wave of brightness. It makes for very powerful reading. In order to get the same impact from reading Catullus' Poems, you would have to go through his entire volume of poems one after the other, and even then you might miss it. It is a fact, I really liked it. I did not expect this, and was so impressed at how well she does this. I find it a pity that this has never been published. PS: I really enjoyed the excerpt; its brightness left me dazzled! Before reading I should have donned a pair of sunglasses!!

Sarah's own poetical, metaphorical writing style is deeply revealed in the above: ... It is made manifest. Most of her 147-page thesis is like this. ... To our knowledge, this aspect of Sarah is illustrated nowhere else in any other of her written works. We see, and indeed experience, her thrilled enjoyment of Catullus' rhetorical gestures. We also see that she is wonderfully sensitive to Catullus' Latin and to the images and scenes in the poetry and to the emotions they inspire in her.

It is clear how thrilled she is by Catullus. And just as clearly wants us to be effected by all this poetic rhetorical effect. Of course, in the process, we see just who Sarah is.

ZMM enthusiasts who want to really see just who Sarah was, should have a good look at both her theses. Even readers who don't know Latin, will have a partial comprehension of the Latin, because so many English words (or parts, or variations), come from Latin. The more you try to find that 'sense' and 'poetic-ring', the more you will started to look for more of it, until the pattern became evident and powerful in total effect!

Dennis Gary recalls '*Dr. Vinke reading short passages of Homer's Iliad <u>aloud</u> in Greek,*'... even though Dennis and his fellow pupils couldn't understand it. Considering Sarah's experience and love of Latin, it would seem likely that she also read various classical works, such as in Latin, to her students, at University of Wisconsin Graduate School, at MSC, and her four years teaching High School Latin.

However, Sarah at some point must have had a considerable change of mind (discussed in our last chapter), about Latin and the Romans, since Mr. Gary adds:

> 'Dr. Vinke, in fact, never made it to [discussing] the Romans. in our [Greek and Romans] Classics course, simply saying on the last day that the Romans were all a bunch of copycats and that all we had to do is substitute the Roman/Latin names for the Greek names and we would have it all.'

In many ways, the extent to which these two theses give insights into Sarah's personality is linked directly to what extent you feel her observations about Catullus are her own observations about life. This also applies in what she says about Horace. What is clear is that sometimes she is deeply moved by how Catullus, and indeed Horace, see the world. And we feel, unquestionably, that she feels much the same things that they do. These ancient Romans clearly had awakened these feelings in her, in such a form that she can articulate them. One must never go too far in this analysis, because ultimately, these are academic theses, not narratives written by Sarah or novels written by her. They are very much formal academic works. All the same, what is one to make of a page 36 sentence such as:

> 'The power of human personality is to be reckoned as another of these riddles of life – that inexplicable quality which makes men great, as incomprehensible and as wonderful as nature. Even though Catullus hates Caesar, he is forced

to recognise this quality in him – the indefinable something... '

Or this:
> 'Epithets of grief: Catullus is keenly sensitive to all the suffering in the world. He protests passionately against the cruelty of a blind fate. immitl fato 64.245, aaeva fore 64.169, acerbo casu 68.1, and there is a cry of anguish everywhere in his conception of death, supremo tempore 64.157, novissimo casu 60.4, For Catullus is so arrogantly alive that death signifies only pathos and bitterness; mutis sepulchr.ls 96.1, mutam cinerem 101.4, pallidulum pedem 65.6, letum miserabile 68.91, miseras inferias 101.2, aaerba cines
>
> Because Catullus seems made for sunshine and because his capacity for pain is infinite, he is distressed at the suffering of others: mieelli passer 3.16, miser (Attis) 63.51, 63.61, miseram {Ariadne) 64.57, 64.140, misers (Ariadne} 64.71, 64.196, misers (mater) 64.119, miseram domum 67.24 ... '

Or this...
> 'Epithets of Chastity. Catullus hardly seems a fit person to be preaching morality. And yet nothing is more evident than the fact that he regarded himself as a thoroughly exemplary person. He protests that he has passed his life puriter 76.19, and that he is castum poetam 16.6, pium poetam 16.5. ... '

Sarah also goes on to list two phrases which give a sense of Caesar's magnificence as a ruler: *magni caesaris* ('great Caesar') *imperator unice* (literally 'the only emperor', but Catullus tends to use this phrase, and indeed the previous one, ironically to mean something like 'the one and only generalissimo'.

We heartily commend to any readers who want to delve deeper into Sarah's personality and her work to look in detail at both Sarah's Horace and Catullus, since here we can only give a flavour of them. What is clear is that Sarah was profoundly moved by Catullus' work and found in it an empathy with many aspects of her own response to the world. This is how she concludes the thesis:

> 'The style of Catullus is the expression of youth, voicing ever-transient sensation and impression, not waiting for time to soften his emotions, or for retrospect to give them the proper proportions. The immediacy of expression makes his vocabulary simple, direct, and colloquial, his sentence is lucid, his meaning clear. It also makes his style extravagant, full of repetitions, superlatives, diminutives, and sweeping generalizations that reflection would have subdued. His epithets are characteristic of the impressionist, responding to the superficial aspects of life more frequently than to fundamentals. His descriptions consist of a few significant features interpenetrated by human personality and emotion.

It is the style of one who feels, not of one who thinks.'

While this final, short paragraph about the nature of Catullus' style cannot be literally true, we see Sarah's point. She is a great enthusiast of Catullus' work, and she particularly praises its emotional qualities.

We can perhaps never know to what extent Sarah herself was a person of emotion rather than of logical thought. At one level, Sarah will always, regrettably, be something of an enigma. But in her analyses and discussions of the works of Horace and Catullus, one often finds remarkable insights into the personality of this amazing woman of Quality ... Insights that are like *gold nuggets* ... *Scattered within* these purely academic theses.

Despite the fact that her theses were on poets of Ancient Rome, not Ancient Greece, we can now better understand the *ZMM* interchange between Phaedrus and Sarah in which Sarah concludes with saying that "*Quality is every part of Greek thought.*"

Chapter 7: Influences On Sarah, Gleaned From 1914 and 1915 Bulletins of Grinnell College.

And The University of Wisconsin Graduate School, For Sarah's School Years, Fall 1919 Thru, Spring 1923.

In the previous chapter, we stated => *It is perhaps not going too far to say that seeking a philosophy of life was very likely a major reason for Sarah to have chosen to deeply study and write about Horace and Catullus at all.* Also, it is clear that Sarah studied these works of Classics more for their philosophy, than for their poetry.

But altogether, it is pretty remarkable that a totally rural Iowa farm girl in the early 1900's could be among the few women to go to college and complete her AB from Grinnell College, 1914. And from this go into public high school Latin teaching from about 1916 to 1920. But she had the personality, intelligence, and grit, and in three short years achieved both her Masters and PhD, in 1921 and 1923 respectively. But still we have the question: When (and why) did she raise her sights on a PhD degree in Ancient Classics! And why the University of Wisconsin, and why Professor M. S. Slaughter, a Professor of Classics & Latin, who taught two full courses that entirely focused on respectively Horace and Catullus?

In this chapter, we try to ascertain what may have been the influences for Sarah to decide to seek an undergraduate degree from Grinnell College – the private liberal arts college in Iowa that has always been famous for its rigorous academic standards and its tradition of social responsibility. As we dig into young Sarah's educational development, we will be alert for the slightest clue as to the various influences, be they Philosophic, Greek Classics, or Roman Classics, as the basis of just how she, some 45 years later in Bozeman Montana, would on a few occasions, use the word Quality.

In our search for why Sarah chose Ancient Classics, we need to remember that in Sarah's youth about a century ago Ancient Greek Classics was a significant area of attention and learning in the United States, and although now rather less so, continues to be into the present day. This awareness had emerged with, and perhaps was to some extent, the *cause* of the founding of this country in the 1700s. The emphasis on the importance of the Ancient Classics in the early and subsequent history of the United States has its origins in the post Renaissance Enlightenment Era, which pervaded the thinking of the USA, especially in its founding fathers, and appears in the countries' documents such as: The Declaration of Independence and US Constitution.

Other examples include:

A) Greek Neoclassical Architecture, as visible on the founding fathers' mansions of Monticello (Thomas Jefferson), and Mount Vernon (George Washington).

B) The Greek Classics Architecture, with prominent Ancient Greek Temple Columns, continues and are quite visible in United States buildings of major universities and government.

C) This is also seen in the time-honoured Antebellum homes of the USA's deep south.

D) In Sarah's day, continuing to today, is the whole university phenomenon of the Greek Fraternities and Greek Sororities, with all their local chapters designated by two or three Greek alphabet letters, or spelled out versions of the same. Examples include: Phi Beta Kappa, Kappa Alpha, Alpha Tau Omega, Phi Sigma Kappa.

E) In high schools, colleges and universities many students took courses in Greek, along with study of Ancient Greece. Such courses would complement the more numerous courses in Latin language, and concurrent study of the Ancient Romans.

In summary: the USA Ancient Greek Classics state of mind (with some awareness of Latin & Ancient Romans) would have been a strong influence on our Sarah as she grew up.

Sarah, who was born only twenty-nine years after the end of the United States Civil War, would have heard plenty about the huge number of casualties caused by the war. And Sarah's Grinnell graduation coincided with the beginning of WWI, and continued into the years she taught Latin and History in High Schools in Iowa between 1916 and 1920. This war doubtless affected her philosophical life outlook, and the adult she was to become. We have already mentioned her general hatred of war.

We now turn to examine the influences on Sarah, using as resource the course catalogues at Grinnell College, Grinnell, Iowa, where Sarah was an undergraduate for four years. Grinnell is just eighty miles, by mainline railroad, east of Sarah's farm and hometown, Dallas Center, Iowa. We also use Published Course Offerings of her Graduate School, University of Wisconsin, where her Masters and PhD Thesis seem to build on the fact that Sarah spent four years teaching High School Latin Language and History in Iowa Public Schools. We examined such course catalogues by Internet searches. In *The Iowa College Bulletins* (Grinnell, we see that Sarah (as Sarah Winifred Jennings) is listed in all four years of attendance and as a graduate. We also see excellent confirmation of their strong classics program.

As we read Grinnell College official publications about their courses, professors, and college staff, we can't help but conclude that the whole campus expects a lot of itself, and this most certainly would be transmitted by osmosis to their students.

This quotation below taken from Grinnell Bulletin Catalogue 1914 gives some insight into these rigorous standards, and a view of Sarah's life at Grinnell, which as in this concurrent Victorian Society, demanded extreme control over the morals of young women.

> The young women of all the departments of the institution are under the general supervision of the Dean of Women. During the past year, the young women of the College organized a Women's Self Government League, having as its object a desire to strengthen the spirit of co-operation and unity, to preserve the social standards of the College and to make the individual lives of the young women more wholesome by sensible living. The regulations formulated and adopted by the young women them- selves include the following points: Study hours on Monday, Tuesday, Wednesday and Thursday extend from 1:15 to 4:15 and from 7:30 to 9:30. Doors shall be locked at 10:00 o'clock and lights out at 10:30. The closing hour on Sunday night shall be the same as that for the four days just mentioned. On Friday and Saturday, these evenings being recreation evenings, doors shall be locked at 11:00 o'clock and lights out at 11:15. There shall be no attendance of students at dances during the school term. Sunday shall be kept free from picnics, strolling, driving and calling. Young women who wish to leave town shall first confer with the Dean of Women. The proctors in co-operation with the women in whose houses the young women find homes assume special

responsibility for their conduct.' Our sources for Grinnell College, both above and below were:

Another article in a college publication says:

> ... the principle of self-governance has always been a foundation of a Grinnell education. And since the opening of the dorms, Grinnell students have been responsible for many decisions about how they would live in their residence halls, and governance structures have long existed to assist that process.'

The Grinnell Bulletin then continues with the Awards, Prizes, and Numerous Large Scholarships ... then a listing of the organizations, and athletic activities ... and soon we get the full impression that this is a hard-working academic institution dedicated to excellence.

We see below, from the Grinnell College Bulletin, how high the college's high school, student entrance standards were:

1. Graduates of high schools that are fully accredited by the Iowa State Board of Education or by the North Central Association of Colleges and Secondary Schools, who have completed a regular four years course including fifteen entrance units from the list hereafter given, with a high average standing and who are fully recommended to the College, will be admitted to full Freshman standing. In adopting this plan of admission, it is the purpose of the College to recognize the work

of the accredited high school, and to accept graduates who have shown a good quality of preparation and intellectual promise and whose record indicates seriousness of purpose and a high quality of personal character. Recommendation to the College by superintendents and principals should be made with reference not merely to scholarship but also to character, and recommendation should be withheld from those who are undesirable or unpromising from the point of view of moral qualities or habits.

2. Candidates from accredited high schools who are not eligible for admission by recommendation, may be admitted on certificate of scholarship and character with out examination, so far as they have pursued the required preparatory studies. For full entrance such students should present fifteen units of preparatory work, as defined hereafter and distributed as follows:

I. Required of all:
English (a) (b)..3 units
Mathematics (a)..2 units
History (Ancient preferred) (a).....................1 unit
Science (Physics preferred) ....1 unit
Total...71 units

I. Four units from the following for the A. B. degree or two units of one language for the B. S. Degree: [Notice huge Grinnell admission requirement for Ancient Languages.]
Greek (a) (b).. 2 or 3 units
Latin (a) (b) (c.). --2, 3 or 4 units

French (a) (b) ....2 units
German (a) (b) ---------------------------------- 2 units

III. Three and one-half or five and one-half units from the following:
Additional Language from Group II................1, 2, 3 units
History, Medieval, etc. (b) (c.)......................... 11 units
Civics .... 1 unit
Economics .... 12 units
Solid Geometry, Math. (b)............................... 12 unit
Trigonometry, Math. (c)................................... 3 unit
Arithmetic, after Algebra (d)............................. 12 unit
Chemistry ....1 unit
Zoology ....1 unit
Botany .... 12 unit
Physiography .... 1 unit
Physiology .... 4 unit
Double Entry Bookkeeping............................... 1 unit
Drawing ---------------------------------------... 12 unit
Manual Training (a) (b) .... 1 unit
Domestic Science ------------------------------ 1 unit

After a <u>full page on required</u> English Language High School Course Accomplishments, the Grinnell Bulletin spells out, for all students, the language graduation requirements, in their choice among four languages. Skipping over French and German we see Greek and Latin. This makes us wonder which? But of course, Sarah most likely completed *both*, of these Greek and Latin Grinnell College language graduation requirements We notice in passing, Grinnell's <u>own</u> huge language *graduation* requirements, which exactly complement Grinnell's own admission requirement, that a High School Graduate MUST have in Languages, even Greek and Latin, as follows !!

GREEK

(a) (b) (Three units) Grammar. A thorough knowledge of the common forms, idioms, constructions and grammatical principles of Attic prose. Books I. and II. of Xenophon's Anabasis, read with special reference to grammatical Drill. Books III. and IV. of the Anabasis read rapidly and with constant practice in sight-reading. Elementary prose composition, based on text read. The *Iliad*, Books I. and II., verses 1–493, read with careful attention to Homeric forms, constructions and meter. Book III. of the *Iliad*, or an equivalent amount read more rapidly. There should be constant practice in sight-reading. The above amount is required as preparation for [Grinnell Course in] Freshman Greek (Greek 1-2) and is equivalent to the Work done in the usual high school course, covering five recitations per week for three years.

LATIN

(a) (two units) Lessons: Grammar; Caesar, four books of the Gallic War; prose composition throughout the year, equivalent to one hour weekly. (b) (one unit) Cicero, seven orations. (If the Manilian Law is read, it may be counted as two orations.) Selections from Ovid, equal in amount, may be offered for not more than three of the Orations of Cicero. Prose composition throughout the year, equivalent to one hour weekly. (c) (one unit) Vergil, six books of the Aeneid; prosody; prose composition, the equivalent of one hour weekly. In lieu of the prose composition, students may present mythology, as much as is contained in Gayley's Classic Myths or Guerber's Myths of Greece and Rome. All candidates for admission must be able to read easy Latin at sight.

In a listing of the 59 Grinnell teaching faculty staff, there were five in the classics. Their President was a Greek Scholar, and would have been president for eight years by the time Sarah graduated. What does this tell you?

We have unfortunately not been able to find out with certainty which courses Sarah took to gain her BA, but most likely she studied the following courses that are quoted in the Grinnell Bulletin.

Specific Requirements for the Grinnell Degree of Bachelor of Arts:

One hundred twenty semester hours, including a major of at least twenty hours and a minor of at least sixteen hours; the candidate must also have completed during his college course twenty hours of foreign language, ten hours of which must be Greek or Latin of half-major grade (See Greek and Latin). Students electing both major and minor from the History, Economics, Political Science group of studies may satisfy this latter requirement with Modern Language. ....

The normal [course] registration for [Grinnell] Freshmen who have no deficiencies is.

The Grinnell Greek course was directed around developing an appreciative understanding of Greek life and of its profound influence in modern times. Mastery of the language is regarded as the primary means of attaining this end, since the vital and significant experiences of the Greeks find expression chiefly in their literature.

COURSES OF INSTRUCTION. 121
Students intending to study Greek should begin it as early as possible in their course, since several years are required to gain sufficient mastery of the language to realize the more important values of Greek study. In the following tabulation, Course A is a prerequisite to a minor in Greek.
Minor: Courses 1–2, 11-12.
Major: Courses 1–2, 11–12, 13–14.
Half-Major: Course 1–2.
A. BEGINNERS' COURSE.
Five hours weekly, thruout the year. The elements of grammar and introduction to Xenophon's Anabasis, accompanied by Greek composition. M., T., W., Th., F., 11:15. Mr. Jones.
1. PLATO, APOLOGY, AND CRITO.
* Five hours weekly, First Semester. This course aims to interpret the life and teaching of Socrates and to make clear his great contribution to modern thought. Especial attention is given to contemporary Greek life and history, in order to make clear the significance of this life. M., T., W., Th., F., 9:15. Mr. Spencer.

2. HOMER, THE *ILIAD* OR *THE ODYSSEY*.

Five hours weekly, Second Semester. The aim of this course is two fold: first, to give an appreciation of the intrinsic beauty of the Homeric poems; second, to give through them an inward understanding of a significant stage in human development. Especial emphasis will be laid upon the interpretation of early ethics, politics and religion. M., T., W., Th., F., 9:15. * Mr. Spencer.

11–12. THE GREEK DRAMA.

Three hours weekly, thruout the year. A careful study is made of at least three Greek tragedies, and Selections from several others are read, as well as a number of translations, so that a fairly complete survey of the Greek Drama is given. The Dramas are treated as a means of making real Greek experience, and the great life problems of the Greeks. M., W., F., 9 : 1.5. Miss Millerd.

13. AN INTRODUCTION TO THE GREEK HISTORIANS.

Two hours weekly, First Semester. A study of the Greek and Persian civilizations as revealed in Herodotus' account of the great conflict that culminated at Salamis. T., Th., 9:15.   Mr. Smiley.

14. GORGIAS.

Two hours weekly, Second Semester. A study of Greek Education. Portions of other dialogues, illustrating the ethical views of Plato will be read. The beginnings of ancient rhetoric will be traced. T., Th., 9:15.   Mr. Smiley.

21. PLATO'S REPUBLIC.

Three hours weekly, First Semester. This course is an introduction to Greek philosophy. Especial emphasis will be placed upon the political aspect of Plato's thought, and upon his contribution to the modern world in this realm. Hour to be arranged. Miss Millerd.

22. THE INFLUENCE OF GREEK ON MODERN LITERATURE.

Three hours weekly, Second Semester. This course will confine itself to the tracing of certain import ant lines of influence. It will consist chiefly of lectures, reports and assigned readings. Hour to be arranged. Miss Millerd.

a. GREEK AND ROMAN MONUMENTS.

(See Art and Archeology). Two hours weekly, thruout the year.

b. THE NEW TESTAMENT.

One hour weekly, thruout the year.

c. COMPARATIVE LITERATURE.

Greek Literature in English. Three hours weekly, thruout the year. This course is intended primarily for Freshmen and Sophomores. A study is made through translations of some of the great masterpieces of Greek Literature, with a view to understanding the significance of Greek experience, and its contribution to the significance of Greek experience, and its contribution to the modern world. M., W., F., 10:15. Miss Millerd.

d. GREEK ART.

Two hours weekly, First Semester. See Art and Archeology. T., Th., 3:15. Miss Millerd.

e. CLASSICAL ARCHEOLOGY.

Two hours weekly, thruout the year. (See Art and Archeology).   Mr. Spencer.
LATIN [Course Offerings.]
[Graduating as a 'Latin – Greek' Major, Sarah likely experienced most ot the following. We note that readings in Horace are mentioned twice, and Catullus once.]
Professor SMILEY, Professor MILLERD, Professor SPENCER,
Mr. JONES. The courses in Latin here offered have in view the following ends.
(1) A thorough mastery of the Latin language and some know lodge of its relation to the English language. (2) A careful reading of representative Latin authors. (3) A thorough study of metrics and such mastery of the general principles of literary art as shall enable the student to appreciate the form as well as the content of the literature read. (4) Some knowledge of Roman religion, philosophy, political institutions and private life. (5) A brief survey of the history of Roman literature—its contribution to English literature and influence upon the literature of Western Europe. (6) The adequate equipment of those who may desire to teach Latin in the high Schools.
Minor: Courses 1-2, 3-4, 11-12.
Major: Courses 1-2, 3-4, 11-12, 13-14.
Half-Major: Courses 1-2, 3-4.
Courses 11-12, 13-14 are primarily for students of Sophomore and Junior registration. Students who expect the recommendation of the department for teaching positions in the high schools are required to take at least twenty-six

semester hours of college Latin, and to maintain thruout all their college work a high standard of excellence in scholarship. It is urged that such students should devote them selves to the study of the Greek language and literature, and that they should elect supplementary courses in ancient history, philosophy and art.

A. CICERO AND VERGIL.

Five hours weekly, thruout the year. The course is open to students who present two units of Latin for admission. Students who have completed this course are admitted to Course 1.

B. VERGIL [sic]. This name is today normally spelt as Virgil

Three hours weekly, thruout the year. The course is open to students who present three units of Latin for admission.

1. CICERO, 'Cato Major de Senectute', 'Laelius de Amicitia';

PLAUTUS, 'Captivi''.

Four hours weekly, First Semester. Open to all Freshmen who have presented four units of Latin for admission. This course must be supplemented by the grammatical training of Course 3 in prose composition. M., T., W., Th., 8:00 and 11:15 and M., T., W., F., 9:15.

2. SELECTIONS FROM LIVY, CATULLUS.

Four hours weekly, Second Semester. Open to all students who have completed Course 1. This course may not be taken independently of Course 4 in prose composition.

3. PROSE COMPOSITION.

One hour weekly, First Semester. Review of forms. Arnold's Latin prose composition.

Required of all students who are taking Course 1. F., 8:00 and 11:15, and Th., 9:15.

4. PROSE COMPOSITION.

One hour weekly, Second Semester. A continuation of Course 3. Required of all students who are taking Course 2.

11. HORACE, 'Odes, Epodes and Satires'.

Three hours weekly, First Semester. An interpretation of the Augustan Age. Lectures on the History of Roman Literature with supplementary reading from Tyrrell's 'Anthology of Latin Poetry'. M., W., F., 10:15.

12. HORACE, 'Satires and Epistles.'

Three hours weekly, Second Semester. A continuation of Course 11. Lectures on the history of Roman literature with supplementary reading from Tyrrell's 'Anthology of Latin Poetry.' M., W., F., 10:15.

COURSES OF INSTRUCTION. 139

13. CICERO, 'Letters.'

Two hours weekly, First Semester. An interpretation of private and political life at Rome during the last years of the Republic. T., Th., 10:15.

14. PLINY, 'Letters.'

Two hours weekly, Second Semester. A study of Roman life and institutions under the Empire. T., Th., 10:15.

21. THE ROMAN ELEGIAC POETS.

Three hours weekly, First Semester. (Given 1915-1916). Open only to those who have completed a major in Latin.

22. LUCRETIUS.

(Given 1915-1916). - Three hours weekly, Second Semester. Open only to those who have completed a major in Latin.

23. ROMAN SATIRE: PERSIUS, PETRONIUS, JUVENAL.

Three hours weekly, First Semester. Open only to those who have completed a major in Latin.

24. TERENCE.

Three hours weekly, Second Semester. An interpretation of all the plays. Open only to those who have completed a major in Latin.

25. TACITUS, 'Annals.'

Three hours weekly, First Semester. Open only to those who have completed a major in Latin.

26. SENECA, 'Moral Letters.'

Three hours weekly, Second Semester. Open only to those who have completed a major in Latin. Courses 21-26 are given M., W., 3:15.

27. Epic, RAPHY.

Two hours weekly, First Semester. An introduction to the subject with a study of inscriptions of various types. Open to those who have completed a major in Latin. M., W., 10:15.

29–30. ADVANCED PROSE COMPOSITION.

Two hours weekly, thruout the year. This course has been given in alternate years and is intended for those who expect to teach Latin in the high schools. (Given 1916-1917). T., Th., 2:15.

31–32. PROSE COMPOSITION.

One hour weekly, thruout the year. A continuation of Courses 3 and 4. Open to students who are taking Courses 11-12, 13-14. T., 2:15.

a. GREEK AND ROMAN MONUMENTS.

(See Art and Archeology.) T., Th., 3:15. b. ANCIENT RHETORIC AND LITERARY CRITICISM.

Two hours weekly, thruout the year. A study of Aristotle's 'Rhetoric' and 'Poetics', 'Longinus' 'On the Sublime', Demetrius' 'On Literary Style', 'Dionysius' 'De Compositione Werborum', Quintilian's 'Institutes'. Large parts of these authors will be read in translation and the reading will be supplemented with lectures. This course is open to Sophomores.

Art and Archology [Course Offerings.]
[Graduating as a 'Latin – Greek' Major, Sarah chose among these courses:]
a. GREEK AND ROMAN SCULPTURE.
Two hours weekly, First Semester.

b. SCULPTURE AND PAINTING OF THE ITALLIAN RENAISSANCE.
Two hours weekly, Second Semester.

The first semester will be given to a study of Greek and Roman sculpture. The second semester will deal with the sculpture and painting of the Italian Renaissance. Little attention Is given In this course to the technique or the particular arts. The principal works are studied by means or photographs and slides, with a view to appreciating the artist's Intention and Its historic significance. (This course is not open to Freshman.)   T., Th., 3:15.   Miss Millerd.

c. MEDIEVAL ART.

Two hours weekly, Second Semester. This course Is primarily Intended to give students planning to take advanced work In any of the Romance languages, a back· ground for the study or life, thought and manners in the countries whose literature Is studied . It is, however, open to other students who find that it is suited to their needs. The work will center around architecture, ecclesiastical, musical, and domestic, as the great art expression of the Middle Ages, working out to the subsidiary and decorative arts characteristic of the time: Sculpture, wood-carving, Ivory-carving, metal-work, painting, illuminating, enamel, mosaic, and stained glass. the object Is not so much to give a history of the development of art-forms, as to Interpret the Ideals, thoughts and aspirations of the Middle Ages in terms of the art of the period. The work will be done by means of lectures, with collateral readings by the students. Miss Sheldon.

d. CLASSICAl. ARCHEOLOGY •.

Two hours weekly, thruout the year. A general Introduction to Archeology will be followed by a study of the various types or the remains of the Greeks and Romans. Open to students who have completed a minor In Latin or Greek….. T., Th., 10:15. …. Mr. Spencer.

c. GREEK AND ROMAN MONUMENTS.

Two hours weekly, thruout the year. An interpretation of the political and religious Institutions or the Greeks and Romans through the existing monuments. Special attention will be given to Greek architecture, the Greek theater, music, athletics, oracles. The course will include a thorough discussion of the history of the development or Roman Law. Lectures and prescribed reading. The course is open to Freshmen. T., Th., 3:15. Mr. Smiley.

Among the English Department Courses we notice these, relevant to Sarah:

13-14. LYRIC POETRY.

Three hours weekly, throughout the year. The course alms to give the student an understanding of the nature of lyric poetry, and an acquaintance with the work of many English lyric poets. A part or the work includes a study and comparison or typical Hebrew, Greek, Latin, French, and German lyrics, read either in translation or in the original language. M., W., F., 10:15. (Not given in 1915-16). Mr. Walleser.

13-14. MODERN ENGLISH POETRY.

Three hours weekly, thruou.t the year. A study or the principles of Poetry, essential and technical, and of certain important poets, chiefly of the Nineteenth Century, such as Wordsworth, Scott, Byron, Shelley, Keats, Mrs. Browning, Matthew Arnold, Clough, the Rossettls, Swinburne, Morris, Noyes. Open to properly qualified Juniors and Seniors. M., lV., F., 10 :15. (Given In 1916-16). Mr. Fletcher.

16-16. SHAKESPERE (sic)

Three hours weekly, throughout the year. The greater part or Shakspere's plays are studied In order, with chief emphasis on the more Important ones. The main object sought Is the appreciation of the plays as literature; but

Shakspere's development, the language, the principles of Dramatic art. and Shakspere's sources receive attention In varying degrees. (Not given in 1915-1916; given In 1916-1917). 'M., W., F., 10:15.   Mr. Fletcher.

In gaining her Grinnell BA Degree, Sarah would have had to satisfy the following overall requirements from the Grinnell Bulletin. Again we notice <u>huge</u> Grinnell graduation requirement in Languages.

Courses required of all Candidates for these degrees:
English, Course A and B .... 6 hours
Mathematics, Course A .... 6 hours
   (Six hours of Greek or Latin in addition to the required language may be offered instead of Math.)
*Laboratory Science .... 6 hours
*History, Pol. Sci., Econ. .... 6 hours
Foreign Language See requirements for degrees 20 hours
*Philosophy, Courses 1,2.................................. 6 hours
A Major study .... 20 hours
A Minor study .... 16 hours

Electives to make a total of .... 120 hours

*Students electing major or minor courses under these general heads may include this requirement as part of the major or minor. ....

o00O00o

A Major Influence On Our Sarah, Was Her University of Wisconsin Major Professor and Thesis Advisor, Moses Stephen (M S) Slaughter.

We now present what we can find about Sarah's University of Wisconsin Major Professor and Thesis Advisor, Moses Stephen (M S) Slaughter who also taught at Iowa College, the original name of Grinnell College

There is plenty of published evidence that Professor Slaughter, throughout his career, was very active in research, writing, traveling widely to give lectures, and advisory help. While Professor Slaughter was teaching at Iowa College, (later named Grinnell College) he is listed to have toured Iowa high schools, no doubt telling about the virtues of his campus, perhaps even to Sarah. We should keep in mind that, Sarah's home town, Dallas Center to Grinnell is about eighty miles by direct railroad, and even possible by horse and buggy tour. Des Moines is on the way some 20 miles from Dallas Center.

Published evidence displayed below also shows he was active professionally in Iowa from the early part of his career. He even went back there repeatedly after he became a professor at the University of Wisconsin: Articles say he served on an Iowa Public High School advisory committee, and he is reported giving talks on the Iowa College campus some three years prior to Sarah's arrival there as a college student.

His motivation for coming back to his old campus would likely have been a combination of => See how the place is doing, visit old friends, give talks at their invitation, and actively recruit Graduate Students for his Latin and Roman Classics research at the University of Wisconsin. With this motivation, we can surely project that this may well have happened repeatedly, even while Sarah was a student at Grinnell. After all, this was in the heyday of railroad passenger service, when it was relatively easy, and moderate cost, to get where needed.

So there were most likely multiple venues where Sarah could have gotten acquainted with Professor Slaughter's apparently quite active and infectious personality, and thus she became interested in his work, and from this, impressed enough to eventually begin Masters & PhD Thesis work with him. Since there are lots of Graduate Schools closer to Sarah's home than the University of Wisconsin, we conclude that Sarah must have specifically gone there to work with Slaughter, especially since she did both her theses with him. Relevant here is the fact that at the University of Wisconsin, Prof. Slaughter taught full courses respectively, on the Roman Poets, Horace and Catullus.

We see many points of resemblance between Prof. Slaughter and Sarah. It may even have been the case that they were rather like kindred spirits. For example, Slaughter had origins as a mid-Westerner, and had extensive work experience on an Indiana farm where he age twelve, was orphaned and was raised by relatives there. And he, like Sarah, went to a small mid-west, private liberal arts college with strong religious heritage (DePauw University, Greencastle, Indiana). His career continued in a western University, where he and Sarah joined forces in academic efforts at the University of Wisconsin. And like Sarah, he was a Protestant Christian church member and anti-war, in that he was not a WWI military combatant, rather he served as a humanitarian worker in the Italian front lines for eighteen months as a top officer in the Red Cross. It is important to note that this was an officer position of considerable responsibility, under desperate life and death war time conditions, that would have proven and greatly developed his substantial leadership abilities. Also, Prof. Slaughter was apparently happily married, which would have met Sarah's approval. But unlike Sarah, he was Graduate School educated in the Eastern Mid Coastal United States, Johns Hopkins.

Because there is plenty of reason to believe M. S Slaughter would have been an enormous academic influence on our Sarah, we feel compelled to devote considerable space to show a few extant publications that tell us of his character, so our readers can feel the full astounding impact of just who he was! This includes a lively approach to life, charismatic personality, effervescent demeanour, and an absolutely first rate academic and professor. To top it off, he was a 20th Century colossus of enlightened leadership! There is no way Sarah could have emerged from three years of his Major Professor and Thesis Latin expert guidance without becoming a version of his image! Such an image of Professor Slaughter, solidly confirmed from Field research at Grinnell and University of Wisconsin, solidly reveals copious testimonials as to his

> " ... interesting reputation as an exceedingly lively and effective teacher of Latin ... it very soon became evident why he was a man much spoken about."

This testimonial from MS Slaughter's early days at Grinnell (~1880's), joined similar offerings continuing up through Slaughter's *Memorial Service Program Booklet* (1924), showing the memorial speeches given by three fellow professors, at University of Wisconsin.

(NOTE: Additional important material concerning Professor Slaughter, as well as Sarah's life, is available on a special supplementary Internet web Page, *'Sarah Vinke Biography Resource Page'*. which Google will quickly find.)

On the whole, there are lots of rather likely connections and major cross fertilizations between Sarah and Prof. Slaughter. An important one of which would have origins in Bryn Mawr (a Women's College), where he (a professor) and his wife (a student and graduated from) both were together for some years. This is surely the long sought connection to Pirsig's memory (which is given in Chapter 4 of this biography) that Sarah had considerably led Pirsig to believe she had been schooled at Bryn Mawr or some other major connection.

> **A Description of Bryn Mawr, From Their Website.**
>
> "From its earliest days, Bryn Mawr has had an international reputation in classical languages. It was among the first institutions to offer doctorates in classical philology to women in the United States. Today, the College is home to a lively community of graduate students, both women and men, who are interested in various aspects of the civilizations of ancient Greece and Rome; and its name is known to classicists worldwide through theBryn Mawr Classical Review, the second-oldest electronic book-review journal, which is received by over 10,000 subscribers around the globe."

Bearing in mind the long-sought connection between Sarah and Bryn Mawr, we recall what Dennis Gary stated about Bryn Mawr:

> 'Sarah assigned to us the Richmond Lattimore translation of the *Iliad,* Lattimore himself taught at Bryn Mawr for several years. The campus seems to have been highly focused on the Greek

classical civilization and the Roman classical civilization and indeed this remains true to this day.

Another significant book that Sarah assigned was Edith Hamilton's *Mythology*. In fact, before Edith wrote this book and others about Greece and Rome, she was headmistress at Bryn Mawr College in Pennsylvania and the dates of her life -- 1867 to 1963 – make her an approximate contemporary of Sarah Vinke's. '

Thus, it's possible that Sarah went to school there, or had friends there, or worked with other faculty members there. But we haven't been able to find out any more concrete information about this.

o00O00o

Professor Slaughter was deeply interested both in the Latin language, and in Roman archaeology: Surely he communicated this interest and fascination to Sarah. Such is evidenced in this extensive academic article on archaeology, in Rome, related to Roman Poet Horace. This following article says Slaughter was then at Iowa College (i.e. Grinnell):

The Acta Indorum Saccularum, and The Carncn Sacclare of Horace. By Prof. M. S. SLAUGHTER, [of] IOWA COLLEGE.

Transactions of the American Philological Association (1869-1896), Viewing page 69 of pages 69-78, Vol. xxvi

In one of the rooms of the National Museum, in Rome, is now to be found the inscription containing the Acta Indorum Saccularum, and the Carncn Sacclare, for which Horace composed the Carrmcn Sacculare. The story of the discovery of this inscription by Italian workmen engaged in constructing a sewer on the left bank of the Tiber, near the Ponte San Angelo, in September 1890 is familiar to everyone.

The fragments of the stone bearing the inscription have been set up on a square pillar, resembling the marble column on which the account was first cut, soon after the occurrence of the festival in 17 b.c. The pillar is between nine and ten feet high and is three and a half feet wide. The inscription consists of 168 lines in majuscule type, and it is very clear and easy to read.

Mommsen's edition of the inscription, undertaken at the request of the Italian government, appeared first in the *Monumenti Antichi publicati per cura della Realc Accademia dei lincci,*. Vol. I, 1891 A reprint was published in the *Ephemeris Epigraphica* for 1891 (pp. 225-274), though the copy was not ready for distribution until some months later. With the Ephemeris copy in hand, I made a study of the inscription while in Rome in the spring of 1894. The fragments of the stone have evidently been set up in their present position since Mommsen's reading was made. The writing has brackets, showing breaks in the stone and consequent omissions of words or letters included in at least twenty-five instances too few letters, showing that the stone has been rather roughly handled in the setting up.

o00O00o

Professor Slaughter was a jaunty and charismatic fellow. It seems likely this jauntiness made a big impression on Sarah; she was of course (or from his influence became) a jaunty person herself. A journalist, hearing the fantastic reputation of Prof.

Slaughter, visited his University of Wisconsin Latin class and expecting to be enormously uplifted wrote:

A Visit To Professor M S Slaughter's Latin Class.

The [this newspaper] reporter visited his Latin class and expecting to be enormously uplifted, but [instead] there was a sweet, laughing gentleman at the desk, where the stern and hoary preceptor should have been. And there was something decidedly engaging about the look in his eyes. So the reporter got a little excited. Moreover, it appeared that the delightful gentleman at the desk - Prof. M. S. Slaughter - was telling a story. *'So Jason gave the serpent aspirin,'* he said, *'and put him to sleep. Then Media ordered her airplane and breezed away.'* I looked inquiringly at the person next to me. *'Mr. Slaughter is telling us an ancient myth,'* he said. *'We'll have to know it for the exam.'*

I was fascinated, and pursued the jovial gentleman from the classroom to his office and was immediately received into his exuberant friendliness: so we chattered down the hill together, and to his house. [Here was placed a photograph of Slaughter. He looked like the elderly Max Planck, famous physicist, complete with petite fragile glasses].

Still fascinated, this reporter followed Professor Slaughter to his house.

It was the warmest, sweetest house imaginable, full of pictures you could be fond of, and old books, and strange little things of brass and cameo and silver, that had been brought from far away, received into the harmony of the place.

''And what is that mysterious object in the corner?' I inquired, when we were sitting comfortably before the fire, pointing to a strange, red thing in the corner. My kindly host smiled suddenly, and rose.

'Oh. That is my most precious possession. I wonder if you would like to see me parade?' So he went to the corner, swung the brilliant red flag of the city of Venice over his shoulder, and marched triumphantly down the room, like a little boy.

"*The city of Venice gave it to me, when I finished my Red Cross work there. I'm fond of it.*' And he put it carefully away again.

I picked up a queer little bronze device from the table. 'That's from Tivoli,' he said. 'Have you ever been in Tivoli'. No? 1t is one of the darkest corners of the earth, to me -- Horace loved it too. You know Horace was a remarkable human poet -- my students are only beginning to find that out.'

And it was there, as he talked more of the old people -- Horace, Horace's Friends, the Italian fountains and hills they loved, that the warmth and living kindness and delicious humor deepened about him. Here was a rare personality.

1 had a sudden thought as I walked away.

'Why, he must be nearly sixty.' And then, '1 don't believe it. He'll never be older than a sigh, or a gay laugh, or perhaps a caress.'

There's an unmistakable similarity between the venerable, life-loving, Classics-loving Professor Slaughter and the charismatic, life-loving lady who Sarah became. It's difficult not to believe that Professor Slaughter made a major contribution to making her into the wonderful lady, a quintessential lady of Quality, she became. We surely see why Sarah sought out Professor Slaughter as her Major Professor, and in the process of her work with him, she surely would have been greatly formed, and reformed into the personality she was to become. What an example to be influenced by!

o00O00o

***The Madison Wisconsin Capital Times*, Monday Dec 31, 1923, concerning Prof. Slaughter,** fills in a lot of blank lines. The fact that this Prof. Slaughter newspaper article was with <u>big</u> headlines as <u>lead article</u> on <u>front page</u>, shows he was deemed an important fixture at Wisconsin, and in the city of Madison, the capital city of Wisconsin. We see that Prof. Slaughter died just six months after he added his signature to Sarah's Thesis on July 1923. He is listed as Professor of Latin, which is the subject matter of both of Sarah's theses and her early career. We note the mention of Bryn Mawr. (This and several other newspaper articles, are from newspapers.com.)

Prof. M. S. Slaughter of University Dies In Rome; 27 Years On Faculty of University. Head of Latin Department. Joined U. W. In 1896;
    Wife With Him at Time of Death.

Prof. Moses Stephen Slaughter, 63, head of the Latin department at the University of Wisconsin, and when left. in September on a year's leave of absence for travel abroad died Saturday at. midnight in Rome,

Prof. and Mrs. Slaughter had arrived in Rome about Dec 11, and Letters dated from Rome written Dec 12, stated that at that time Professor Slaughter was in ill health. Death came Saturday night; after a severe illness of four days. Mrs. Slaughter the only immediate survivor, was with the professor at the time of his death.

Prof. Slaughter was born in Brooklyn, Ind on Oct. 30 1860, the son of John and Sarah Slaughter, and received his bachelor's degree in arts from De Pauw university in 1883. Following attendance for several years at Johns Hopkins university where he obtained his doctor of philosophy degree, Prof. Slaughter spent two years in universities at Berlin and Munich, Germany.

On June 28, 1898, he married Miss Gertrude Elizabeth Taylor, of Cambridge, Ohio. Two daughters were born, both of whom died ... within a year, at the ages of 14. and 16 years.

At Bryn Mawr, at the Colleagiatc Institute at Hackettstown, N. J., and at Iowa college, Prof. Slaughter taught before joining the faculty of the University of Wisconsin in 1896, with the title of professor of Latin.

Prof. Slaughter holds membership in the Latin American. School of Classical Studies, at Rome, the American Philological association, in the Archeological Institute of America [also president], in the Classical Association of the Middlc West and South, and is a member of Phi Beta Kappa honorary scholastic society. He was member of Delta Kappa Upsilon social fraternity and of the university club at Madison. 'The Story of Turnus," written in 1896, is Prof. Slaughter's chief literary production, but he has contributed to numerous literary and literary periodicals. Pamphlets and articles on Horatius [Horace], Virgil, Lucretius, on the Luci

Saccularius and numerous book inscriptions have all so been written by Prof. Slaughter.

Prof. Showerman stated that the remains would probably be 'brought to Madison for internment at Forest Hill in a lot where those of his daughters, Misses Elizabeth and Gertrude are interred. Prof. Slaughter was a member of the First Congregational church.

o00O00o

So we see that young Sarah Jennings was a product of farm country Western Iowa US, imbued with her country's Ancient Greek 'state of mind', itself an outgrowth of the Post Renaissance Enlightenment Era. The schools that Sarah attended were permeated through and through, with Ancient Greek and Roman emphasis. Grinnell, with its Christian Religion emphasis and unusually high academic standards, excelled in the Classics. Here she surely learned of Ancient Greek *Arête* (ἀρετή), *utter, most striving, excellence*, and in its basic sense, means *"excellence of any kind"*. From this she must have set her sights on graduate school, selecting Prof. M. S. Slaughter, a prime Classicist and a charismatic, kindred soul. This lead Sarah to the University of Wisconsin, allowing her to eventually become a Professor at Montana State College.

And now we see, the formative steps of Sarah, which lead to her saying to Robert Pirsig:

'*I hope you are teaching Quality to your students.*'

Chapter 8: 'You're Quality, Mr. Gary!' Sarah As Teacher And Inspiration Of Montana State University Student Dennis Gary.

Dennis Gary, who was born in 1938 in Chicago, Illinois, is the most important source in this book along with Pirsig himself. Like Pirsig, Dennis actually knew Sarah Vinke, being taught by her at Montana State College (MSU) starting in 1956 to 1960.

Dennis first emailed Henry Gurr on 25 October 2009. This is the first part of Dennis's email:

> Dr. Gurr:
> On a whim I Googled 'Sarah J. Vinke' the other day and was linked to one of your webpages, concerning the book *Zen and the Art of Motorcycle Maintenance (ZMM)*.
>
> I was a student of Professor Vinke. I attended MSC from 1956-1960, getting a BS in Secondary Education with an academic major in English. I took the second quarter of Oral and Written Communication from Dr. Vinke in the Winter Quarter of 1957 at Montana State College, now Montana State University. Later, at the urging of Jack Barsness, another professor at MSC under whom I studied magazine article writing and short story writing, I took Shakespeare and Greek and Roman Classics from Dr. Vinke. I believe Pirsig arrived at MSC in 1959, but by that time my remaining course of

study was pretty much cast in concrete, so I never really got to know him. I read *ZMM* years ago and delved into it again the other day. .. Below, I have written my memories of Professor Sarah Vinke and the MSC English Department for the years I was there as a student and an English Major.

Henry was, needless to say, absolutely delighted to hear from Dennis. As Dennis Gary explains above, he himself took Oral and Written Communication from Sarah during the Winter Quarter of 1957, from January to March. He took Shakespeare in the autumn of 1958 and Greek and Roman Classics (in English translation) in the spring of 1959.

Mr. Gary has many different memories of Sarah, some vivid, some more hazy, and of course he acknowledges that there were interactions that he had with Sarah which he's forgotten about over the considerable period of time since they took place.

That Sarah had a profound effect on Dennis's life is incontestable. We are grateful as biographers that Dennis has made himself so freely available for providing information about Sarah both in the years when Henry Gurr was researching her life and in the period since we embarked on writing this biography.

Perhaps it's best to let Dennis recount his own memories of Sarah as he recalls them.

I was born in Chicago, but when I was eight years old, my family moved from Elmhurst, Illinois to the town of Bozeman in Montana where my father, Ronald Gary, took over the family ranch near Gallatin Gateway close to the foot of the Gallatin Canyon. Our family moved to Bozeman in the summer after I completed the third grade in Elmhurst. I started the fourth grade in Bozeman.

My father gained a MSC Bachelor of Science in Electrical Engineering in 1928. My two aunts, Margaret and Josephine, on my father's side, were also graduates of MSC. I think there were two reasons behind my father's decision to return to Montana. Firstly, he was working in Illinois as a consulting engineer and he wanted to do some other type of work. Secondly, the house in Elmhurst which the family rented was being taken back by the owner who was returning from Oakland, California, after World War II. Additionally, the lease of the ranch to Ernest Monforton, who owned the adjacent ranch, was up.

I was eighteen when I started my studies at MSC. Among my many professors, was Sarah Vinke herself. Studying Oral and Written Communication under Sarah Vinke was one of the most bizarre learning experiences I ever had. I usually got As from her and I never had to give her a jar of watermelon rind pickles. There was a rumor that if you gave Sarah a jar of these, which were her favorite pickles, you would get an A. I think that, playfully, Sarah sometimes suggested this, but I can't remember. It seems obvious to me that Sarah's mind was highly original and that she found the intellectual confines of teaching at a university frustrating in many ways. The paradox was that she had a profound interest in academic matters but was also very much a realist with an entertaining, positive and pragmatic knowledge of the world itself. I remember, for example, that after teaching us a class on Aristotelian logic, Sarah told us that 'None of this works in real life.' We must have looked as if we didn't know what she meant by this and so Sarah elaborated by saying: 'If you don't believe me, try Aristotelian logic on your date on Saturday night in the back seat of your car!' I also remember, on a different note, that she once spoke about The New York Sunday Times and said 'Most of my colleagues think of this newspaper as being akin to the Bible but don't believe this because all The New York Times does is support our liberal prejudices.'

Dennis Gary was always grateful for Sarah having been one of his professors and at times de facto adviser, but he acknowledges that it was only through a stroke of destiny that he signed up for her section of Oral and Written Communication in the first place. He says:

I remember, that Winter Quarter, that the class sign-up schedule had a designation for the Student Major and certain sections were intended for those of us who were majoring in Education. Sarah Vinke's class was supposedly directed at students who were majoring in Education. I myself was majoring in Education with an academic major in English, and, so by a sheer accident of fate, (because of how these sections were designated at MSU) I became one of Sarah's students in Oral and Written Communication. I've always felt since then that my being taught by Sarah was somehow meant to be my destiny since the system of designating sections for particular majors was never tried again. I've always been grateful that it was my destiny that this is what happened.

Dennis explains that as well as his course in Oral and Written Communication, he attended Sarah's classes on Shakespeare. As he recalls:

> Sarah used to reserve the faculty lounge in the student union building and ask us to meet her there for her Shakespeare class. This was a more relaxed place, with more comfortable chairs and a generally more relaxed ambience, compared with a regular classroom. She felt it was a better environment for discussing Shakespeare as we could discuss him over coffee and, if we chose, could smoke. Sarah herself used to smoke and she would carry a carton of Marlboro's sticking out of her purse. I think she saw Shakespeare, in a thoroughly non-academic way, as the great poet and playwright of life whose work was completely rooted in the world of the living, rather than the world of the ivory tower. I remember very vividly that once in a Shakespeare class she said:
>
> > *All great drama consists of blood, guts and sex; nobility of expression and thought is just frosting on the cake.*
>
> I also remember that in one Shakespeare class, a day after having asked us to write a description of a scene from Shakespeare's *Richard III,* she threw our papers into the waste paper basket, and then, to our surprise, produced sheets of butcher paper and crayons and had us attempt to draw the scene instead. She told us that spectacle is a visual experience and that this is why she wanted us to express ourselves in that way.

Dennis continues:

Sarah Vinke certainly knew her Shakespeare. I found her inspiring and exciting as a teacher and I never felt that she only had a cold academic interest in Shakespeare's works. I think she would have enjoyed living in Shakespeare's day and attending one of his plays at the Globe Theatre in London where no doubt she would have had confirmed in the reception of the audience to the plays, that great Drama was indeed mostly blood, guts and sex. What I do know is that I had no trouble getting an A in the summer of 1961 when I studied Shakespeare several years later at the Oregon Shakespeare Festival in Ashland, Oregon. Nor, for that matter did I have any trouble in courses about Shakespeare and Renaissance Drama apart from Shakespeare when I was earning my Master's Degree at the University of Oregon. I remember very vividly when I was at Oregon that I was urged to use my copy of the Harrison edition of Shakespeare instead of the Craig Edition, even though the Craig edition was a departmental adoption of Oregon. The professor who was teaching me at the time felt that the Harrison edition was superior editorially. [And] Who had picked the Harrison edition for us to study at MSC? The answer was Sarah Vinke!.

Dennis Gary recalls that he and Sarah got on pretty well and that she used to respect the fact that he was generally on time. She respected this fact so much that once, as he recalls, when he was actually late for once due to a snowstorm making it impossible for him to get to the university campus on time, he raced up the stairs of Montana Hall of the university.

When I pulled open the classroom door, the class greeted me with a burst of laughter and a round of applause. Sarah chuckled, 'Great timing, Mr. Gary, she said. 'I had only just remarked that the sky must be falling: Mr. Gary isn't here.'

Dennis also says:

I wasn't studying Classics at MSU and I certainly didn't know Classical Greek but I do remember very vividly that as part of a course which Sarah was offering in Greek and Roman Classics, taught in English translation, Sarah occasionally reading or reciting in Greek. Sarah read aloud short passages of Homer's *Iliad* in Greek. I suppose she felt that her very enthusiasm for Homer and Greek would be interesting to us even though we couldn't actually understand what she was saying, and this was certainly true. Sarah didn't read lengthy sections in Greek -- perhaps just a minute or two -- with the goal of letting us hear what Greek sounded like. Meaning was left with the English translations. As I have written, when Sarah got to the end of the quarter, she told us [in our Greek and Roman Classics class] that we hadn't made it to the Romans, but they were all a bunch of copycats anyway. Consequently, I was surprised concerning both her PhD Theses featured Ancient Roman Poets, and their writings in Latin, rather than Greek topics. I don't remember her reading to us any passages in Latin.

I have known several English professors who specialized in a field of literature they thought would get them a professorship -- not a field they were interested in. Once they got tenure, they sought to move into areas of interest.

In Shakespeare, Sarah pretty much left the reading to her students, except when giving examples, interpretation, etc. Her enthusiasm for teaching and her energy as a teacher were infectious and brought a powerful incentive to me to do the very best in my studies and to see my studies not just as a cold but necessary grounding in academic subjects, but in a vital part of my thinking and my life.

So from Dennis we learn, despite her Latin oriented PhD Thesis work, Sarah must have had a decided teaching preference for Greek, as opposed to Latin. Dennis continued remarks, also support this very important conclusion:

Sarah assigned to us the Richmond Lattimore translation of the *Iliad* which was new at the time and which she told us she felt came closest to capturing the flow of classical Greek. She obviously had a remarkable knowledge of classical Greek and a great love of the subject. She once remarked in passing that she had travelled by train through Greece after World War II.

Dennis then recalls:

In the 1960s, when I was at the University of Oregon and a Master's degree candidate, a fellow student saw me with the Lattimore translation. He was from Princeton and he expressed his surprise that anyone from Montana State would have even known about it. Well, anyone who thought that we at MSC were not lucky enough to have great teachers who inspired us, clearly did not know that we had Sarah Vinke as a teacher. I think it's also worth mentioning that the writer Carolyn Alexander, writing in her recent book *The War That Killed Achilles*, uses the Lattimore translation, except for the final chapter where she explains that she had to use her own translation because of copyright problems. Sarah's far-sighted realization of the significance of the Lattimore edition seems to me yet another example of her acuity and perceptiveness when it came to teaching.

Dennis continues:

Another significant book that Sarah assigned was Edith Hamilton's *Mythology*. In fact, before Edith wrote this book and others about Greece and Rome, she was headmistress at Bryn Mawr College in Pennsylvania and the dates of her life - 1867 to 1963 – make her an approximate contemporary of Sarah Vinke's. I remember that on January 19, 2010, I was at the Borders Bookshop on Union Square in San Francisco and Edith Hamilton's *Mythology* was on display.

The Richmond Lattimore translation is still in print [as of 2016] by the University of Chicago Press with the cover of the book decked out with rave reviews from rival translators. Lattimore himself taught at Bryn Mawr for several years. The campus seems to have been highly focused on the Greek classical civilisation and the Roman classical civilisation and indeed this remains true to this day. There seems, in fact, to have been a close connection between Sarah and the Bryn Mawr campus. It's possible that Sarah went to school there, or had friends there, or worked with other faculty members there.

Dennis's memories of Sarah, vary from those that focus on her teaching, to more personal memories.

Clearly, both Sarah and he regarded their relationships as something of a friendship. As Mr. Gary recalls:

When I was a few months from graduating, I went to see Sarah to ask her whether she would act as an employment reference. When I asked her this, she seemed to be delighted to be asked. I remember that I asked her why she preferred to be called Mrs. Vinke at MSU rather than Dr. Vinke, as I knew she had a doctorate. What she said was, 'Well, Mr. Gary, the reason is because it was a lot harder for me to get a husband than a PhD and he didn't last nearly as long.'

If I remember rightly, Sarah had been married to a Professor of Agriculture at MSC, who passed away several years later. Our conversation continued and she asked me to tell something more about myself, in particular where I was from. I told her that despite being born in Chicago, I had essentially grown up at 421 West Main in Bozeman and on the family ranch two miles past Gallatin Gateway. I also told her that my father and two aunts were graduates of MSC. She seemed very surprised by this and said: 'You mean you've gone all the way through MSC without telling anyone on the faculty this, about your father and your two aunts?' I replied by saying that it didn't really have anything to do with me. Sarah said in response to this : 'It doesn't have anything to do with you, Mr. Gary, but I think it's wonderful that you wanted to succeed here at MSC on your own without telling any of us on the faculty about your father and two aunts being graduates here. You'd be surprised, Mr. Gary, at the pressure put on the faculty by alumni of MSU to give their children top grades.'

Dennis says he has always regarded this as one of the most significant conversations he ever had with Sarah. Some of what follows here has already been quoted above, but it's so important that some repetition is helpful as, apart from anything else, a vigorous reminder of just how great Sarah's influence was on people. As Dennis says:

I don't remember exactly what I said in response to her remark about alumni putting the faculty under pressure to give their children top grades, but I do remember very vividly that a few moments later Sarah smiled at me and said, and these were her precise words, and of course these words have attained much greater resonance with me since I read *Zen And The Art of Motorcycle Maintenance* in about 1989. Anyway, what Sarah said to me was: '*You've got character, Mr. Gary. You're quality.*'

In my bewilderment I asked her what she meant by the word Quality in this respect because I associated the word with things like laundry detergents, brands of coffee and Buicks. I remember that Sarah went off on a discussion about character and Quality, but unfortunately I didn't grasp what she said, still less remember any details, which seems to me a great shame when after all, there has been so much discussion since then in the media, triggered by the importance of the word quality in Pirsig's legendary book, about what quality actually means. Nor did I ask her if she'd tell me more about Quality; I wish I had.

As we've seen, Dennis recalls:

I remember pondering her statements, that I had character and quality, on many occasions during the next few weeks. I felt, and this is difficult to express, but it really is how I feel, as if I'd been given an enormous charge or responsibility or indeed the authority to do something significant with my life. I recall Pirsig's comment in *Zen and the Art of Motorcycle Maintenance* about Sarah herself when he said that her message were perhaps Delphic in nature. What did she really mean by what she said? I basically don't know exactly. I think the truth is that there is something of the inscrutable in such multi-faceted and complex characters as Sarah Vinke. It's almost as if they take a kind of relish in saying big things but not elucidating and it may be that in fact the elucidation wouldn't be helpful anyway because it would just demean and in some ways even reduce the big pronouncement. Perhaps the truth is that one has to make of the big pronouncement whatever one wants to make of it and one should be patient and not too demanding in terms of trying to find out exactly what the person making the pronouncement meant.

Dennis also says:

After all, it's the big statement that matters and we have to draw our own meaning from the big statement. I remember also, for example, that Sarah once said to me, that when you teach Shakespeare you must always teach *Hamlet* last or you'll never get onto another play. I believe this is because of the play's complexity - its many levels of meaning. Looking backward, it has a plot similar to *Oedipus Rex* by the Greek playwright Sophocles. Looking forward, it embodies the psychoanalytic theory of Sigmund Freud. who bases much of his theory on the Oedipus Complex. Likewise, it is the ghost of Hamlet's father who commands him to kill his mother's second husband who is also Hamlet's uncle, not Hamlet's father. In Shakespeare's day you did not trust a ghost. This is partially because the audience was split between members of the Church of England which did not believe in ghosts and Catholics which still did.

Dennis also remembers the following:

Dr. Vinke told me she was the third woman to be hired at MSC, joining Beatrice Freeman Davis and Kay Roberts. I had met Beatrice through my grandmother when Beatrice was retired and invalided, working on a never completed book. Kay Roberts I had met in passing because she was the wife of Arthur Roberts, Drama coach and American history teacher at Gallatin County High School (now Bozeman Senior High School).'

I remember the 1930s as date for when Sarah was hired by MSC, but this may be an error since we know Sarah first came to MSC in the 1920's and she returned 'to stay' in 1946. I think she said something to the effect 'When I came to Montana State to stay . . .' There is confusion as to correct spelling of Sarah's married name: On the Montana Hall roster it was 'Vinke,' but in catalogues and schedules it was 'Vinki.' She had an explanation, but I can't remember it.

At any rate, when I told Sarah that my grandmother Gary was friends with Beatrice Freeman Davis, Sarah replied, 'That settles it. Your grandmother must have been a very intelligent woman. Beatrice had no truck for fools.' In fact, my grandmother had spent only a few months on campus with the view of qualifying to teach elementary school which did not require a four year degree at the time. Then she dropped out to marry my grandfather. When I knew her she was bow-legged and had varicose veins -- possibly the result of having seven children. She stopped at that point upon the advice of the family doctor. I saw a picture on the wall of my grandmother's house of the handsome young woman she had been.

I do remember that the first few years I was on campus both Sarah and Jack Barsness had corner offices in Montana Hall and you could look out the windows and see much of the campus and indeed down to Main Street and the steeple of Holy Rosary Catholic Church. But by 1958 or '59, they were in cramped windowless offices in the interior of Montana Hall because the larger offices could house two or three instructors as the faculty grew rapidly. Sarah also had a cot in her space to lie down on. I think Pirsig may have been assigned to help her get up.

Concerning MSC's Montana Hall offices. In a loger email Dennis said:

Sarah and Jack had offices with windows looking out the campus with mountains in the background on the second, or possibly third floor of Montana Hall, initially but with the influx of new hires such as Pirsig, they were assigned smaller, inside offices with no windows and several of the newer instructors got the larger, windowed offices [where they were assigned 2 or 3 instructors per office]. There were plants in Sarah's office, but also on various windowsills in the hallway and other offices. These also be Sarah's doing because she could be seen almost anywhere watering a plant.

Curiously, I once saw the salaries paid full professors at Montana State in the 1950s and realized that in 1964, when I first got a contract from a small high school in the Sacramento, Ca, delta, it was for $6,200 for the first year, more than professors like Vinke at MSC received in the 1950's.

I remember that Montana State forced English Professor Titus Kurtichanov to retire and perhaps Sarah Vinke as well in the early 1960's, because MSC could hire two instructors for what it was paying each of them (a total of 4 instructors in this case).

Dennis rounds off this series of recollections by recalling:

...in the following year, in the darkness of my attic room at a boarding house in Klamath Falls, Oregon, after a day teaching High School English I would lie awake in my room wondering exactly what kind of charge, inspiration and responsibility Sarah had given me when she exclaimed, spontaneously: 'You've got character, Mr. Gary....You're Quality.'

In *ZMM* Pirsig mentions Peter Voulkos Ceramic Vases at the DeWeese home: Dennis has these memories:

I knew the Voulkos family in the late 1940s and in the 1950s. Peter Voulkos, whose vases Pirsig mentioned in *ZMM* and who was a student of Robert DeWeese, became famous for his ceramics, etc. and founded the School of Ceramic Art at the University of California, Berkeley.

His family lived about a block from my grandparents in Bozeman and his mother used to come over to have my grandmother read and explain to her mail she had received that was written in English since she could not read English. The Voulkoses were Greek. (Spelled as Voulkas in *ZMM*, which must be in error.) I encountered Sarah at the Voulkos home once .... [Here's the story]

    Pete ran up to me on campus, saying, 'You may not remember me. I'm Pete Voulkos. I've met you several times, once at my mother's house. I'm down here from Helena and nobody I currently know on campus, knows where she lives, or how to get there. I need this anvil taken to her house as soon as possible and you know how to get it there. When I got down to the Voulkos house and lugged whatever it was in, there was Sarah, visiting. I was surprised at the time, but now, realizing Sarah's interests am not now.

[From an Ancestry.com search result =>] It looks like Freddier Rose's mother Mary was the Mary Voulkos in the family I knew. I don't know whether it was at the reception at the Voulkos home after Mary or Margaret got married that the groom's friends stole the bride. The party became so raucous that some neighbour called the Bozeman Police who issued citations much to the chagrin of the family.

I had, in fact, met Pete twice, once when my parents and I were in Helena Montana, visiting my father's cousin, Agnes Gary. Agnes told us that there was a Brey Institute devoted to the making of pottery, and my parents saw it as a possible place to buy plates cheaply, replacing some that were cracked.

Wrong. We stepped into this building that looked like a warehouse, but with some folding chairs at one end. There were two muscular guys one working on what we learned was a kiln and the other an anvil.

One of them stepped forward and introduced himself as 'Pete.' Then gesturing to the other guy said, 'and that's my associate, Rudy Autio.

I raised my hand and asked Pete if his last name was Voukos, and was he from Bozeman. Pete was startled, saying 'How did you know?'

I replied that he had a striking resemblance to his brother Manuel. My parents were upset, whispering to me, 'How many times do we have to tell you that little boys are to be seen, not heard.'

My response was, 'I noticed the resemblance. You didn't.'

The other time when I was running an errand for my grandmother to ask Mrs. Voulkos if she had one of my grandmother's pans. There stood this guy, who turned out to be Pete, taking a picture of himself using a delayed reaction camera with Manuel's sailor hat on.

At any rate, Pete put the anvil in the trunk of our family Buick. When I got down to West Main, I had a real struggle lugging the heavy anvil up the walk and onto the porch, I being all of 5'6' and weighing all of 120 pounds.

Stopping to catch my breath, by now being in the doorway of the Voukos's living room, I spotted Sarah Vinke sitting in a circle of other people drinking coffee.

Sarah spotting me calls, 'Come on in Mr. Gary and sit down and tell us about yourself, what courses you're taking, what do you think of them, do you like them.'

I replied that I needed to get back to the college library.

Sarah's response, 'The library can wait.'

Suddenly, Sarah had let me know how important this young ranch kid was.

Dennis adds:

I feel that my characterization of Sarah as multi-faceted is verified by the above mentioned MSU archives, as well as what I drew from my anecdotes. She was very much the scholar, as well as the populist, and certainly a women's movement pioneer. Also, Sarah believed that country kids deserved a good education, too. My parents had some cultural interests based on life in Chicago during the 1930s and 40s, but still it scarcely included the Greek classics or Shakespeare.

Sarah was a world traveler. The archives documents on her tour of Europe certainly bear this out. It is interesting that she quit teaching during her marriage. Her devotion to Louis Vinke fits in well with her devotion to Shirley Luhrsen, and indeed to all of her students, etc. I wonder if, as with Shirley in the 1940s, the lack marriage of a female faculty member was a problem back in the 1930's. Also, we have the evidence of the thank-you letter from the Mississippi

Freedom Democratic Party. Her financial support of that organization indicates Sarah's willingness to support liberal, not necessarily very popular causes. She supported the empowerment of underprivileged groups such as black people.

Many names in the archive [MSU Library Folder Re Sarah] relating to the American Association of University Women (AAUW) meeting, are familiar to me. Alice Oliver taught at Gallatin County High School, probably Spanish and/or French. Peculiarly, Spanish was canceled for lack of interest at GCHS. Having spent much of my life in California, this now seems ironic.

Many other last names on the AAUW attendance list are familiar. Many of the sons and daughters of faculty members were at Gallatin High when I was.

Henry Gurr asked me about Sarah's use of the word 'Quality' in relation to Pirsig. I suspect that Sarah refuses to be categorized, that she both talked about and acted out Quality [without using this word], though acting it out without labeling her actions or intellectualizing them. The only time I remember her addressing Quality by name was in that appointment where I asked for a reference.

Once she told us, 'You must shake your fist at fate. You mustn't let the gods think they are getting the better of you.' Let me give an example of how she applied this to herself: At the point of getting one of her degrees, she had had her purse stolen. In response, she withdrew her last twenty dollars from the bank and went out and bought the biggest, ugliest woman's hat she could find.

Dennis also remembers:

In our Oral and Written Communication class, Dr. Vinke told us to 'Take very good care of the textbook, *Effective Communication*, and only bring it to class when asked, so that it would be in good condition when we went to sell it on the used book market', because it wasn't 'worth keeping.' I said to Jack Barsness that I found that strange since Howard Dean had dedicated the book to her. Jack said the reason for the dedication was that the manuscript had been rejected by the publisher the first time it was submitted and Mr. Dean was moaning and groaning and wringing his hands. Sarah said, 'Stop your whining Howard, give me that manuscript. I'll take it home and fix it.' When resubmitted, it was accepted by Prentice-Hall. But Jack said Sarah was right, the book still wasn't worth keeping.

Dr. Gurr sent me Sarah Vinke's article, 'Self-Criticism in Speech,' which was about in-class speech instruction and helping students be at ease and better able to accept the criticism of fellow students. He asked me if what Dr. Vinke's article stated fit my experience.

What speech I took from Vinke was incorporated in the Oral and Written Communication course. I am trying to remember what procedures she used. I know they were not just one speech after another. A perhaps irrelevant memory is of the female student who at the beginning of her talk Draped a cat cadaver floating in formaldehyde in a sealed clear plastic container over the speaker stand, but did not refer to it at all during her speech. When asked about it afterward, the student said that we were told the importance of using an attention getting device and that it had certainly caught our attention. (By the way, it was commonly thought you should keep close watch on your pet cat during the term dissection was being taught in science courses.)

The methods Dr. Vinke advocates in her 'Self-Criticism in Speech' sound like something she may have done, but I have no clear memories of it, something perhaps complicated by the fact that I took a good, though more conventional speech course my senior year at Gallatin High, which included being the announcer for a fifteen-minute radio show recorded in class but broadcast over a local radio station; so I still got nervous giving talks, but accepted it as natural and as something that went away with time.

On one occasion, when Dr. Vinke was going to a conference for a week, she assigned speeches and asked me to go each day to get the key to her office from the department secretary, pick up her roll book and a tape recorder, and to call on the students in turn to give their talks. I remember that there was more to it than that, such as writing comments and handing them to the speaker, the speaker answering questions, etc. At the time, I was concerned about being considered the teacher's pet, but did as instructed. In retrospect, again, was Mrs. Vinke sending a message to me about my future?

Apparently, Professor John Parker was also interacting with Vinke. He used to give open book essay tests in Major British Writers (a practice I later used in ninth grade college prep courses). But more to the point, he set a term paper deadline several weeks before the end of the quarter and then had us present our papers orally to the class. The class was supposed to take notes during the presentation and hand them up to the speaker, after which he [the speaker] could comment on them and take questions from the class and Parker. At the beginning of the third term of British Writers, Parker informed us that his procedure for having us deliver term papers orally was an adaptation of a procedure advocated by Dr. Sarah Vinke of the English Department. Incidentally, I discovered that Parker enjoyed off-color humor, so I used to build a reference to something bawdy into my term papers. It worked every time.

Dennis also remembers actually attending a party at Sarah's home. As he explains of the experience:

I've been in the house Shirley Luhrsen describes in Henry Gurr's telephone interview with her as being that of Dr. Vinke. I've eaten those dishes she describes, seen and heard that piano. I can't remember who played it but was asked if I would like to (I don't play.) I can't remember who all was there or what the occasion. But sometime before the party, Sarah walked into a class I was in, not her own, and handed me an envelope saying, 'Here, this is for you.' Inside was an invitation. Only one or two other students in the class got an invitation. Another student nudged me, saying 'That's' a real compliment' as Sarah walked out. I was staying in my fraternity's house at the time. What a contrast.
    I don't think I have much more on Sarah's home. It may have been a duplex arrangement. Not so much cluttered as tightly organized, a place for everything and everything in its place. I may have also been concerned with getting back across town to the

fraternity house for dinner as we were fined for missing it.

I've been trying to remember what Sarah said about church, probably to me in her office. It was something to the effect that the importance of Sunday attendance was to get away from the cares of the workaday world and commune (she did not say with what or whom).

Shirley tells you of Sarah's trouble getting around with a cane, during her final years at MSC. Montana Hall did have an elevator, but it was so slow you would have to allow fifteen minutes to get the elevator to go three floors and back. Rolling open the door took strength as well.

Shirley alludes to a Bozeman production of *Henry IV* and Sarah explaining the stir it caused in the community. What I remember fits this well: I have studied the Henry plays under Sarah; and under Angus Bowmer, at the Oregon Shakespeare Festival, who at the time was producing *Henry IV, Part I*. While I was there, Bowmer himself played the part of Falstaff that summer. Also, Waldo McNair at U. Oregon covered this and related plays. In the play *Henry IV*, the character Falstaff is engaged in leading Prince Hal astray and frequents the 'house' of Mistress Quickly and Doll Tearsheet. He also drafts rich men's sons into his army and then lets them buy their way out using the money to hire his barfly cronies. In order to get credit for slaying an enemy soldier, Falstaff stabs a dead man, saying, 'The better part of valor is discretion.' One can imagine how all this went over in small town Montana seventy or more years ago. I think Sarah alluded once to the local production and its problems, but I can't remember anything specific.

Teaching veterans on the GI Bill could be an added problem even when I was in school, because many were still taking advantage of the GI Bill rather than going to class out of any love of learning. Also, of course they were somewhat older and more experienced in the way of the world.

Shirley's mention of WWII veterans brought back this memory: Once when Sarah stepped in on a minute's notice to substitute in Major American Writers for Paul Grieder, and was certainly filling in time, she asked how many of us even knew what Moby Dick was. Before anyone could chime in about it being the name of a book and a whale, a veteran chimed in that it was a venereal disease. It didn't faze Sarah who just laughed with the rest of us, placing her hands on her knees, and then went on.

Dennis adds:

After leaving teaching in 1968 following a nervous breakdown, I spent a year in Stockton CA, working as a social worker in Old Age Security, not a good way to recover. Then I entered an Alcohol Rehab program in Sacrament, eventually getting a job as a hotel timekeeper in Sacramento.

Concerning Mr. Gary's experience: Readers will doubtlessly know that teachers in all levels of American public schools are now—and have been—under tremendous pressure. After years in the classroom, they often suffer their own form of 'battle fatigue'. Perhaps, not as severe as in war, but no less real. And the better teachers are the ones who suffer the most because they keep trying to hold the students and themselves to very high standards. These teachers don't give up, despite often impossible circumstances. And our modern society doesn't help them much. There are of course parallels here to what happened to Pirsig, as reported in *ZMM*.

Dennis continues:

> After that, I was unemployed for some time and lived in a boarding house run by Dorothea Puente, who as things turned out, became a notorious serial killer in Sacramento. She may even have come close to killing me, because on the day I moved out, as a parting gesture, she offered me a 'nice, cold glass of ice water.' Several hours after that I was vomiting and had diarrhea, then felt weak, but exhilarated, as my body had purged the toxins.
> Just imagine, two important women in my life: Sarah Vinke and Dorothea Puente.

Dennis continues:

> By inclination, I am a literature person, not a philosopher, although someone with a degree in philosophy has told me that my interest in linguistics puts me in the same ball park. I have only once been on (the back of) a motorcycle, and that for less than thirty minutes, twice in my life. I am more of a house plant than an outdoors man, though growing up on a Montana ranch necessitated learning about nature. I have walked the streets of Bozeman, wandered the buildings of Montana State College, learned in the classrooms of

Sarah Vinke and visited her office, fished from the banks of the Gallatin River, climbed Mt. Blackmore, and been in Cottonwood Canyon. All these things are in, or referred to, in *ZMM*. Like Pirsig, I have looked out the windows of Montana Hall and seen the Madison range. I wondered then how Sophocles and Shakespeare could have made it across such vast expanses, to this cultural oasis, Montana Hall?

I sought Sarah out several years after graduating when I was back in Bozeman briefly, not knowing whether she was dead or alive. I found her address on Arthur Street and knocked on the door. No one answered. Then I noticed a door bell and rang it. A woman answered the door, and I explained who I was and that I wondered if Mrs. Vinke still lived there. She replied that Mrs. Vinke did not, but said it was okay that I had asked.

I was living here in San Francisco when Pirsig's son Chris was murdered. I can remember taking a bus that went past the Zen Center and over to Haight St. to view the scene of the crime. Somehow, it seemed the right thing to do.

Years before, while passing through Bozeman, I entered Montana Hall, while it was empty. It certainly had the feel described by Pirsig in *ZMM*.

I do remember Sarah's response when a classmate of mine handed her a wedding invitation was one of delight, but with a comment to the effect, 'Who would have thought that an old bag like me would ever again be a member of a wedding party.'

A similar incident, was a Mountain Retreat Excursion dinner presented by the Gallatin Canyon Women's Club: I was recruited by Sarah Vinke to drive because my familiarity with Gallatin Canyon, Karst Camp, the Flying D Ranch, and Spanish Creek, Cherry

Creek, and Hell Roaring Creek, gave me a better chance of finding the place, than the others who were in the group. So there I was with a hand-drawn map and a copy of written-out directions in my hand.

I borrowed the family Buick from my parents, and the group from MSC piled in. There were several individuals I did not know and several members of the faculty from the Montana State College History Department whom I recognized. One of the History Department professors playfully commented that he hoped we didn't get into an accident because there would be no English or History Departments left if we did.

After everyone had arrived, Sarah showed up last. Leaning on her cane, she came walking up just as I was wondering if we should go looking for her. Sarah got into the front seat and closed the door thinking that from there she might assist me with directions. On the way up to Deer Creek, Sarah and I sat in the front seat with another woman between us; this may have been Shirley Luhrsen, but I cannot recall for sure. I met her in a very peculiar way. The arrangement was that I would wait in the parking lot across the street from the back of Montana Hall in the car described. This woman showed up, tapped on the door, and said, 'Dennis?'

I don't remember her introducing herself as Shirley, but I do remember the [robin's egg] blue cowboy boots she was wearing. In my mind I am trying to establish who, of the several other persons on the trip, sat in the back seat of the Buick. I think that Verne Dusenberry, Robert Dunbar, Alton Oviatt, Merrill Burlingame, and Pirsig were the possible members of this traveling caravan. I am not sure; this is, of course, all lost in history—no pun intended. I imagine there was room for four or five.

So off I drove on Highway 191, electing to take the old 191 route through Gallatin Gateway and cross the Gallatin River before turning up Gallatin Canyon. I chose to use the old Highway 191 as I felt it would be easier to keep my bearings by recognizing the many landmarks such as the Spanish Creek, Flying D Ranch, Hell Roaring Creek, Cherry Creek, and many more.

The roads up to Deer Creek were really country roads, not much more than unmarked dirt trails, branching off for no apparent reason. While some of my passengers had been there before, several had not. It is difficult to explain where you are going to someone else if you haven't personally driven the roads before.

At any rate, I had a sense of triumph when I pulled up a trail and there were the Deer Creek Cabins.

Unfortunately, our dinner was being prepared at another camp that was a number of miles away. However, it was announced that the dinner was being brought over to Deer Creek. This was a real relief to me considering the strain of driving to Deer Creek from Bozeman.

We spent the night at Deer Creek after a big dinner. I shared a cabin bedroom with one faculty member, with single beds on different sides of the room. Considering the long drive I had just made, I slept very soundly and woke up to a breakfast that was prepared by the women on the trip.

Later on in the day, the faculty men organized a softball game. Not being into sports, I did not join in; but I watched briefly. It was interesting to see grown men with PhD's batting and running bases around the informal diamond. There also was a tennis net strung between trees on either side of a clearing. I walked a little way up the trail at the side of the cabin and contemplated crossing the log over the creek; but lacking the sureness of foot and balance, I just sat and relaxed beside of the creek. [In her own Deer Creek writings, Shirley Luhrsen states that the 'tennis' net was in fact for badminton.]

Later on that evening, the group that had come in the Buick left at my suggestion. On the way up, I had elected to take the old Highway 191 because it gave me the needed orientation to landmarks; yet, coming back I suggested the new highway which bypassed Gallatin Gateway. This would get us to Bozeman faster, and had the advantage of giving the faculty a quick look at the Nine Quarter Circle Ranch, another noteworthy location. Sarah remarked as we passed one ranch that her husband Louis Vinke, had been involved with it. I felt like I was quite a tour director.

It was dark by the time we got back to Bozeman, and I suggested that I would be happy to drive each person to his or her door. One wanted to be dropped off behind Montana Hall, and the others I dropped at their homes. They seemed pleased with my willingness to cater to them, but I must admit that I had an ulterior motive: as a student at Montana State College I was curious about my professors, who each day appeared out of nowhere and disappeared into nowhere. By taking them home, I would find out more about them and where they lived. When my driving duties were completed, I contemplated calling the Phi Sigma Kappa house and getting a bed for the night. But with just a twenty-minute drive ahead of me, I instead headed back to our ranch near Gallatin Gateway and my own warm bed.

Currently, I am living in a room in a residential hotel, Herbert Hotel, in San Francisco and making do on what I get from Social Security retirement and a small annuity, courtesy of Wells Fargo, which took over Crocker Bank in 1986. Life on the jagged edge, I sometimes call it. Most of what I have written of my recollections of Sarah was typed in the H2O Café on Polk Street in San Francisco, surrounded by drug dealers, prostitutes, the disabled, and a smattering of businessmen, artists, professional people and students.

We have both greatly enjoyed working with Dennis on this project. We agree with Sarah wholeheartedly; we most emphatically feel that Dennis is Quality.

-o00O00o-

NOTE1: Readers may read more of Mr Dennis Gary's considerable writings Re Mrs Professor Sarah Vinke, by Googling some combination of => Dennis Gary, OR *Howard Dean, Nemesis to Robert Pirsig while Teaching in the MSC English Department.*

NOTE2: CAUTION: Readers who access Howard Dean's Book (steps below), should, after this page comes up, scroll to the bottom, since the first book pages are there.

NOTE3: Readers may see a selection of some 22 pages of Howard Deans Book, by Googling =>
   APPENDIX I: EFFECTIVE
   COMMUNICATION, Howard Dean, Prentice-Hall, 1953

Chapter 9: One Witness Talks To Another --
The Dennis Gary Interview With David Swingle.

Dennis Gary's contribution to any investigation of Sarah Vinke's life would be remarkable and extensive purely based on his own personal experience, but he provided another, almost equally exciting insight into Sarah. This was when, on August 3, 2014, he interviewed David Swingle, who was also an alumnus of MSU at Bozeman. Dr Swingle had many excellent recollections of Sarah to offer.

[NOTE: To find an Internet Link to this entire interview, & other related information, please Google > *Sarah Vinke Biography Resource Page*]

Dennis was eager to talk to David Swingle because he knew that David had also known Sarah and it turns out that David was himself profoundly influenced by *Zen and the Art of Motorcycle Maintenance.*

At the time when Dennis interviewed David, David was an official instructor and advisor in Museum Studies in the Museum of the Rockies at MSU. David was born in the year 1942. David didn't know Sarah nearly as well as Dennis did, partly because David was only a child at the time he knew Sarah. David's sister Diane, along with her family, was a member of the Episcopal Church in Bozeman and David's family knew Sarah socially. They asked Sarah if she would become Diane's godmother, and she was happy to do so. David recalls that when he was about eleven or twelve and around the time his sister Diane was confirmed, Sarah would often attend Sunday dinners with the family.

As David recalls:

> 'Sarah was very nice to me when I was a kid. She wouldn't talk down to me. She would talk with me. She would ask about my ideas and I can't recall her hectoring me at all. But I never had her for a class because when I finally got to the university, she no longer taught there.'

In the interview, David recalls that Sarah had a deteriorative spinal condition. As David says: 'Yes, she had a profound dowager hump, as I recall. She was probably very arthritic. As I remember in her house, she used one, if not two, canes.'

Prompted by this, Dennis himself recalls what he had not thought important to mention before, perhaps because Sarah's living presence made such a major inspirational effect upon him: that Sarah was close to an invalid.

> Unfortunately, Sarah's physical condition was literally deteriorating in front of us. I cannot remember her actual height, but she was not tall. It is a little hard to remember a teacher's height when so often you are a sitting student and the instructor is standing in front of you. By my

senior year she could be seen using a cane or crutches on campus.

Dennis prompted from David some interesting comments on the nature of people who taught at MSU in Sarah's day. David himself subsequently became a faculty member at MSU and remarks:

> I've been around this campus for a long time and I've seen lost souls who show up out here on some kind of teaching contract, a tenure or a non-tenure contract. The MSU community even now is so different and the values of the university are better than they used to be. But the values then, in the days of Sarah Vinke and Pirsig, were not really established or they were the values of people like Sarah who had standards that were very hard to meet. I think many people who taught there, and very likely Pirsig too, found it very hard to do their best work in an academic community that perhaps wasn't very congenial to them.
>
> I think perhaps the community gave opportunities for people like Sarah to teach and earn a living and accommodated their very iconoclastic attitude towards their subject. I also think that people like Pirsig were just really academic cannon fodder and had to work extremely hard for the freshmen they were teaching and marked papers that were often probably fairly illegible and maybe didn't make a great deal of sense. I can see why Pirsig became obsessed with other things and why perhaps he saw Sarah Vinke's comment about

the importance of quality as a kind of saving grace, and saving salvation, at a time in his life when he wasn't really enjoying his work very much and found his life fairly meaningless and full of drudgery. I mean, in that circumstance, you can really see, can't you, why he would find the idea of Quality as a goal of some great resonance and importance.

Dennis Gary's interview with David was lengthy and wide-ranging, although David's knowledge of, and recollections about Sarah are fairly limited and everything he said we are setting down here. David also made some interesting remarks about *Zen and the Art of Motorcycle Maintenance* and his comments are surely especially important as he himself subsequently became a faculty member at the very university where Sarah taught and where Pirsig was inspired by Sarah. This is how David describes how he first got to know *Zen and the Art of Motorcycle Maintenance* and the kind of influence it had on him, his thinking and his life.

> Well, how I was first introduced to the book *Zen and the Art of Motorcycle Maintenance* is kind of weird. My wife and I first taught in Detroit, on the edge of Detroit in a pretty backwards school situation where we actually had a lot of influence because we cared – bothered to do anything there. And then we moved to San Francisco where she was in the American Conservatory Theater while I was teaching school, and she went overseas with a

USO tour for a year, which gave me even more latitude to really deal with my teaching, and when we got back together we were really concerned about how provincial the Bay Area students were.

This is about the time that the movie *Deliverance* had come out and so Bay Area kids, kind of left-wing high school kids, were sure that the inland areas were full of bow-hunters killing outsiders. They had a very negative view of the rest of the country, very isolated. So we decided we'd form a traveling school in the summers. We bought an Air Force surplus bus and our students formed a co-operative and they raised all the money. No matter how wealthy they were, they had to raise all the money, without having Aunt Bessie write the check. So we would travel doing community stuff, community works during the summer. And sometimes we'd travel a bit during the school year on weekends and we'd travel out of California. Also we'd travel into rural areas of California, and so they'd get a much better view of reality.

Because I knew Montana well and had a place here in Bozeman, we'd come here. We had one student along named Rick Rodriguez. Rick was a big, heavy-set kid, but he was one of the brightest students I ever had. I could deal with Twain, Melville, or anything with him on pretty much a peer basis. While we were here in Montana, Spring, 1969, we took him to the MSU Student Book Store; of course, it was just a playground for Rick and the others. They loved it. He bought a copy of a weird book called *Zen and the Art of Motorcycle Maintenance,* and he said, after I asked him, 'Yeah. This book is written about this campus.'

So I thought, oh, good here's another one of this type, because there were a number of books out bashing inland campuses, about how backwards they were and so forth. So I avoided reading the book because I thought 'it's just another trashing of a poor campus, poor in quality and poor financially.' But then he said, 'No, you really have to read this.'

So I began to read and I came across Sarah Vinke and so I became more personally attached to the book. And I bought my own copy and struggled on through the first parts of it. As things turned out, at about the same time when I got onto the second part of the book, I was transferred from Advanced Placement English right out into heading Industrial Arts. So they told me I was running an 800-student Industrial Arts program. And so I was yanked out of what I had been teaching and put in the shops out behind the school. But because we needed some extra money, I also began teaching night school, too. So I taught for the junior college (College of Marin), where I originated a course in Auto Mechanics for Women.

As I prepared a curriculum for it, I recalled reading the second part of *Zen and the Art of Motorcycle Maintenance,* which really deals with the matter of logic and causality. It's so clear and so vivid. What I did was take cuttings out of the book *[ZMM]:* actually literally cut a book up because this was pre-computer and photocopied the paste-up. So the course was designed for mostly divorced and widowed women who had to deal with automobiles and they were getting ripped off by dealership service managers and private mechanics all over the place. For tuition and living I'd worked as a mechanic for years and I saw horrendous problems with this. So I would use quotes from the book. I'd actually cut the book up and put it on a Xerox machine and run it off for them so they'd have it in class, and we really got used to the idea that there's nothing 'magical' in the machine.

The Sutherland family, in *Zen and the Art of Motorcycle Maintenance,* is always concerned about getting there, not about how a machine runs and not how to prevent trouble. So because of *Zen and the Art of Motorcycle Maintenance,* I was able to really stress preventive maintenance. Check your tires. Check your oil. Don't burn the car up unnecessarily. And when you deal with a service manager, here are the questions you ask. But they really liked the book and some of them would go back and read the front of the book. So I found the book tremendously useful. I think other teachers could still do this.

Since that time there's been a real change in public thinking because of computers. Computers are like what Pirsig was writing about in his manuals, I expect. You have to do it right, or it flat-out doesn't work. Computers aren't intuitive, not even Macintosh's, which are closer to being intuitive. If you don't enter the right date, you don't get the right result. Now,

Google is beginning to use a kind of generalized thinking like a human does, but you have to search correctly or it won't run, not because its evil or that information technology can't help you, but because you didn't do it right. So you have to go in there and you have to analyze what you did stage by stage.

When Pirsig is dealing with a fuel/air mixture (a carburetor mixture on a motorcycle), he analyzed the plugs or he'd look at the carburetor setting or realized if he changed altitude… I think there's one part in the book when they're coming into Miles City which is a higher elevation than the Dakotas and the bikes aren't running well because the air density has changed. And Pirsig goes through what he did for carburetor adjustment. But the Sutherlands won't go through it; they'd rather just blame the machine. They had a BMW motorcycle, a much better cycle than the Honda that Pirsig had. They'd blame the machine, instead of becoming logical. They could only behave in frustrated irrationality.

I taught with a guy in San Rafael called John Kenward. And John Kenward was a close friend of the Sutherlands, and he had lived in a commune with them. A communal situation, I believe in Minneapolis. Unfortunately, John has been dead now for twenty-five years. But he would tell me stories about the Sutherlands and said that Pirsig got it absolutely right; that they were very nice people, but they really wouldn't figure out how anything worked, including the household they were in. They refused to solve simple plumbing problems. I remember he mentioned that. She would try to make bread that was supposed to rise but it wouldn't and she said they couldn't figure out the yeast mixtures.

On the other hand, there was Pirsig, who was able to logically sort out a situation to get through it. And I've always been fascinated by his comments and his views on his son as he tries to intuit how his relatively silent son is interpreting his trip. A Honda 305, the motorcycle Pirsig was riding, is actually quite a small motorcycle, and with the load they had, it must have been really uncomfortable for Pirsig's son Chris on it.

Thinking about life generally, we're much better nowadays about tolerating variation and novelty in our fellow beings. The 1950s were very much a time of polarity. You were either conventional or you were a Commie. There wasn't really much time for people who deviated from the norm, but look now at the number of street and sidewalk ramps we have and special facilities for the handicapped. It's a simple matter of tolerance. Nowadays we try to deal with people who are different and help them and we acknowledge their disadvantages. People with limitations are, quite rightly, encouraged and allowed to thrive. I think we are now a much more democratic society and my guess is that Pirsig's book significantly helped to further this process. Who knows, after all, how many readers bought copies and then passed the copies around to their friends? I think you can easily see how that would create maybe four or five times more readers than the ones who originally bought the book.'

On the matter of Quality, well, I often think of this in terms of planned obsolescence, which was a big deal when we were young; the idea that organizations would design products that were actually deliberately manufactured in order to go wrong at some point so consumers would have to buy some new products.

Now, this wasn't an approach to life, I think, that was seen in the nineteenth century or the earlier part of the twentieth century. In the nineteenth century particularly, the sheer quality of products such as furniture and machinery was stunning even though technologically speaking their machines don't really compare in terms of technological sophistication, with what became available in the later twentieth century. I know quite a lot about mechanics and I've worked as a mechanic and I can attend to a wide range of cars including Porsches which are a complicated kind of car, yet now even a basic car is a much better vehicle in every sense than a Porsche was thirty years ago. Cheap new cars are faster, handle better and are more reliable than the expensive cars of two decades back. A Porsche used to be a great car. Now the Porsche is no better than the average new sedan.

Automobiles, and the quality of appliances, and the quality of computers; these factors have all evolved faster than anyone could have imagined even a few years ago. My Masters degree at San Francisco State University was in Educational Technology in 1970. We used to envision having teaching machines that would never get tired and now we have them and computer based curricula work very well. I think we're in better times now, despite the twenty-four deluge of bad news. I think people are better. I think ethics are better. I think Pirsig's ability to weather the terrible circumstances of his life, including the death of his son Chris, have made him one of the many models of people who got through the 1950s – which I think was the lowest time in US history – and managed to blossom despite having lived through that time. I saw something on the television recently about an actress who was blacklisted in the 1950s for twelve years – yes, twelve years. – at the height of her career simply because she had gone to a Communist Party member's funeral and given a eulogy and as a result she got blacklisted. I think things are better now. And I think Pirsig's book did indeed play a part in this and I think his emphasis on Quality is vitally important.

Altogether, Dennis Gary seems to us, to have elicited some interesting comments from David Swingle; comments that help to set Pirsig, *ZMM*, and the United States intellectual climate of the 1950s in perspective. We have the sense that in the interview Mr. Gary conducted with Dr. Swingle, the fact that they had both been students at MSU, and had both known Sarah, made them highly effective collaborators in their combined summoning of important memories of Sarah, and of the atmosphere at MSU back then.

Chapter 10:Quality: A Dialog Between The Authors.

This chapter is based on a dialog, which took place via Skype between Henry Gurr (HG) and James Essinger (JE). The subject is Quality in the sense that Sarah famously gave to the word. The dialog has been edited for clarity and coherence, Skype conversations not necessarily being known for either. Additional material has been added to the dialog by both of us since the Skype took place. Where the dialog included quotations from memory, these were replaced by the exact passages. Here, as generally in this book, we use the abbreviation ZMM for 'Zen and the Art of Motorcycle Maintenance'.

JE - Henry, we already know from your material earlier about the background of how you began reading Pirsig's famous book and began thinking about it. In this Dialog we're going to be talking about the concept of 'Quality' in terms of how Sarah Vinke and Pirsig used the term.

HG - James, let me please say right away that, as I've mentioned before, I have serious concerns, and grave misgivings about any long discussions concerning the word Quality: Let me give some background which I think will help readers understand what I'm worried about. *ZMM* readers will remember that the word Quality was used, evidently first by Sarah, and then at her prodding, taken up by Pirsig. From all we have learned about Sarah, we see she is a wonderful person, full of energy and goodness. Pirsig said of her: 'A brilliant teacher.'

Yes, Sarah was a real artist at teaching. She was such an imaginative, creative person, that, as we've seen, her students called her 'The Divine Sarah'. However, there is plenty of evidence she really didn't much use the word Quality, or much talk about it. And there is thus plenty of reason to believe that Sarah would refuse to intellectualize about Quality. Instead, she lived and breathed Quality, and urged those around her, especially students, to do the same. Similarly, in *ZMM*, Pirsig does not even use the word Quality, until near the middle of his book. The first use of word Quality is near the end of Chapter 14 of *ZMM*. The next three uses are Sarah's, in chapter 15.

Let me emphasize: For the first half of *ZMM*, rather than 'talk about (or use word Quality), Pirsig tells us where and how good things physically happen to him, and then his qualitative response(s). This writing pattern continues for all of *ZMM*; we see it is his method and is apparently on purpose. Also, we see all this is done in his first half of *ZMM* without the word Quality. Here are some examples of 'good experiences' from just his first three pages of *ZMM*.

> *The wind, even at sixty miles an hour, is warm and humid. When it's this hot and muggy at*

eight-thirty, I'm wondering what it's going to be like in the afternoon.

We are in an area of the Central Plains filled with thousands of duck hunting sloughs, heading northwest from Minneapolis toward the Dakotas. This highway is an old concrete two-laner that hasn't had much traffic since a four-laner went in parallel to it several years ago. ... I'm happy to be riding back into this country. It is a kind of nowhere, famous for nothing at all and has an appeal because of just that. Tensions disappear along old roads like this. ....

But now in July [red-winged blackbirds] *they're back and everything is at its alivest and every foot of these sloughs is humming and cricking and buzzing and chirping, a whole community of millions of living things living out their lives in a kind of benign continuum. You see things vacationing on a motorcycle in a way that is completely different from any other. In a car you're always in a compartment, and because you're used to it you don't realize that through that car window everything you see is just more TV. You're a passive observer and it is all moving by you boringly in a frame.*

On a cycle the frame is gone. You're completely in contact with it all. You're in the scene, not just watching it anymore, and the sense of presence is overwhelming. That concrete whizzing by five inches below your foot is the real thing, the same stuff you walk on, it's right there, so blurred you can't focus on it, yet you can put your foot down and touch it anytime the whole thing, the whole experience, is never removed from immediate consciousness. ....

We are just vacationing. Secondary roads are preferred. Paved county roads are the best, state highways are next. Freeways are the worst. We want to make good time, but for us now this is measured with emphasis on 'good' rather than 'time' and when you make that shift in emphasis the whole approach changes.

It was some years ago that my wife and I and our friends first began to catch on to these roads. We took them once in a while for variety or for a shortcut to another main highway, and each time the scenery was grand and we left the road with a feeling of relaxation and enjoyment. We did this time after time before realizing what should have been obvious: these roads are truly different from the main ones. The whole pace of life and personality of the people who live along them are different. They're not going anywhere. They're not too busy to be courteous. ... The discovery was a real find.

I've wondered why it took us so long to catch on. We saw it and yet we didn't see it. Or rather we were trained not to see it.

Conned, perhaps, into thinking that the real action was metropolitan and all this was just boring hinterland. It was a puzzling thing. The truth knocks on the door and you say, 'Go away, I'm looking for the truth,' and so it goes away. Puzzling. ....

So here, in just the first three pages of *ZMM*, are examples of *how* in the first half of his book Pirsig creates, page after page of inspiring and challenging words in *ZMM,* discussing the shades and meanings, and goodness and quality of experiences *without using the word Quality*. Thus, overall, Pirsig clearly sees Quality as something that can only be understood and recognized in a specific application and in specific circumstances. And that outside a real world experience or application, the concept of Quality cannot usefully be defined, or even in words usefully much talked about. As Pirsig says in *ZMM:*

> *'Once you begin to hear the sound of that Quality, see that Korean wall, that non-intellectual reality in its pure form, you want to forget all that word stuff, which you finally begin to see is always somewhere else.'*

For these reasons, we must accept as negative the fact that our *Dialog on Quality* will unfortunately be a lot of mere word-talking about Quality. And as we do this, we have to remember this is not the Pirsig approach, nor even Sarah's. But on account of the fact that Sarah's and Pirsig's meanings for Quality are very complex, subtle, and tenuous, even vague, I agree we should proceed with this *Dialog On Quality*. But as we do this, I think we should try to remember, as Pirsig put it, that

> *'all this talk about Quality, isn't Quality.'*

Correspondingly, we will bring out how Pirsig, without the Q word, nevertheless 'creates an overall, philosophy of excellence in all endeavours, life choices and outputs.' In this Chapter, we will try to offer concrete real world examples of what 'Pirsig's idea of Quality *embodies.*'

JE – Yes, I accept what you say, but I still don't see why I or we should feel inhibited in talking about what Quality actually means, all the same. I suppose we will just have to accept that we have a healthy disagreement on this subject; I'm not sure it's necessarily good for a book if the collaborators agree on everything.

By the way, in reading *ZMM* about Quality, I realized that Pirsig himself was aware of how obsessed he became with the concept of Quality and Pirsig does admit that he has a fairly obsessive mind. Would you argue that a writer of his calibre needs to have an obsessive mind...?

HG – Perhaps so. ... But I would say it was really Phaedrus that was the obsessive one, and not author Pirsig, as he was writing *ZMM* years later. I say this because, for me obsessive means out of control, 'his fanatic intensity' as was Phaedrus at Bozeman and U Chicago. For author Pirsig, far better words would be: Persistent, tenacious, unrelenting, resolute, forceful: But ultimately, as the creative writing of *ZMM* is done, control and discipline are also seen.

So Pirsig in *ZMM,* can be better described as extremely tenacious in his quest for truth. So, having three times been prodded by Sarah to pursue her idea of Quality, Phaedrus tenaciously, and unrelentingly, went into a deep examination of the idea, and it was Pirsig finally writing these discoveries into *ZMM* in some very exciting, and indeed immortal, prose. The result was no less than a new foundation for Western Philosophy where, strange to say, there was none previously. Essentially Phaedrus' resolute pursuit started when he realized that he himself did not know, at a deep level, what Quality actually was. But given his penetrating insightful mind, he ended up with a profound paradigm changing foundation for Western Philosophy and Culture. Other people, never having Pirsig's tenacity or Phaedrus's tenacity, had for over 2000 years failed to realize (or do anything about), major and disastrous fault zones in current day Western Philosophy, Science, Mathematics. As Pirsig wrote:

> *Analysis* [reason, logic, math, science, etc], *however, seemed to have something wrong with it that prevented it from seeing the obvious. ... The cause of our current social crises, he* [Phaedrus] *would have said, is a genetic defect within the nature of reason itself. And until this genetic defect is cleared, the crises will continue. Our current modes of rationality are not moving society forward into a better world. They are taking it further and further from that better world. Since the Renaissance these modes have worked. As long as the need for food, clothing and shelter is dominant they will continue to work. But now that for huge masses of people*

> *these needs no longer overwhelm everything else, the whole structure of reason, handed down to us from ancient times, is no longer adequate. It begins to be seen for what it really is—emotionally hollow, aesthetically meaningless, and spiritually empty. That, today, is where it is at, and will continue to be at for a long time to come.*
>
> *We have artists with no scientific knowledge and scientists with no artistic knowledge and both with no spiritual sense of gravity at all, and the result is not just bad, it is ghastly. The time for real reunification of art and technology is really long overdue.*

So here we see what was pushing Pirsig, compelling him into high-caliber action, were these disastrous defects, in science, and ultimately our western society. He saw these as huge problems, crying to be fixed, hence his tenacious and seeming obsessive pursuit of Quality, which he saw as the answer to it all.

JE – What exactly is it about the concept of Quality that you think came to concern, fascinate, and obsess Pirsig?

HG – In *ZMM*, we first learn about Pirsig's preoccupation with Quality when Pirsig re-visits his old Montana State University campus, and walks into Montana Hall and discovers his old office. [As we've stated earlier in *A Woman of Quality*] it's very likely that this visit really did happen. As Pirsig relates the experience, he suddenly starts having a long series of very strong memories, and very emotional memories.

In particular, he remembers it was Sarah that said to him, as Phaedrus, in her enigmatic way, *'Are you teaching Quality?'* And after Sarah asked this, for the third time, he started thinking about it, and he realized he really didn't know. For him it was a giant enigma, and I remember in the book, he says he stayed at his desk puzzling over it until nine in the evening. And when his wife called him and asked him what happened, he told her he would be right home. Then in his obsession, he forgot even about that. And it wasn't until three AM that he decided to go home, totally stumped on what Quality was about.

Now Pirsig, as Phaedrus, clearly had a very, very active mind and would indeed pursue questions and problems, tenaciously to their very end until he got an answer. Ultimately, that's what caused him his psychological breakdown. But his pursuit of Quality, working on it, and turning it over, and coming back to it, and working on it; and working with students on it, and getting them to write about it, was just the beginning of a very long chain of intense activity that persisted essentially until the book *ZMM* came out. His teaching in Montana was in 1959 to 1961. His motorcycle trip which was written into the Zen book was in 1968, and the book itself came out in 1975. What is that... fourteen years? It took this long for Pirsig's tenacity to reach an answer that was acceptable to him.

JE – Yes, about that. I'll be asking in a minute about what you think Quality is. But just getting back to Pirsig for a moment, when the Sarah incident happens in the book, the book's tone seems to me to change dramatically. The book begins really... well the book's fascinating all the way through... but it begins as quite a homely, friendly account of a journey, a motorcycle journey, which then starts to get interspersed with deep and fascinating philosophical ruminations, which Pirsig calls Chautauquas, and tells us why he uses this name for them. I personally find it an extremely satisfying name for this philosophy discussion of his.

Once he brings Sarah in, though, the tone of his thinking starts to change. There is more of a sense of puzzlement and to a certain extent, a hard-driven, anguished search for this truth of what this Quality might mean.

HG – Absolutely. And it's very perceptive of you to see this major shift in the book. He uses the first half of *ZMM*, to use your words: 'Create many thousands of inspiring words in *ZMM* discussing (without this Q word), what Quality means to him, and what the idea of Quality *embodies*' But after Sarah's enigmatic '*Are you teaching Quality?*' question, Pirsig tells us that

> *That was the moment it all started. That was the seed crystal... The one sentence 'I hope you are teaching Quality to your students' was said to him, and within a matter of a few months,*

growing so fast you could almost see it grow, came an enormous, intricate, highly structured mass of thought, formed as if by magic.

So, yes indeed, this is where *ZMM* changes 'tone': Starting here Pirsig tells us of his ever heightening pursuit of just what means Quality. To paraphrase Pirsig: *'He was actively in pursuit of something now.'* He is tenacious and relentless ... but not obsessive ... in seeking answers for the Remainder of *ZMM*.

ZMM enthusiast Lee Glover, a correspondent of mine, pointed out yet another major shift in *ZMM*, just after the one you point out: This is at the mountain top, where fear of physical rock-slides and fear of a mental rock-slide, abruptly force the Narrator to abandon any higher climb, and start down. Here, the reader immediately realizes that the *ZMM* narrative metaphorically abandons his ever higher idealistic philosophic investigation. Thus we have:

BEFORE MOUNTAIN TOP: Ever higher discussion of: Idealistic, philosophical, theory-laden, pie-in-sky, Savior Phaedrus.

AFTER MOUNTAIN TOP: Moving ever downward to: Practical, useful, down to earth, everyday things of the ever Practical Narrator who says:

'You go up the mountaintop and all you're gonna get is a great big heavy stone tablet handed to you with a bunch of rules on it... That's about what happened to him [Phaedrus] *.... Thought he was a goddamned Messiah. Not me, boy. The hours are way too long, and the pay is way too short. Let's go.* [down].

JE – What do you think motivated Sarah's mention of Quality to Pirsig, as reported in *ZMM* Chapter 15. From the testimony of Dennis Gary, who of course was taught by Sarah, and thus knew her well – 'You're Quality, Mr. Gary!', we can infer that the word Quality was one she used, at least on a few occasions, and perhaps in her own private meditations.

HG – James, this is a big puzzle, because as far as we are aware, beyond her conversations with Dennis Gary and Pirsig, Sarah seems NOT to have much mentioned the word Quality to anybody else or written it into her published articles of which we are aware. But, with the testimony of Dennis Gary and Pirsig, we see just how Sarah introduces the word 'Quality' and what it potentially could mean. With this, Sarah herself started a new and expanded understanding and usage for the word Quality. And it is *this* vastly expanded meaning that is used throughout the second half of *ZMM*. Now after *ZMM* came out, readers asked a host of questions, which forced Pirsig to do a tremendous amount of further thinking. His answers were written into his book *Lila*.

Now in *Lila,* Pirsig breaks Quality into two different parts. One of them he calls Static Quality, which is everything we know and feel and understand. In his Railroad Freight Train Analogy, he calls this Static Quality, which is the *contents* of the railroad train on the track of Quality. He means by Static Quality, that which is fixed, it's given, it's here. Thus, Static Quality is essentially all of our knowledge, all of our thoughts right up to the split-second of the moment, called 'right now'. So, Static Quality is what is in our minds, as well as all our history of our lives, and the history of our civilization. This means Static Quality is, for example, everything that's in my mind, everything that I've read in books, all my knowledge, how to get up in the morning and brush my teeth and how to read a book, and Static Quality is everything that's on my web pages. And for Pirsig in his analogy, the freight train analogy, Static Quality is the whole entire contents of the box-cars in the 120 car, two mile long, railroad train.

JE – So are you saying that Static Quality is what's in your head?

HG – Yes, everything that's in my head and everything I see around me. Now to make a restricted definition, Static Quality is everything that's around me, that's already in existence, that I'm *aware of, or can be aware of.* Now...

JE – I don't really get this. If you're saying that Quality is just thoughts in your head, I don't see how that tallies with Sarah's insistence on Quality as a particular positive attribute of something.

HG - It might become clearer if I explain what Dynamic Quality is according to Pirsig's thinking. While Static Quality is everything that already exists in your mind. It's already what's in the freight train box cars; it already has happened. In contrast to Static Quality, Pirsig introduces Dynamic Quality, which is the *action* of our mind finding and opening up the next split second of our life. Pirsig calls this 'the cutting edge of reality', which could also be called the cutting edge of new awareness, or the cutting edge of life's next experience. In his railroad train analogy, Pirsig says of Dynamic Quality, 'it's the very front skin of the freight train locomotive'. Thus Dynamic Quality is that which is actively and always moving forward, just as the very front of the freight train engine is always cutting, Dynamically, into new territory. And just as soon as this cutting edge has happened, we now have into mind thoughts and memories. And these thoughts plus memories, are now Static Quality, because they now exist, in your mind. Static Quality is the very thing that builds into your memory and knowledge, a split-second after Dynamic Quality has caused its leading edge to go wherever it goes, as Pirsig says: *'Following the* [railroad] *track of Quality'*.

JE – I understand this but it seems a bit abstract to me. It doesn't seem closely related to what you've described of Quality as being people's way of using their brains to solve problems. Which, by the way, has always seemed to me, from the moment you mentioned it to me, a wise and interesting way of understanding Quality. I mean, I personally feel that this biography of Sarah needs to be very clear in what its concepts are and maybe really clearer, than Pirsig sometimes is. And basically what you say is that Quality is indeed people using their brains to solve problems and it's the result of evolution giving people brains that allow them to solve problems.

That struck me as being a very wise and useful and comprehensive way of understanding Quality, because it links very well to Pirsig's ideas in the early chapters of *ZMM* exploring technology, about how understanding technology and making technology work to bring you benefits, is a really important thing to do.

I think Pirsig's view on technology was particularly accurate. He was writing in the late 1960s, and *ZMM* was published in 1974, which was close to a decade before the modern computer age really got going in the way we understand it. I mean the microchip hadn't even been invented then. But Pirsig was saying basically that when you have powerful technology you have to know how to use it and know what to do, to make it give it its very best performance, and it seems to me that is exactly how we relate to computers today. And so I think Quality as a manifestation of how human beings use technology to solve their problems is a very, very, pertinent definition -- OK, maybe not definition, we are supposed to avoid the word definition -- but way of understanding Quality, and I'm really, I'm much more comfortable when Quality is spoken in those kind of terms than when it's spoken of in more abstract terms that I don't really understand.

HG – Yes, let me pick this up in the following way. Your meaning of quality, 'quality of', as relates to 'product or service', is just one meaning, and a very restricted one. But Sarah and Pirsig's meaning vastly expands the meaning of Quality. Their Quality refers to a perception of an 'immediate participatory relationship', which is an action of our mind: Quality, especially Pirsig's Dynamic Quality, is our brain's ability to <u>automatically</u> perceive problems and proceed to solve those problems: And this is another way to say what I said above about Pirsig's Dynamic Quality, as 'the cutting edge'. Now it's important to see how these two ways of describing fit each other, and also fit with the achieving of 'The Good'. Including as a by-product, good answers, and good results in the very process of all of our lives: Thus Dynamic Quality includes, but also goes way beyond, just quality technology products and quality services.

Doing what our brains are designed by nature to do, our minds <u>on-automatic</u>, can solve problems and in the process, instantly recognize *better* and *best* solutions. Now it is important to see that, this solving problems is fully equivalent to Pirsig's Dynamic

Quality, as 'the leading edge of reality': And is indeed how I earnestly urge our readers to think about Quality in action. In summary: As I understand Pirsig in his book *ZMM (*augmented by *Lila),* is this => Quality, especially Dynamic Quality, is our entire, holistic mind - body's nearly automatic problem solving response to life coming at us, and it's always dynamic, and is happening every split second. As Pirsig says in the quotation below, Quality is the cutting edge of creating our reality, itself:

> *Quality,* [is] *the leading edge .... The cutting edge of this instant right here and now is always nothing less than the totality of everything there is. Value,* [i.e. Quality is] *the leading edge of reality. ...* 'All of it. Every last bit of it.'

JE – OK, now I understand this.

HG – To take a concrete example: in this Dialog you are sometimes posing questions for me. Now in response (and this is the action of Dynamic Quality) I have to perceive your question. I have to prepare and formulate answers in my mind, then my audio system must change those apparent thoughts in my mind to English words, then English sentences. then these sentences must come out with a voice, in a clear enunciation, with clear, complete, direct answers which carry wholly my meaning, feeling, and understanding of what I want to say.

Now, that's Dynamic Quality. That's my brain problem-solving, providing answers, on the fly, to what's coming at me in this conversation. Saying it differently, I'm in a 'go state', 'primed' for high-quality action. An extreme version of this, can happen in a highly creative state called 'flow',

So, now once these thoughts have come into my mind, these thoughts, plus everything that has happened before, in my whole entire life, by Pirsig's statements, become Static Quality. This is how I understand Pirsig in *ZMM* and *Lila*. Just as soon as Dynamic Quality's done its job, you now have in your mind 'added contents' to your Static Quality.

Here, I'm suddenly reminded of an example of Dynamic Quality in what Pirsig told his students about writing when he was a teacher at Montana State College.

> *Now, in answer to that eternal student question, How do I do this? that had frustrated him to the point of resignation, he could reply, "It doesn't make a bit of difference how you do it! Just so it's good."* [Dynamic Quality] *The reluctant student might ask in class, "But how do we know what's good?" but almost before the question was out of his mouth he would realize the answer had already been supplied. Some other student would usually tell him, "You just see it."* [Dynamic Quality] *If he said, "No, I don't," he'd be told, "Yes, you do. He proved it." The student was finally and completely trapped into*

making quality judgments for himself. [Dynamic Quality] *And it was just exactly this and nothing else that taught him to write.*

This of course, is what they should achieve, in any and every aspect of life.

Ultimately, this message is Pirsig's overall goal in *ZMM*. In fact, in his public discussion *Art and the Metaphysics of Quality,* Pirsig says another example of Dynamic Quality:

'Art is [any] endeavor. Whether it's gonna come out right or not. It's still Art. It's what you do. It's who you are as a person that makes it Art or not Art.'

JE – Yes, I understand that. And now I can relate to the idea of Static and Dynamic Quality in the following terms. The distinction between the two types of Quality works very well in the relation to the history of technology, because after all the issue of technology you could argue is simply the answers that we human beings have come up with to solve a particular problem. Which is at the heart of why the technology exists.

HG – Yes, I'd agree with that.

JE – If you go to the Science Museum in London or the Science Museum in America and look at the old telephones there, you will find that telephones a hundred years ago look very different to the telephones of today. For one thing, our telephones today use tiny electronic microphones. In the past they tended to use granules of charcoal to actually create a field which would affect the diaphragm and pick up the sound.

So you could argue that Static Quality is the solution that we've come up with in the past.

This Dynamic Quality, to use the terms you use, is like the leading edge, basically the leading thinking edge, Pirsig's 'cutting edge of reality', in the *minds of the creators*, of new technology solutions that are coming up. Now that makes sense to me. My challenge, and then reward, is that sometimes during my reading of *ZMM*, Pirsig is often really in tune with what I totally relate to as far as what Quality means. For example, at one point in *A reader's guide to Zen and the Art of Motorcycle Maintenance,* he says, and I think this is a really important point he makes:

> *I think it [ZMM] practises what it preaches. I remember thinking to myself as I wrote it, 'If this is going to be an essay about quality you had better not fail to provide an example of it in the writing itself.'*

HG –Yes. Moreover, in *ZMM*, absolutely every word carries its own weight. This comes from the demands of Quality, plus Pirsig's good writing mind, plus constant demand of the publisher to keep costs down.: In ZMM these factors are very important, but you have to look close to see this truth => *EVERY* word carries its own weight. There are NO wasted superfluous words in ZMM !! .

Changing the subject, I'd like to add-on-to my above comment Re Pirsig's abovementioned public presentation *Art and the Metaphysics of Quality*. I'm remembering this talk was perhaps thirty minutes long, and he's focusing on Quality in doing art. First off we realize, that he's talking about art such as what artists make, a painting, or a drawing, or art could of course be the composer making music. Early in his discussion he says:

> *Quality is right in front of everyone's nose all the time. Some see it, some don't, but once one sees that Quality clearly and takes it as a guide for his whole life, then he becomes an artist, a real artist, regardless of what he happens to be doing at the moment.*

So, we see Pirsig's 'doing art' (ie Doing Quality), applies to *any and all actions of any person, no matter what that person is doing.* He continues, first with a passage from *ZMM,* then adds a bottom line thought:

> *Art is high-quality endeavor.' That's all that really needs to be said. Or, if something more high-sounding is demanded, 'Art is the Godhead as revealed in the works of man.' ... In the MOQ, those two statements are identical, and if you can get from one to the other you will have*

understood *Zen and the Art of Motorcycle Maintenance.*

Thus, he says

> '*it's who you are as a person that makes what you are actively now doing either art or not art.*'

Of course, Pirsig is all along pointing to the actions of Dynamic Quality. He says:

> *If it's really Art, then it is automatically being done with Dynamic Quality. 'Art by a two year old is Dynamic.'*

JE – So, you're saying that his definition of art, I mean, would you say that his definition of what is and what isn't art must boil down to whether it's any good or not?

HG – Yes, especially because <u>whatever our brain does is automatically good, and Quality, and thus Art</u>!! And again we notice '*Art*' in the title of the book – ZMM.

JE – Yes, that's a very important thing for you to remind us of, or to point out. Now we've come to what I think is a really crucial moment in this discussion and it's this, because I would agree with Pirsig, as a literary agent myself and as a writer. I'm only too familiar with the fact that some writing I get submitted is Quality and some isn't. In fact, the quality of writing I get seems to *stand on its own,* and it doesn't really seem that related to, for example, whether the person is a nice person or a friendly person, or whether they can even spell very well, or any other personal factor, except perhaps how articulate the person is.

What I find is that some people can write to a level that I would say is Quality and some can't. That's just the way it is. It's possible to help someone who can't, to write better, but there also needs to be some natural talent.

Now, I think that one of my jobs here in this biography of Sarah, as your collaborator, is to play devil's advocate, not because I want to be deliberately provocative but because I think that's one of my jobs. One of the things I still feel strongly about is this, I know that there is no easier way to annoy a devotee to Pirsig's obviously brilliant book than by saying to them, 'Well, would you please define Quality'. Of course, I know a *ZMM* devotee will refuse to do this, but it still seems to me that to wish for a general statement of what Quality means is important. Nobody could really deny that the content of Quality isn't vitally important in human culture.

HG – Yes, and of course this is, in essence, why Pirsig wrote *ZMM*. And considering how very difficult it is to understand and live Quality, I would further assert that to properly learn and understand Sarah's and Pirsig's Quality there is no other alternative than to completely absorb all Pirsig's book *Zen and the Art of Motorcycle Maintenance*. Ditto his *Lila*.

JE – Yes, and we want to get back to Sarah and Quality in a moment. But do you not think that a legitimate criticism of Pirsig's use of Quality, even though I certainly believe it was a very profound and useful term to focus on, is that it's subjective? And when he says of his own book, *this had to be a good book*, or rather when he said '*if I was going to write a book about Quality it had better be a Quality book*', then that makes a lot of sense to me. But really, no-one can prove *objectively* that Pirsig's book is any good, although I think it is, but only that there is a consensus of opinion that it is and that many millions of people have bought it – is this not a basic problem with the concept of Quality? That deciding what constitutes Quality (or not) is UN-scientific and highly subjective? Doesn't this, as an objective, material based experimental scientist, bother you?

HG – Here is my first kind of response to something like this question: This 'subjectivity problem' is just exactly the whole problem of life. It hardly matters what we are doing, we are constantly making choices, and decisions, and actively deciding what is good to do next as we go along. And these choices and decisions are pretty much based on subjective judgements, necessarily accomplished by our problem solving brain. This is Pirsig's Dynamic Quality and hence his cutting edge approach to reality. Moreover, our silent thoughts to ourselves and communications with other people tend to be vague, fuzzy, and ambiguous. At best, we get only a partial grasp of ... 'what's going on'. Consequently, we can only roughly think (or communicate) what we really mean or nail down what we really know ... about anything.

It took me a long time to realize (when teaching my students), that *all communication is ambiguous*, because words themselves are ambiguous. I'm searching for the correct term here – more than ambiguous, words can have many dual meanings. And it is for the perceiver, in this case the students, to figure out what the meaning is, and if they get hold of one meaning and it turns out to be wrong, they need to recognize that, and then look for a better, different meaning, and respond to that. All of life is ambiguous this way, and we've got to realize it. But it gets worse: All of our thoughts and judgements are subjective, and UN-scientific! Yes, subjective for everything we are involved in. Thus, we have to achieve an understanding how to live with this 'subjectivity problem'. And even this understanding of the subjective problem, is none other than a subjective understanding.

So ... one way or another, all of us, most especially students, must realize we are always dealing with the problems of subjectivity, ambiguity, and multiple meanings. And we have to, on our own, make it all work, within our own human limitations. In summary: It isn't just the human process called Quality that is subjective. Our choices and decisions, in fact for all of life, are mostly based off subjective judgements. We mostly don't have the time, and in many cases don't have the skill, to make scientific, logical judgements. In other words: Our mind in action, Pirsig's Dynamic Quality, is making our judgements and decisions, most of which are done "on the fly" and are subjective.

Now, in ancient times, Greek philosophers decided that what we need to do is become very definite, very explicit, to write things out. And *be very logical, and 'UN-subjective'*.

They are the ones that set up two ideas (really ideals). On the one hand, there's objective experience (and corresponding knowledge). And on the other hand, there's subjective experience (and it's corresponding knowledge). Called dualism, these two forms of knowledge are to be kept completely separated. And the whole drive of our Western Civilization, and specifically Western Philosophy, come down to a demand for very clear, explicit objective (i.e. scientific) answers to everything. And they decided there should be NO subjective anything: NO wishy-washy, fuzzy, opinionated, wilo-the-wisp, subjective, allowed anywhere. This had two effects: 1) Our own subjective knowledge not only is said to have no value (no Quality), but 2) The separation of subjective from the objective, has led to a complete separation of the person's own self, from their own world. And worse, they don't even know this. And to a large degree, this is where I was, up until the time I started reading Pirsig and Barfield.

All of this Pirsig discusses in *ZMM*. He points to the positive benefit of objective thinking in our science and then technology, and our modern civilization. On the other hand, Pirsig points out how there's a whole bunch of negatives that have come to pass with this 'evil dualism': All the while he is discussing the negative effects of the separation of the person from their word, he is showing us the operation of Quality, AND is showing how to become a <u>reunited, whole person</u>! Pirsig tells us that the drive for clear specific *Objective (i.e. Logical, Analytic, Scientific)* answers isn't enough. We must ALSO have *Subjective* answers and *Subjective Judgements* coming from Dynamic Quality. We have to recognize that, at rock bottom, all our human experience is subjective, but all the same, this is our *only* guiding force. Dynamic Quality based *Subjective Judgements* (so called by Pirsig) are always up front (*cutting edge of reality*) guiding us in everything we do (Dynamic Quality). And this includes even the scientist's so called objectivity. Here remember, I am a dyed in the wool career scientist. All of these are major points of both *ZMM* and *LILA*. And we've got to accept this, and *on our own,* we've got to work inside of it.

Concerning *subjectivity* (not to be confused with subjective judgements), we must carefully note what Pirsig says in *ZMM*:

> *He* [Phaedrus] *noted that although normally you associate Quality with objects, feelings of Quality sometimes*

> *occur without any object at all. This is what led him at first to think that maybe Quality is all subjective. But subjective pleasure wasn't what he meant by Quality either. Quality decreases subjectivity. Quality takes you out of yourself* [i.e. your Subjectivity, and], *makes you aware of the world around you. Quality is* [thus] *opposed to subjectivity.'* [Hence, for example your Quality response can reduce your Subjective Self-awareness (ego), and you can then make better Objective Observations, as in maintenance, or science.]

Later, Pirsig has this to add:

> *Quality should not be considered subjective, Quality should be considered as reality itself.' That's very important. And if you can get that reality itself which is free from subjectivity, free from ego, you have Art.*

So these are my and Pirsig's answers to your question: 'Doesn't this, as an *objective* scientist, bother you, that Quality in judgement is highly *subjective*?'

JE –. What I think you're saying really is this: *Let's not be surprised that our understanding of Quality is a subjective process, because actually Quality (and all of life), is precisely that.* And now I would like to return to a subject we've already discussed: Why is it, in your opinion, so dangerous and foolhardy to try to define the word Quality?

HG – I'd like to answer that by using an analogy. There is the concept of God that's been around us for a very long time: God, a creator of the universe, a God that is the author that keeps this whole world running, a God that ensures that he fills all of us with the desire for life, and to keep on wanting to be good productive persons. Now such a creature or being, in reality, is so unperceivably immense and so *all-encompassing*, for example, the whole universe, that just as soon as we attempt to say what that is, we have *reduced* the size of who God is, or can be. *As soon as you try to talk about God you have reduced and distorted the very thing that you're trying to talk about.* So you have to realize you don't try to talk about God with a capital G. Some of us just feel and notice God's presence, or at least feel the presence of something, or some being, and then this can be pointed to. Also, you can look at other people and see they are feeling much the same thing, forming a basis for discussion, again by pointing.

Now ALL of this inability for defining or discussing God applies by analogy to the notion of Quality. In the above, sentence by sentence, replace God by Quality! And, in agreement, with my 'why we should not try to define (or talk about), the word Quality' is a Pirsig statement in *ZMM*:

> *'Now, to take that* [Dynamic Quality], *which has caused us to create the world and include it within the world we have created, is clearly*

impossible. That is why Quality cannot be defined. If we do define it, we are defining something less than Quality itself. '
(Pirsig's '*create the world*' will be explained below.)

Earlier, in *ZMM*, Pirsig had been even more specific:

'*Since the One (Quality) is the source of all things and includes all things in it, it cannot be defined in terms of those things, since no matter what thing you use to define it, the thing will always describe something less than the One itself. The One can only be described allegorically, through the use of analogy, of figures of imagination and speech. Socrates chooses a heaven-and-earth analogy, showing how individuals are drawn toward the One by a chariot drawn by two horses. . . .*'

Also, here is a related Pirsig statement from *ZMM* that says we really should <u>*not even try*</u> to talk about what Quality is:

'*... since any description of Quality is a kind of definition and must therefore fall short of its mark. ... [and] statements of the kind ... which fall short of their mark, are even worse than no statement at all, since they can be easily mistaken for truth and thus retard an understanding of Quality.* '

JE – Yes, this all seems to me to make sense, but at one level I think it's just dodging the issue. I mean, it's as if for example, someone said to me 'hey

James, don't try to define love, just enjoy it' well I'd say 'OK I take your point, but I'm a writer. My job is to try to produce meaning: that's my profession.' And I certainly would feel that I was entitled to make some attempt at defining what I thought love was. Of course, there are different kinds of love. As far as Quality is concerned, I would say this, and we've already touched on this in our book earlier on ... I'd say that 'the way Sarah was using the word Quality was a very special and exciting and philosophical and spiritually enriching way of using the word, as opposed to the way that we used it in common, everyday language to mean a product or service of a high standard.' But just the same, I think defining, I think using the word 'quality' [lower case q], to define a product or service of a high standard is also a perfectly reasonable and logical way of using the word.

And I would also say, by the way, though, that although manufacturers will have ways of saying which mathematical measurements will constitute a quality [product or service], and what doesn't constitute quality, I still think that there is probably a lot of subjectivity in their definitions. But, all the same, that's a different use of the word than Pirsig's or Sarah's Quality.

JE – Moving on to the way that Sarah is using Quality, it seems to me that she is talking about using the word Quality to indicate, or to suggest, some marvellous worthfulness of some aspect of life that we feel is really working and is really meaningful and is really pleasurable and makes our lives feel great and fantastic, rather as exemplified in the very last paragraph of *ZMM*, which is:

> *'Trials never end, of course. Unhappiness and misfortune are bound to occur as long as people live, but there is a feeling now, that was not here before, and is not just on the surface of things, but penetrates all the way through: We've won it. It's going to get better now. You can sort of tell these things.'*

That very last paragraph is one of the finest pieces of writing I've ever read. I mean American literature has a tradition of doing great final paragraphs and that's one of them.

HG – James, I'm getting chills down my back at hearing that stunning final paragraph. I want you to know that.

JE – Yes, it is a great final paragraph. I do think, as I say, that American literature has this great tradition of wonderful endings. The ending of Harper Lee's *To Kill a Mockingbird* is breath-taking and marvellous, and so is the ending of Jack Kerouac's *On the Road*, a book that was in fact published on the day I was born: September 5, 1957. To me, the ending of *ZMM* is, in effect, a one-paragraph philosophy of life. It's basically saying that things in life should be and can be pretty good, that life can be pretty amazing, even if we live in a world where things are not always going to plan, but that a spirit of gentle optimism is appropriate. And Pirsig's ending paragraph is something that I think is very exciting.

However, this ending makes me immediately remember, that after the book was famous, Pirsig's son Chris who of course, features heavily in the book, was tragically killed by muggers in San Francisco. Pirsig must surely often have thought about that dreadful event in connection with the last paragraph of his book. He must have often thought about Chris, when he mentions that difficult things will happen.

But as a writer, I would agree that there is no useful way that you could define the Sarah Vinke kind of Quality, simply and ultimately, because, words are inadequate really. As a writer and literary agent, I do quite a lot of fiction coaching. I tell my clients there are four levels of reality [in writing of fiction]. 1) There's where you just tell somebody about something. 2) Then there's where you use vibrant and evocative, sensuous language to show it to them in an evocative way. 3) Then there's movies, where we can actually see the actors doing the action. 4) And then there's doing the thing oneself, which is the most alive level of reality of all.

So basically, we as writers can get closer to 'reality', with these four levels, all the while realising that words can only ever really evoke reality, they are not a substitute for it. We just have to do the best we can.

HG – It is for *every person to realize* what you're saying about words and writing is exactly true. *This is the fix that we're in the middle of.* And all persons, whether writers or readers, must, *on our own, perceive in ways that adjust and compensate for this inadequacy of words, and nevertheless find what the writing is pointing to.*

JE – I want to now shift the focus. I think it's quite right to give this attention to Quality, after all it was Sarah's big contribution to the book. But I want to just focus on Sarah for a moment and say the following... I mean we've already explored in this book quite a lot about her life and what happened in her life. Clearly, one of the drawbacks to writing a biography of Sarah is that there isn't much material about her, partly because by the time she became famous she had only had a few more years to live. Moreover, she doesn't appear to have left a lot of testaments or letters or anything like that. There's also the fact that in *ZMM,* Pirsig himself, is rather sparse in telling about her life and what she thinks Quality meant. So, let me ask you a question. What do you think Sarah would think of our discussion if she was hearing it today?

HG – First off, she would say: 'Yes, it's good to struggle with this.'

JE – Do you think she'd find what we said pertinent to her own view of Quality? Can we really know what her own view of Quality was?

HG – All we have are Pirsig's and Mr. Gary's, statements about when she said the Q word to them, which is not much to go on. But more importantly, from Sarah's actions, we can conclude that she would say something like this: '*Quit all this talking and thinking about Quality, just start doing it. Get out there and take action, in real world circumstances.*'

JE – And what kind of action do you think Sarah would have wanted the person to take do you think? I mean, I agree with you, it's a very good answer.

HG – Let's bear in mind Dennis Gary's, in my view, extremely important recollection about how Sarah said that '*all great drama consisted of blood, guts, and sex,*' and her insistence that her students '*use colored crayons and butcher paper to draw a dramatic spectacle.*'
    Sarah was surely saying, 'All those words that my students wrote, were just head trip intellectualization that didn't (couldn't possibly), evoke enough real visceral emotion. So I want you, my students, *to feel the emotional difference,* when you *draw these real-body experiences in color.*' In summary, Sarah's answer to questions like yours James, would maybe be met with this: 'Now I'm going to show you, with *dynamic action* in your *own mind and body*, these directly experienced, feelings, and resulting emotions.' In other words: '*Quit*

talking. Don't even think the Q word! I'm going to have you take action ... to <u>really</u> see ....

JE – Yes, I agree that's one of the most interesting pieces of testimony about Sarah there is. And in fact, it occurs to me in some ways that sometimes our struggling with understanding Sarah and her attitude to Quality is not entirely unlike struggling understanding Jesus the Christ, and his attitude to life. This is because these are both way back in history, and there's a limited amount of testimony, and one has to try and make the most of it one can. Moreover, it seems to me a very profound statement about Shakespeare, which again, makes it even more hypothetical, which I'm sure Shakespeare himself would agree with it.

Unfortunately, because of the way Shakespeare is taught academically or taught in schools, the plays are taught as something that children find a bit boring really, as if they're some sort of dirge to read through them. The way Shakespeare is taught, students often don't experience the fact that Shakespeare's plays are full of life. And what Sarah was really saying is that Shakespeare's plays are blood and guts and sex, which is after all what life is. We are physical creatures who have blood and guts and who, also when we reach certain ages in our lives, have and want sex as well.

Sarah's really saying, in effect, that plays, most especially those of Shakespeare, are the core of what life's all about. And I suspect that if we'd asked her what she meant by Quality, I think her answer would have been: 'Don't talk about it, go out and do it [i.e. Quality].' Which is all very well, but it doesn't *really help us actually do Quality* except by extending our own ideas onto what we think it means. Which may have been exactly what she would have wanted us to do. Still, I think, she would love the idea of living a life where Quality was one's goal, where having Quality friendships and relationships was what really mattered, along with loving art in the most elemental and primal sense, not as an intellectual pastime, but as something to adore and to be passionate about.

HG – Agreed. ... But I want to pick up where you said 'Loving art.' ... I think Sarah's idea of using colored crayons derived from her passion to want her students to *notice inside themselves what was happening in the immediacy doing of art*, as contrasted with the mere writing of words. And she purposely set this up to be an emotional hit, by purposefully having them write words first, then just as purposefully *throwing their honest, effortful, just-completed work into the trash. Right before their eyes. Worthless garbage.* She wanted the contrast of direct, eye-hand visual involvement. And in this immediacy, she wanted her students to *notice the feelings and the emotions of doing art, to show, feel, experience,* what Shakespeare meant - Blood, Guts, and Sex.

JE - Of course, this whole class scene as told by Mr. Gary, is very much telling us where Sarah was in Quality, without her in anyway saying so. And not 'saying so', we may take as her 'way'. I'm sure that Sarah would have thought that there was Quality there. And so really, I think we're accepting you can't define Quality, but we're coming to the conclusion that it's a very real thing to focus on and above all, a very exciting thing. It's not a kind of academic, philosophical term, it's really a way of relating practical philosophy to the glory of life.

HG – Exactly! Thank you! And this brings me back to what I was trying to relate earlier, when I was talking of God. When we are faced with terms like God or Quality, any attempt to define it, or any to attempt to discuss it, makes it smaller and can leave only distorted impressions.

JE – Yes, it's true.

HG – But we can always *point to Quality*. But *if and only when it has already happened.* This is what Pirsig does in *ZMM*. Throughout his book: he points this direction; he points in another direction, then points in yet another direction, because each one of those 'pointings' helps to get the reader into the correct mental space, and correct frame of mind. But get this: After Pirsig 'points', the reader must still complete the rest of it, *on their own, by their own purposeful mental efforts*. This is because the reader *always must still complete the communication*, for the very reason that communication is just limited this way, and most especially in communicating either the concept of God, or Love, or Pirsig's Quality. The idea of Quality means you're going to, and this is Sarah's approach, *meet life head-on* and *be in it.* These are the first aspects of Sarah.

Now another aspect of Sarah comes from Shirley Luhrsen, who was a student of Sarah's and later a professional teaching colleague. We quoted Shirley's repeated emphasis that Sarah surrounded herself with beauty ---

> 'a lovely oriental rug' – 'She let me play her grand piano on her beautiful blue-bordered Oriental rug, browse her book cases and let me take a couple of them'

and other examples, in Sarah's wonderful apartment.

And Shirley, rather than talking about concepts re Quality, simply implied Quality was everywhere in Sarah's apartment.

Shirley tells us that the whole entire ambience in Sarah's apartment is genteel and has a certain degree of organization, but a certain degree of purposeful clutter. And Shirley discusses how Sarah would invite Shirley (as a student and later a young teaching professional) to come to my apartment and play my piano. In effect, she is saying 'participate, enjoy, absorb, in this, the qualities of my apartment. All these are, I assert, Sarah's 'Quality-In-Action', rather talking about the meaning of Quality, itself.

Also, we must remember, Quality was everywhere in what Sarah did with her students to help them and to point and move them. Like, for example, Mr. Gary when he was in class, she took all of their writings that they put their energy in and threw them in the trash. Threw them in the trash. Shock in the face, for the very reasons that you've got to get to your *raw emotions*, you've got to get to your *blood and viscera here...* 'We must draw it, in color.' Whether drawings, or an apartment, Sarah's way was: We must surround ourselves with Dynamic Quality.

In addition to the above, we have the numerous newspaper reports, of how Sarah would take leadership action, in AAUW, and Professional Societies. Also in giving out the Louis Vinke Livestock Show Awards, or giving public talks about Greece, and WWII relief efforts, or the virtues of the United Nations, an unpopular topic in Montana.

There were numerous other ways Sarah would take action, step-in (even take charge) and help Shirley as a young woman. This is also illustrated in Dennis Gary's story of how Sarah took charge to help fellow Professor Howard Dean rewrite his book and got it accepted by a publisher, when Dean

> ... was moaning and groaning and wringing his hands about the rejection [of his *Communications* book]. Dr. Vinke told him to stop his whining, that she would take the manuscript home and fix it for him.

JE – She was an amazing woman and I think an incredibly positive person.
I think really this whole Dialog has helped me understand something I was never really sure about. I never really understood why there was such a resistance to defining Quality, but now I understand it.

HG – Again, it's like attempting to define God, you've got to realize ... just as soon as you try to start talking about it ... you are diminishing the very thing you're trying to put into words. But we do have Pirsig's method of 'pointings', such as we see in *ZMM*.

JE – Well, yes, but as you know, I still tend to think the attempt is worthwhile, though that fact that hardly anyone is persuaded to believe or disbelieve in God by logical argument suggests that the attempt may be futile. It may simply be that words are inadequate to describe some things usefully. God, love, sexual experience, Quality: These are all terms to which words can never do much real justice, which isn't to say that writers aren't entitled to try.

HG – Even Pirsig reports finding out in Korea, in a dramatic way, the limitations of words. In *ZMM* he says:

> '*He* [Phaedrus] *comments on how amazing it is that everything in the universe can be described*

by the twenty-six written characters with which they have been working. His [Korean] *friends nod and smile and eat the food they've taken from tins and say no pleasantly. He is confused by the nod yes and the answer no and so repeats the statement.'*

In fact, some of the limitations of words and ideas, and what he's going to do about it, are taken up by Pirsig just five pages into *ZMM*'s Chapter 1:

'In this Chautauqua I would like not to cut any new channels of consciousness but simply dig deeper into old ones that have become silted in with the debris of thoughts grown stale and platitudes too often repeated. Now the stream of our common consciousness seems to be obliterating its own banks, losing its central direction and purpose, flooding the lowlands, disconnecting and isolating the highlands and to no particular purpose other than the wasteful fulfilment of its own internal momentum. Some channel deepening seems called for.'

JE – If someone has an amazing experience with someone they love, has an amazing passionate afternoon with them, there's a limit to how well you can describe it in words. Ernest Hemingway once said very memorably to a friend who had had an amazing experience, 'if you talk about it you'll lose it'. This seems to me a wonderful thing for Hemingway to have said, and I think it's truly and profoundly relevant to this Dialog. ... Similarly, when we try to describe an amazing sunset, or a momentous religious experience in church, ... words are a ... ineffectual .... paltry .... are an invention of human beings that have big weaknesses. But language is a necessary compromise in order for us to communicate things to each other.

HG –Absolutely... plus I have few more words here... Yes, all we can do is live with these limitations, and breathe Quality: AND we can point at Love, Sunsets, Religious Feelings, even Quality, and use whatever words we have: But we, and whoever is listening to us, have to realize in very big ways *why those words are limited*. It's like enjoying the sunset, you just participate and be-there and don't disturb it. And if you want to relate this to other people, the best is to invite them to sit beside you and do the same. This, I believe. is Sarah's 'way'. To repeat what I said earlier about what Pirsig's said in his transcript:

> '*Art. ... It's what you do. It's who you are as a person, that makes it Art of not Art.*'

Now to Sarah Vinke's use of the idea Quality and the word Quality, let me add-in some thoughts that build from Pirsig's Railroad Train Analogy: Dynamic Quality is the cutting edge of ourselves, and our society, and indeed the whole universe. So, Quality, particularly Dynamic Quality, is the cutting edge of our whole reality, and that's what Pirsig got a-hold of and worked on and worked on and worked on. And this cutting edge, called Dynamic Quality, is an <u>automatic</u> problem solving ability we have in ourselves, and it most certainly is an important part of our being. Pirsig says it's the leading edge of the freight train engine, that opens up new territory, but just as soon as that territory is entered, just ever so slightly, the thickness of a coating of paint, it becomes Static Quality, in those boxcars following along on the track of Quality. For example, to the contents of those boxcars are added our newly learned, skills and knowledge.

JE – Henry, I want to ask you this. After you began to really understand the book, would you say that your life has been significantly different ever since?

HG – Well, if my friends were observing me, from the outside, I don't think they would notice any difference at all. But my wife, although she's read *ZMM* and respects it, simply hates the fact that I spend so much time with it. I'm suspicious that it takes me away from her, so every time I work on *ZMM* (or anything on my computer) it's a negative from her standpoint. …. But for me, *ZMM* had such a profound and life-changing effect, that I've chosen to spend much of the past ten years, nearly a full-time effort, to research *ZMM* further. A large portion of this effort was to develop and maintain my Internet Website, which has lots and lots of general research material about *ZMM* and about Pirsig.

JE – When you say 'researched the book', you mean looking into background material relating to the book and looking into material spinning off from the book?

HG – My *ZMM* Research eventually expanded into these areas. But my original idea was to travel those same *ZMM* Route Highways so well described by Pirsig, and attempt to find, photograph, GPS locate, and document the actual physical places he describes. My own '*ZMM* Trip' started at the University of Chicago 9 June 2002 and arrived at the San Francisco Golden Gate Bridge 8 July 2002, thirty days later. I took a total of 1901 photographs, and on a follow-up research trip, Summer 2007, I took an additional 800 photos. Of these, 915 photos have been selected to be shown in my photo-book *for Zen and Art of Motorcycle Maintenance*. By viewing these photos, a person can re-live what the Narrator and Chris saw on their 1968 trip. Not any *ZMM* travel passage has been left out. In essence, I did *ZMM* literary field research and that's kind of funny because, you know, I'm a physicist. What am I doing involved in literature?

JE – Well, let's look at something for a moment... so can you answer that question which is a fair question? You are a physicist, and, by contrast, *ZMM* is of course a work of literature and popular philosophy, perhaps. So, why do you think it made such a big impact on you?

HG – To answer to your question why did it make such a big impact on me... Well, this has come out in various ways, but give me a second to get my thoughts together. Let's see, so why *did ZMM* make such a big impact on me?

First off, you see, at the time I'd actually read the book, I'd already decided to get out of the world of physics experimental research and to get into the world of education and physics teaching. I thought that our world needed more education to help with the huge crises of humanity, as I was seeing it, and still do. And one of the biggest crisis for me back then, was nuclear weapons and the threat of nuclear annihilation. Indeed, ever since 1960 in graduate school, this has been a big black cloud hanging over me. So, in 1975, I got into teaching to try to make a contribution. This has continued to the present day, and in essence, that's why I'm here. The details of why and how I did this are on line, on my University of South Carolina Math Department, the homepage:

I got into teaching to find better and more satisfying ways for students to learn physics. ... As a new teacher, I was looking for answers, and did a great deal of research on teaching techniques, psychology, invention, creativity, flash-of-insight, and how our mind works. These were interests of mine ever since I had been in High School. The majority of my research findings were put to work in the classroom, and I was making progress. I've already stated some of my history at the beginning of this biography, so I'll summarize the big ZMM impact events, mental blindness, and openings for me:

In 1985, when a student handed me a copy of *ZMM* and I saw the title, I instantly remembered I had seen a review of *ZMM*. I believe it was in *Science Magazine,* some three or so years earlier. I also instantly remembered what I said to myself upon reading the review: 'I've got to read this book. It has what I want to know about.' But the review left me with no indication of what the book would actually be about. So when the student handed me this book, I said: OK, now I've got my chance to read it. And as I said earlier, my first several readings were *not* a very big impact. In other words, in my first several readings of *ZMM*, I was basically blind to Pirsig's important messages.

Now it's not the first time such a serious and major blindness has happened to me. This is an important story, with important messages as to how we are so often blind to the very thing we are looking for.

My initial lack of perception of Pirsig's important messages is ALSO illustrated in how I was brought, kicking and screaming, to understand another very important author whose name is Owen Barfield. His main book is *Saving The Appearances* ... a most remarkable paradigm changing book. Just as remarkable in many ways, and in agreement with, what Pirsig is pointing out to us: Barfield was, in essence, talking about the flash of insight and implications. A very good friend of mine, Harold

Kelley, handed me a copy of *Saving The Appearances* saying: 'Look, we've talked about these flash-of-insight matters for three or four years, what's in this book I know you want to know about.' But you know what? I gave him that book back, three times. Each time saying 'I can't get anything out of this'. Finally, the blinders fell from my eyes, and I was now able to *see* what Barfield was driving at. …. I mean … to *really* see the penetrating insights in Barfield's *Saving the Appearances,* whereas previously *I didn't at all* see Barfield's panorama of human's 'Evolution of Consciousness'.

The same was true for my first several readings of *ZMM*: *I didn't at all* see important ideas and answers I was *already looking for*: And remember, these were what I needed for good teaching, such as => good psychology, good understanding of the human mind, creativity, a flash of insight.

I was already looking for those things when these two books (ZMM & Barfield) got handed to me. *These topics were actually IN these two books and were what I wanted to learn, but I did NOT really see their presence.* Now, when it finally took hold …. What I was looking for was right before my eyes, in both Barfield's and Pirsig's books! As Pirsig says in *ZMM*:

> *It was a puzzling thing. The truth knocks on the door and you say, 'Go away, I'm looking for the truth,' and so it goes away. Puzzling.*

JE – And what was it you were looking for?

HG – Many things, including an understanding of how the human mind not only works but how it develops, from child to adult, and how it learns. How it creates new concepts, thoughts, and words. How an understanding of invention, creativity, and the flash of insight provides clues for good teaching and how students can best learn. What are students' diversions, dead-ends, roadblocks, and how these can be avoided. It was problem-solving and physics understanding. Yes, all this is in *ZMM*, plus how our mind works. The social and societal implications of all these, and history.... Plus, I was especially interested in Inspiration, which is another word for Insight, or sudden Flash of Insight, which in *ZMM* are called 'Crystallizations'.

In fact, perhaps on purpose, Pirsig is repeatedly mentioning examples of his own *sudden mental arrivals,* even *reversals* of previous conclusions, as he *suddenly comes to realize a new idea, or relationship, previously un-available.* I believe that, these are there for us (and my students) to <u>actually *see* practical insight examples</u> of the Narrator, when he is following, naturally, his own track of Quality. To <u>see these</u> as we read ZMM, we should watch for such words as => *sudden-/ suddenly* (26), *realize* (31), *oh* (7), *all right* (6), *came to (~me)* (2), *comes to (~mind)* (18), *insight* (3), *flash* (4), *wave of* (8), *crystallization* (12), *discover* (68), *reality* (81), *think of* (5), *think about* (7), *state of*

282

mind (4), *flash of illumination - is so intense* (1)......
I'm running out of examples ....

> ((NOTE: To learn more about Mental Arrivals, when a person's problem is resolved by a Flash of Insight (or Similar): Please Google Search for Web Page =>...*An Anatomy of An Idea Come to Mind! By Henry Gurr*...... After this page comes up => Please Do > Top > Edit > Find > ... *The Light Came On* ...))

JE – I understand, I understand. Why do you think no-one had ever come up with answers to these big issues with the same clarity and accessibility that Pirsig does?

HG –Well, there's lots of other thinkers who *do* discuss these *same* 'big issues' with the *same* clarity and accessibility that Pirsig or Barfield do. And you know what happens? Every one of those authors gets basically ignored. ... Repeat ... They get ignored. Even Pirsig has basically been ignored. I mean, has the world changed because of his work? I don't think so. Owen Barfield has been basically ignored, as has the author Michael Polanyi, another great writer on similar topics. These, and many more important thinkers are out there, but largely they get ignored, even by the professional, academic philosophers who ought to know better.

JE – Is it really fair to say that Pirsig got ignored when... I don't know how many copies of his book have been sold altogether, but it must run into the tens of millions?

HG – Yes, but you ask a man in the street about Pirsig and they're not going to know about him. But if you ask the man in the street about, oh, I don't know, Aristotle or Plato or the Bible, they're definitely going to know about them.

JE – Yes, OK, that's a very fair point.

HG – Professional academic philosophers, as a group, tend to ignore writers such as Pirsig, Barfield and Polanyi. As a matter of fact, and I've already said: These academic philosophers also ignore 'subjectivity', the flash of insight, and things that are related to the flash of insight, because these do *not* involve thinking in words. Academic philosophers, generally, *only* trust language, logic, mathematics, and 'objective thinking'. And they do *not* trust anything that just 'happens' in their mind or arrives from their 'subconscious' … or 'just appears' 'miraculously' … like a flash of insight, which totally, illogically, 'comes out-of-the-blue'. Both Barfield and Pirsig have much to teach about this very 'illogical' flash of insight, really an aspect of Dynamic Quality. But the whole subjective idea of Dynamic Quality provides even *more putative reasons* for these supposedly 'philosopher objective thinkers', to reject and ignore Pirsig. Similarly, for Barfield, and Michael Polanyi.
    And this brings to mind Thomas Kuhn's *Structure of Scientific Revolutions*, which does a *very* good job at explaining the ins and outs of how and

why, at first the majority of practicing scientists, as a matter of multiple demonstrated facts, reject and ignore new scientific discoveries. It took me a long time to realize that what Dr. Kuhn was saying *also* applied to why Pirsig, Barfield and Polanyi get rejected and ignored.

JE – Well, so how do you feel about the fact that this book that you've spent maybe twenty or thirty years of your life thinking about and devoting so much time to has not been read by most people? Although in all fairness, I must say, that when I've mentioned this project to people, most of them have heard of the book.

HG – How do I feel? Naturally it's a bummer. It is almost certain that all my earnest years of effort will be basically ignored, for the same reasons that Pirsig, Barfield, and Polanyi are basically ignored. I was talking to one of my more astute fellow physics teachers about my being 'ignored', which was clearly happening in the aftermath of my many talks to the American Association of Physics Teachers.

Here is his advice. *'Henry, you have to do what you have to do.'*

Here is Pirsig's similar answer to the same problem:

> *'Writing it* [i.e. ZMM] *seemed to have higher quality than not writing it.'*

To me, the Quality Track says: Ignored or not, a person must keep on trying anyway.

Now responding to your 'Many people have heard of *ZMM*'. But, how many of them have actually read it?

JE – Yes, I see what you mean. Well, I'm an example of that sort of person because I'd heard of the book, but I hadn't read it until we began working together. I remember many years ago glancing at the first page and being struck by the very first sentence, but that would have been a very long time ago, maybe when I was a teenager. The book was published when I was seventeen years old so I didn't really read it then. I think many people have heard of *ZMM* without actually reading it, in much the same way, for example, that many people have heard of the stories contained in several of Charles Dickens's novels – *Oliver Twist* and *David Copperfield*, for example, without having read the books. I mean, is that not the fate of any philosophical writer, that their readership is comparatively limited compared to say, a popular novelist?

HG – I think that's fair to say in general, that Pirsig is more blessed as among philosophical authors. He's probably one of the most and widest read, perhaps the most.

JE – I think that's probably true. So, can you account for your lack of understanding of meaning of *ZMM* for the first three years after you read it and then why the book made such an impression once you did get what it was all about?

HG – Well, I must emphasize that this is a very big message about us as human beings. There are things that we are looking for, things that we want to know, but we still can't see them. This "perceptual blindness + blockage", and how to solve it, is in essence what Kuhn's book is about. And this blindness is not only our fix, but also something that we have to learn about, and learn how to 'get-around-it'. Pirsig, and Dr. Kuhn help us understand how we are locked in our own little head, and then suggest to us what we must do to make a breakthrough, and actually open up the territory that we're already in. …. As I've mentioned Pirsig saying:

> *'It was a puzzling thing. The truth knocks on the door and you say, 'Go away, I'm looking for the truth.'*

JE - I just want to cut in there and say that this is an issue which preoccupies me as well but in a different way. As a writer, literary agent and publisher, I'm clearly involved with the fact that we're locked in our own heads and have no choice but to be locked in our own heads as human beings. This is a great problem I do think about quite a lot, because it very much explains to me why novels are so important. Because novels are a way of communicating the kinds of things about human experience that couldn't really be communicated any other way.

I mean, you could argue that a telephone directory contains lots of information about people's phone numbers and addresses and things, and it's obviously a very important and practical document, but a novel contains, a good novel, contains information about what it's like to be human, and frequently in fact, people don't discuss those things or articulate them unless they're reading novels or, in some cases, writing novels. And I think there are two things to say here. I think, first of all, unfortunately the nature of a philosophical book means that there's a limit to how popular a work of philosophy can be because of its very nature There's not that many people who are interested in philosophy as something they want to read about it.

But I do want to say in Pirsig's defence, that I do, in fact, tend to see it as a successful philosophical work, partly because Pirsig is very good at writing dramatic novel scenes. I mean the scene where he goes back, or maybe it's in his dream or imagination, it's not really clear, but the scene where he goes back to Montana State University and revisits the room where he met Sarah is actually a very good example of very gripping and dramatic first person narrative. And I think it's important to communicate that although the book is sometimes obscure, most of it is replete with meaning and fantastically well-written. There are times when it is obscure, but then it may be the case that all philosophical books are occasionally obscure when the writer perhaps can't fully communicate easily, as is also true of novels, what he means. But most of *ZMM* is very nicely balanced (to use the terminology we've developed), and I like the kind of experience, of what he makes of the experience. And I love the fact that at one level this is a road novel, and it's at one level a novel about a guy on the road who rather than stopping regularly to shoot pool, or play juke boxes or play a fruit machine, or one-arm bandit, instead, his hobby is unpretentiously thinking about life, and that's why I like the book so much. So I think it's important to say it's not an academic book...

HG – True, but while *ZMM* truly is a philosophical novel, we should emphasize to our biography readers that *ZMM* really comes across as a mystery novel with an exciting cliff-hanger, who-dun-it type thing. Of course, the philosophy happens to be in there, but the reader has a choice whether to pay that much attention to it. So the impact for the reader, can be an exciting novel. They just read it that way.

JE - I agree. In some ways that's a very pleasant way to read it because, I love the book for so many reasons -- I find the philosophy in it really exciting and very interesting -- I also love the accounts of the scenery, which are actually some great accounts of scenery. Now am I not right that you actually retraced Pirsig's journey?

HG - Yes, in 2002, I retraced, and researched the Pirsig and Chris *ZMM* book travel route: My research goal was to find the physical location of each of Pirsig's travel location descriptions (scenes), take photos of each, as well as mark the locations on a GPS. Of these photos, 832, two photos for each page of *ZMM*, are now posted on the photo gallery of my website.

Which reminds me, *ZMM* is also highly rated as a travel book, a travelogue, because of Pirsig's excellent descriptions of travel and travelling.

JE - My interest is why, at a time of your life when you did finally get what the book was about, as you understood what the book was about, why it had such a lasting impact on you?

HG – Just to reiterate what I've already said… *ZMM* had what I was looking for. This book supplied what I wanted (and needed), for my teaching! Also ZMM supplied, and continues to supply vital nourishment for my personal life, such as already discussed refreshing answers to the deadness of Nihilism, and to build a foundation under Western Philosophy and Thinking. These are the reasons ZMM had such long lasting impact on me: However, and a HUGE however => Initially, *I did not see any of this!* AND *this is a very big point for all of us:* For three years, and across multiple readings, I was basically blind to the fact that *ZMM* had what I was looking for. I've realized later that I was blind to the meaning partly because I simply did not really expect *ZMM* to have 'What I was looking for'. Ditto for Barfield's *Saving the Appearances,* despite the fact, I had been

<u>repeatedly told</u> by Harold Kelley, '<u>This book has what you are looking for</u>.'

And our readers should strongly keep in mind: a) All of us, repeatedly, get 'stuck' this way. Pirsig calls this 'Value rigidity', and b) the only way out of stuckness is to keep on trying, 'with everything you got'. And b) Both Pirsig and Thomas Kuhn's books offer us *'Study Guides in escaping Stuckness and Perceptual Blindness'*.

JE – Can you be more specific about what you were looking for?

HG - I was looking for many things. For example, I was looking for better techniques of teaching. I was looking for better understanding of how the human mind works. I was looking for ways to help students get motivated into true academic study. I was looking for ways to help if they were perceptually blind to a particular physics topic. I was looking for good ways of helping students learn how to write and to point out to students that we're not going to give you technical instruction on how to write, you just look at it and if it's good, that's good writing. I had my students do a tremendous amount of writing because I think it helped them solidify into their mind what they were thinking, and solidify in their mind what they had learned in physics. I'm firmly convinced that writing up their Lab Reports will help them discover the parts of physics that they don't know or understand well enough. And then work on needed improvements.

Now all these things I was working on with my students, are similarly what Pirsig was constantly working on in ZMM. And the reason I know that Pirsig's methods and his explanations are indeed very successful, is my own personal experience, as well as my fifteen years working with Nobel Prize Winner Fred Reines. He was my thesis advisor (major professor) when I was doing my PhD Thesis, and then 15 years my employer during my early career in experimental neutrino physics research. I observed what Reines did, and his explanations for what he did. Clearly Reines knew what he was doing.

For young people, Reines advised the following approaches: His methods fit ZMM, and besides his methods were quite successful and lead him to a Nobel Prize! =>
->A) Even if you are ignorant, or don't have training or other knowledge, start working on your next big project and ideas anyway!
->B) Don't worry about being at a disadvantage compared to an experienced expert:
->C) This is because "A Beginners Mind" clearly has its own advantages, especially when it comes to forming new unusual break-through ideas!
->D) Start your new work immediately, with your best ideas first, and with whatever resources you have at hand.
->E) Solve problems as you go, and in process, you will quickly find, and learn what you need to know.
->F) Work very hard, and "Be in the Flow!

->G) Get on with what's top priority, and most importantly => Don't allow any diversion from your top priorities!

In summary: This is the Fred Reines '*way*'! This is what works, step by step! Moreover, such methods support and verify Pirsig's thinking in *ZMM*:

Overall, these are the very reasons I had over half my students read *ZMM* in the years 1995 to 2001. I'm very sure they learned many things from it, including how to achieve a flash-of-insight discovery that can make the physics lesson crystal-clear. What to do when you're stuck, what to do when you don't have the information you need and how to get unstuck. For example: in *ZMM*, the narrator is constantly thinking about maintenance. He is forever feeling the cycle's warmth and vibrations, listening to the sounds of his cycle, and what is good, and what needs attention. He is trying to identify clues as to what could be the cause of the problem he is suspecting. How to make a discovery. How to solve a problem, any problem. Moment by moment, what are the best choices. How to move forward with your life. The book is all about that and it gives example after example of this in motorcycle maintenance; and it gives example of this again and again with his interpersonal relationships with the people he travels with, he visits with, and most particularly, with Chris.

A continuing thread in *ZMM*, illustrates how the narrator is stuck in his ability to relate as a father to his son, and then, what is the glorious new opening, the climax of the book on the ocean-side cliff. This is the climax scene, how the father and son get a breakthrough, as to what was their relationship trouble, and how they can get back together again. Just a marvelous, totally unexpected, come-around, solving a problem, essentially a flash of insight, and getting a hold of what it was that prevented the *ZMM* Narrator from becoming re-united with Chris, and knowing what to do about it.

In summary, these were the things I was looking for, and found in *ZMM*. Also, these revelations, were what I wanted my students to see, experience, understand, and adopt in their own life.

JE: I understand. I understand, yes, I would agree. That's again why I think there's a lot of very powerful, novel-type techniques used in the book. The book was clearly, to some extent, of its own age, although of course it has survived. Pirsig's book is now, not long before it would have been written fifty years ago. What do you think about the impact the book made in its time? What do you think was special about the book that made it particularly relevant to what was going on in 1974 when he published it?

HG – What was happening in the 1960s and 70s we've mentioned in this biography already. These times are troubling no matter what. We'd had two world wars, the actual use of two nuclear bombs on whole cities of people, plus now, the threat of the vastly more destructive H-Bomb, fifty minutes away on an Intercontinental Ballistic Missile. Then there was the pointless, gruesome, morally wrong US war in Vietnam (shown daily in the living rooms, on the then new TV), with a resulting deep distrust of our government, even the universities, with the students riots, and hippie rejection.

And, although there's tremendous material success in the United States with all its wealth, there's much empty meaninglessness in the thinking of the US that, essentially, comes from Nihilism. This is a philosophic view that has permeated our Western Culture: That there is no meaning in this world, that we're just this bunch of atoms, randomly rattling around, following the laws of physics, and the tooth and claw of biology.

Starting with the aftermath of WWI, somehow with pure logic, philosophers, using their understanding of science, concluded that our lives, even the universe, has no meaning. ... Not only my whole nation ... I personally was stuck in this gloomy meaninglessness of Nihilism. And it was very demoralizing: I felt there was no meaning to our existence. It doesn't matter a damn what we do or don't do anything.

In the 1960s and 70's this point of view all came to a focus, and was terribly disheartening: .... We make no contribution to this world, we have absolutely no effect, and after we're gone, the slate is erased clean, it's like we were never here! .... It is important to realize that these Nihilistic conclusions, are the flip-side of => 'our lives, are just following tooth and claw biology and being nothing more than atoms randomly rattling around, following the laws of chemistry and physics'.

Now, these supposed 'scientific' conclusions, the Nihilistic conclusions mentioned above, are an absolutely wrong interpretation of both science and the previous history of Western Progress, and Pirsig is here to tell us this. Ditto for both Owen Barfield, for Michael Polanyi, and another I just remembered: John K. Sheriff's *The Fate of Meaning,* a title which says it all.

The striking agreement of Barfield and Pirsig covers a wide range of topics, and all the more valuable since their conclusions are apparently independently discovered. I add in Polanyi and Sheriff, but the areas of agreement are more limited.

Now, these first three authors were new openings for me, and (as I discovered only later) solidly confirmed by the fourth. I could see a new breath of fresh air. Owen Barfield said, 'What do you mean there's no meaning? Just look around you... at a mother holding her baby for example.' And yes, I could finally see Barfield's right, it is profoundly true, our world is filled with meaning and purpose.

Now, another thing that these three authors give, most particularly Owen Barfield and Pirsig, is the rock bottom truth of the whole idea of constructivism. Which says: Our problem solving brain, <u>automatically</u>, constructs, builds up, throughout our daily activity, our complete world in our own minds. A conclusion called "constructivism", leads, in turn to the understanding that the whole universe as we know it exists <u>only</u> *in our own minds*. This same conclusion is also implied in all of *ZMM,* where *Dynamic Quality is the cutting edge of reality'* and *makes our reality*. *'All of it. Every last bit of it.'*

The first use of the concept of constructivism was in psychology, people constructing in their own minds what they think someone else is thinking. Then physicists adopted this term when they realized that students constructed ... in their own minds ... physics. This was when physics teachers eventually realized that they can't "teach" physics. Rather, the physics teacher must properly present the physics material to be learned in such a manner that their students can (on their own) build up accurate physics knowledge in their own mind. Not only must the student build a physical model of physics in their own mind, but also, at the *same* time, build an *understanding* of physics. In other words, students are teaching themselves and the teacher must supply the materials that best promote this!

This same idea (technically called Philosophical Constructivism OR Constructivist Epistemology) is important for ALL of us to understand. Along with our normal ongoing perception of the world around us, our brain is (<u>automatically</u>) forming memory traces of everything we see and think. Simultaneously, these on-going 'perceptions and stored-memory-trace-content altogether' actively (problem-solving brain again), mentally combine to 'construct' our general mental model of the world around us. This 'constructed general mental model of the world around us (then stored in memory) is the very 'thing' that, in the ongoing future, is turned around and used for decoding (second by second) our next perceptions, thoughts, and future actions.

Now, the more I think about it, the more I realize that this truth applies to absolutely everything that comes into our mind. We construct the universe around us from the get-go. It's all constructed, created, <u>automatically ...</u> by and in our own human brain ... in our own human mind. This is how Pirsig puts it in *ZMM*:

> *The Quality which creates the world emerges as a relationship between man and his experience. He is a participant in the creation of all things. ... Quality is the continuing stimulus which our environment puts upon us to create the world in which we live. All of it. Every last bit of it.*

Now, in our mind, how is this actually being done? We can best understand all this with the physics model of Princeton Physicist J. J. Hopfield: He created a Mathematical Theory that showed for a biological brain, that Single All At Once Optimal Solutions To Surrounding World Complex Input, is indeed possible and indeed likely. Thus Hopfield says essentially, that our human problem solving ability (such as in a Flash of Insight, AND an action Pirsig calls Quality), is a natural property of our God given brain. From this we can see, that Pirsig's Dynamic Quality, is an ability, really an <u>automatic and intrinsic property</u>, of our own physical biological human mind. And from this it naturally follows, that the Hopfield Theory strongly supports what Pirsig is saying, and conversely. All this points to just how it is that our brain, as a physical system, can <u>automatically</u> discover good answers, i.e. good solutions, to what I would call 'life's problems coming at us'. Pirsig calls this the result of Dynamic Quality, and these solutions (some of which are perceptions insights, thoughts, and future actions) are to be ALSO understood as *constructing*, in our mind, the whole universe! As Pirsig says. *'Every last bit of it.'* This quoted phrase is asserted four times in *ZMM*, so Pirsig surely must really mean this.

From this our readers should go on to realize that Philosophic Constructivism is the general foundational undergirding of *ZMM*. This is most apparent when Pirsig uses the word *'construct' specifically with this meaning, NINE times in ZMM*, quoting Albert Einstein and Henri Poincaré along the way.

And I believe Pirsig's *'create the world in which we live'* applies (at most) to the <u>part of the universe</u> that is created (brain constructivism) in … our own mind … which is all we can ever know. This again is Pirsig's Dynamic Quality constructing the universe in our mind. This in turn creates *all of our knowledge*, which Pirsig calls Static Quality. In *ZMM,* Pirsig summarizes how important this constructivism is:

> *'The sun of quality,'* he wrote, *'does not revolve around the subjects and objects of our existence. It does not just passively illuminate them. It is not subordinate to them in any way. It has created them. They are subordinate to it.'*

A recent insight came as I was in final editing in a fifth re-read of the above => In modern times, at the beginning Western awareness of, *'we invented it'*, and *'it's all in your mind'*, to a large degree, actually helped generate the nihilistic gloom and despair! Because => If the human mind invented it, then shock, there are no God given rights or wrongs, and morality can't possibly inherently exist, nor thus have any values, or meaning. Nihilists say *'life is without objective meaning, purpose, or intrinsic value'*. These of course, altogether, defeat any human meaning for life. Pure gloom. In fact, it was these very feelings and conclusions, clearly known .to be wrong to Pirsig, Barfield, Polanyi, and most certainly Sheriff, that in a large measure, motivated their writings. ...

Now, the ', <u>wrongly</u> understood, provided an undercurrent justification or a base, for the Nihilistic View. But these four authors provide a much need antidote for the nihilism error and trap. But, better said, their work ended up being, a complete reversal of all the nihilists' conclusions!

As Pirsig said:

> *A 'Copernican Inversion ... Nothing changed as a result of this revolution, and yet everything changed.'*

Here I'm reminded, that in essence, Thomas Kuhn's *Structure of Scientific Revolutions* in its own way is also A Handbook On How To => 1) understand perceptual blindness, 2) assist new insights (epiphany's), and thus, 3) for persons who experience mental blockages, 4) promote needed 'Copernican Inversions'.

However, in contrast with the badly mistaken and highly destructive Nihilist views, constructivism properly understood, reverses each and every one of those above gloomy, pessimistic conclusions, and shows that value and meaning are a very real, constructive, happy, fulfilling results. Also, it is seen that the Nihilist Trap, is self-made. Thus Quality can point the way out, in that a person *decides* that life has meaning and purpose, and proceeds to *take up the very actions, that enhance* that outcome, for themselves and their larger community.

In summary, Pirsig supplies the antidote: ...

> *'Quality is the continuing stimulus which our environment puts upon us to create the world in which we live. All of it. Every last bit of it.'*

Here, I'm reminded of William James' famous free will decision: *'My first act of free will shall be to believe in free will.'*

William James became very depressed as a young man from his study of science, creating a 'crisis of meaning'!. He was unable to function, and was sick in bed for some three years. Although the name had not yet been invented, he was stuck in the Nihilist Trap. His decision started his way out. The *ZMM* narrator reports Pirsig (as Phaedrus), was similarly afflicted:

> *'his past despair over abstract questions of existence itself that he had abandoned in defeat.'*

Thus, these are my answers to your question: How was *ZMM* particularly relevant to what was going on in 1974 when Pirsig published it? I happen to think these answers also apply to most persons in the 1970s and will continue to apply for a long time into the future, possibly a thousand years.

JE – And the thing about Pirsig's book, it seems to me, is this… he's saying that the coherent and warm and human and well-thought and, indeed, Quality thoughts of a human being making sense of life and the world are what life's really all about. He's *NOT* just saying 'I'm Pirsig, my opinion is what really matters.' Instead, through his own examples of *embodiment*, he's giving us the opportunity to *find these meanings for ourselves,* and above all, he is saying, in effect, that out of all the chaos and confusion of the world there are opportunities to retrieve, and to enjoy, and to live with real meaning.

Recently, I was watching the trial of the United States murderer James Holmes, a young man who went into a cinema in 2012 and shot and killed twelve totally innocent people and injured seventy. I suppose my own antidote to the James Holmes nightmare scenario was really found in a press conference I watched on YouTube a few days before this Skype interview I'm having with you, in which the prosecutor and his colleagues had a press conference in Colorado, I'm not sure the city, with many of the victims of Holmes there, and it was a very warm-hearted press conference.

The prosecutor basically said, 'Well, we did try to get the death penalty for him, but not all the jury wanted that, and I respect what the jury said.' But what came out from this was not so much that point which is just a question really of what the punishment should be, but this…you got a sense that the victims and prosecutors had become friends and there was a community of people who'd either suffered directly because they'd been victims themselves, or had suffered by intimate proxy because a member of their family had been killed or injured, or like the prosecutors, they'd suffered through professional proxy because they'd vicariously suffered with the victims. There was a sense of real meaning and potency in this community.

And for me, that's in many ways exactly the feeling, albeit stemming from a very different source, that Pirsig's book gives me. It gives a sense that we are a community of human beings and that disinterring meaning from the world is something that can be done. And this of course leads on, for me, to this very idea of Quality. And you may well want to say some more things, but I think I'd like to move on to that when you've said what else you want to say.

HG – Well, I think all these things are what people need to think and feel about. ... And examine the possibilities for their own lives. Just as we already discussed, these are all the needed properties and outcomes of a good novel. And are of course what Sarah would have us do. And if our readers want to dig in deeper, then of course they've got Pirsig's *ZMM* Chautauquas. I truly believe that persons reading Pirsig will achieve a constructive philosophical grounding for their lives. It certainly turns out this way for lots of readers, including myself.

JE – Exactly. Having discussed Sarah's role in triggering Pirsig on Quality, I want now to give you a chance, yourself, to say what Pirsig's Quality means to you and what the concept has done, has meant to your life...

HG – OK, first off, let me say that there are several *different ways* of understanding Quality in Pirsig's book. In my earliest readings, I concluded that Pirsig's Quality, in essence, is a Mystical force that rules the universe. It's not physical laws (like Newton's Laws of Motion and Gravity), that run the universe, it's Quality. This (as in the case of Owen Barfield), is similar to a personal belief that: 'What came first in the universe was universal mind, and this makes and controls everything …'

JE - Can you explain what you mean when you say Quality rules the universe?

HG – Pirsig says it well, at the mountain climbing climax with Chris: They're just about there at the top, and he proclaims:

> *'Quality is the parent, Quality creates the subjects and objects of this world.'*

And if you read that one way, he's saying Quality makes physical objects, and *in physical objects*, called persons, Quality goes on to create subjective experience, and runs other body processes, such as …..

JE – Can you elucidate that, on what that means, can you describe what you mean by that in everyday language so that people understand what you mean?

HG – This is the first way of reading ZMM Re Qualit*y* => Let's consider, making a human baby, a physical object with all kinds of wonderful properties. The first way you might read Pirsig's book is this => It is Quality, a Mystical Force, that makes babies, just as it is Quality that makes a universe full of atoms, molecules, chemicals, biological cells, and biological creatures, etc. All made by, and of, Quality.

JE – Yes, I understand, I want this to be discussed not in these rather metaphorical terms but in what you actually mean by that. Do you mean ... when you say Quality makes babies... do you mean that Quality (among much else) *IS* the evolutionary force and dynamic that gave the mother's reproductive systems, and this in turn *IS* the real parent of the baby?

HG – Yes... and... even more mystically, it is Quality, *operating within the mothers (and father's) organs, and atoms and molecules,* that make the baby. In Pirsig's language that's Quality. Quality did all that. This is implied in *ZMM* where Pirsig writes out his own version of Lao Tzu's *'Tao Te Ching'*. (Our readers may read it at the end Chapter 2 of our biography). .... From Pirsig's *'Tao Te Ching'* version, I saw my first Mystical Interpretation of meaning of Quality, and additionally why I thought 'Quality ran the Universe'. We've already quoted that passage in this biography, Chapter 2, but here are the specific words that say to me ~'Quality Created, and Ran, the Universe':

It [Quality] *is the origin of heaven and earth.*

in the world itself and not simply the human brain. ... "

[NOTE: Please think carefully here: For Barfield, similar to Pirsig, this "world" or "universe", has it's ONLY existence in our mind! The "world" or "universe" outside of ourselves (such as we commonly think of it) may, or may not "be there"!]

In the quotation above, we have to realize that Barfield's 'changes in the world' are achieved (just in our own mind) by mental arrivals he calls 'inspirations', which step by step, over eons of time, create his 'evolution of human consciousness'. Pirsig's version of this is already mention in quote above and means the mental arrivals he calls 'crystallization', also, like Barfield's Inspiration, are steps in constructivism in action: To illustrate this, we repeat what Pirsig says:

> *The birth of a new fact is always a wonderful thing to experience. It's dualistically called a "discovery" because of the presumption that it has an existence independent of anyone's awareness of it.*

So, in summary, *ZMM* was a tremendous relief to me. It helped me out of the Nihilism trap, along with Barfield's *Saving the Appearances*. These two books worked together to help me escape deadening, demoralizing, Nihilism. Both authors were providing me with answers for my teaching, which we've already discussed. Both books were certainly helping me, solidify the whole idea and truth of constructivism (as a theory guide), which was already emerging as an important, useful conclusion, coming out of all my research about best ways of teaching.

Through my reading of *ZMM,* I learned to think like this: 'You're stuck, work on the problem as much as you can, try to find out as much about it as you can, and then *quit and wait.* As Pirsig says, in effect: there's just no way your motorcycle isn't going to get fixed, because if you give your brain enough time, your brain <u>automatically</u> will find an answer. Just wait, it will come. These are ideas that have emerged more and more strongly, as I work in this entire territory. For me, this is a very satisfying understanding: It's a point of arrival I've been working on ever since 1987.

And also my life has been impacted in the sense that I've changed my behavior to being more accepting. I found myself wanting to make time to pet my dog Suki, and to enjoy the world right now, and not to be in such a damn hurry. I was brought up in what they called this WASP (White Anglo Saxon Protestant) way of demanding a lot out of myself, which included for me a kind of Victorian mind-set upbringing => 'I'm a doer, and I'm in this world to get something done, no matter how hard or tough is the work!."

With *ZMM,* this changed: We're not here just and only to accomplish something big. We are also here to 'be' and 'to be in the present'. We're here to notice the moment, and take in this moment and react accordingly. This is the importance to me ... my experience in connection with my dog 'Suki' ... the prodigious importance of 'being present in the moment'... relax, rest, look around, and consciously enjoy just being here.

JE – Yes, and I think that very much fits in with Pirsig's own enjoyment of the cross-country motorcycle ride he has, after all, he didn't need to write the book in that way. He could have written it purely as an abstract discussion of philosophical ideas that interested him. I think, moving towards wrapping this up, we haven't really said much about Sarah. Now, that's partly because Sarah's thinking influences Pirsig which influences us, so we're really continuing in our own way, perhaps continuing her heritage to some extent. But do you believe that Sarah originated this idea of Quality, this more metaphysical approach, this special interpretation of the word 'Quality', or do you think she got it from the Classics?

HG – First of all, Sarah was truly a Classicist, and this was surely the origin of her own meaning of Quality. But to illustrate this, let me take up your perennial question 'Why didn't Pirsig ask Sarah for a definition of what she meant by Quality'. In *ZMM*, this question in essence DID get asked in mid Chapter 28, as the lead-up to University of Chicago:

> *He had asked Sarah, who long before had come by with her watering pot and put the*

idea of Quality in his head, where in English literature quality, as a subject, was taught. .. 'Good heavens, I don't know, I'm not an English scholar,' she had said. 'I'm a classics scholar. My field is Greek.' ... 'Is quality a part of Greek thought?' he had asked. ..'Quality is <u>every</u> part of Greek thought,' she had said, and he had thought about this. Sometimes under her old-ladyish way of speaking he thought he detected a secret canniness, as though like a Delphic oracle she said things with hidden meanings, but he could never be sure. .. Ancient Greece. Strange that for them Quality should be everything while today it sounds odd to even say quality is real. What unseen changes could have taken place? ...

From this, we clearly see that Pirsig essentially did ask Sarah what was her meaning of Quality, but from what Pirsig says, we have every reason to believe, the answer was to not be sought in Sarah herself, but in the Ancient Greeks: Which Pirsig did extensively pursue, as he reports on in *ZMM.*, most especially at the University of Chicago.

Also, in *ZMM*, after Sarah's initial prodding, Pirsig reports his extensive study of Quality, starting with his asking his classes to '*Write a 350-word essay answering the question, 'What is quality in thought and statement?*' all the while, he was deeply pondering Quality. In *ZMM*, Pirsig recaps:

> *This was the beginning of the crystallization that I talked about before. .. Others wondered at the time, 'Why should he get so excited about 'quality'?' But they saw only the word and its rhetoric context. They didn't see his past despair over abstract questions of existence itself that he had abandoned in defeat.' If anyone else had asked, What is Quality? it would have been just another question. But when he asked it, because of his past, it spread out for him like waves in all directions simultaneously, not in a hierarchic structure, but in a concentric one. At the center, generating the waves, was Quality.*

So he did ask students '*What is Quality*' and gave a full report. And from this, we may deduce he could have also asked Sarah. But, perhaps by the time he was writing *ZMM*, Pirsig realized that you can't tell someone what Quality is, you can't put it in words, and you just better not try. So, he chose to write *ZMM* the way we see, by 'pointing' to Quality, and did not try the low Quality shortcut of 'just telling' us those questions Sarah may have been asked, nor 'just telling' us the answers she may have given.

In other words, whatever Sarah may (or may not) have said about Quality or the Ancient Greeks, he perhaps deliberately chose not to mention her views of such. Instead, in the *ZMM* narrative, he fully reports, step by step, his own research into and development of his own understanding of Quality … Stating from his complete ignorant confusion to final synthesis at the end of *ZMM*. Thus, we never hear of Sarah's thoughts, while Pirsig uses his whole book to help us, page after page, to gradually see what Quality really is. And what we see and experience of Pirsig's Quality is most likely, after all, true to Sarah Vinke's Quality.

Let's remember that Pirsig knew Sarah quite well and knew what Sarah did in her own life, which was that she lived Quality, and if necessary, would point to Quality, in her own teaching. Pirsig knew he didn't have to ask what she meant by her prodding; all he had to do was watch, and learn. Of course, he may have been too proud to show his ignorance. However, I tend to believe that, in general, Sarah most likely didn't attempt to discuss Quality or say what it was: She would, in effect, just simply point to it and push people towards it, as she did her own students, such as Dennis Gary and Pirsig. Obviously, she did, on occasion, use the word Quality, as with Mr. Gary and Pirsig.

Now getting back to my 'We can assume that the word Quality was Sarah's own distillation of her very extensive Ancient Classics training, especially from the Ancient Greeks.'

Above we saw Pirsig's *ZMM* report:

> *'He had asked Sarah, who long before had come by with her watering pot and put the idea of Quality in his head, where in English literature quality, as a subject, was taught. .. 'Good heavens, I don't know, I'm*

not an English scholar,' she had said. 'I'm a classics scholar. My field is Greek.'
'Is quality a part of Greek thought?' he had asked.
'Quality is <u>every</u> part of Greek thought,'

And this passage for Pirsig, must have great meaning, because he essentially repeats this in a crucial media interview, as you see below:

INTERVIEWER: 'It's interesting that she [Sarah] was a Greek Scholar, [and] that you've gone back and traced the roots of ....
PIRSIG: *'Yes, If you are going to up-end all human understanding, you've got to go back to the beginning.* [And] *our Western understanding does really start with the* [Ancient] *Greeks really. God knows why .... God doesn't know how they got started on that particular questioning which led to their love of reason and their ability to analyze things, ... it was lost ..... The Romans never really picked up on it. But I asked her the question: 'Did Greeks, the Ancient Greeks, was that* [Quality, Arête] *a part of their thought?' And she said 'It was every part of their thought.'* [Here RP is talking in a whisper for emphasis, then burst out loudly and happily next sentence:]. *And SHE had a sense of Quality. A brilliant teacher.* [Her students] *called her 'The Divine Sarah.', that was her first name. And the students who'd had her said, 'When your got done with the class with her, your head just went round and round and round.' She's that kind of person,* [who] *would bring it out of herself and*

present it to her classes. I think I was her last student. She retired just after that, and I missed her greatly.

In this passage we should particularly notice
- a) Whispered for emphasis, Re Quality: *'It was every part of their thought.'*
- b) *Then burst out loudly and happily:*
- c) *'And SHE had a sense of Quality. A brilliant teacher.'*
- d) *'They* [her students] *called her 'The Divine Sarah.'*,
- e) [And repeating his letter to me, finishes with:] *"I missed her greatly'.*

So this is clearly Sarah's great influence on Pirsig, and this Greek Classicist understanding must have come from her whole upbringing, plus her Grinnell College, plus University of Wisconsin Graduate School, where she most particularly focused on the Ancient Roman Classics in her Masters and PhD Theses. Now, it is unlikely that her specific use of the specific word Quality would have appeared in any of her academic training. It most certainly wasn't in mine. But it just occurs to me (AHA) that the Ancient Greek word 'Arête' almost certainly Sarah would have learned academically in many of her courses, and (I just realized, AHA again) Sarah may well have read (even owned), the *same* little book I owned and read in my Engineering School Western Civilization class => H. D. F. Kitto's *The Greeks*. A book so widely used in colleges and universities, that it achieved *'standard text'* status. These are big reasons that this book was *the very exact one* that Pirsig mentions in *ZMM*, as follows => :

> *His search for it* [virtue, and how Sarah's Greek origin sense of Quality, might be thus be related to Ancient Greek Rhetoric] *takes him through a number of histories of ancient Greece, which as usual he reads detective style, looking only for facts that may help him and discarding all those that don't fit. And he is reading H. D. F. Kitto's "The Greeks", a blue and white paperback which he has bought for fifty cents, and he has reached a passage that describes 'the very soul of the Homeric hero,' the legendary figure of predecadent, pre-Socratic Greece. The flash of illumination that follows these pages is so intense* [that the images of] *the heroes are never erased and I can see them with little effort of recall. ... Kitto had more to say about this areté of the ancient Greeks. 'When we meet areté in Plato,' he said, 'we translate it 'virtue' and consequently miss all the flavour of it. 'Virtue,' at least in modern English, is almost entirely a moral word; areté, on the other hand* [in Ancient Greek]*, is used indifferently in all the categories, and simply means excellence.'*

Thus, we may conclude that Sarah's use of Quality comes from her whole self, and was correspondingly her *own* distillation of her whole Classical Academic training, and from all this, translating the Ancient

Greek word '*Arête* into the nearest English equivalent *Quality*. So it must be taken that this also is where she learned this *most essential Arête* (Greek: ἀρετή), *utter, most striving, excellence,* in its basic sense, means "*excellence of any kind*", and as quoted above, "*describes 'the very soul of the Homeric hero'.*". And from this, why she pushed and prodded Pirsig, '*Are you teaching Quality?*'

Concerning Sarah's above statement: We have also seen how several times, Pirsig said she was *joking*, and his response back to her was similarly *joking, tit for tat.* But clearly, the way Pirsig writes the story, he wants us to understand that Sarah kept prodding him in her own wise mysterious, unique way until he was in a corner and forced to do something about it. After Sarah's third prod, he finally sat back and asked himself '*What the hell is Quality?*' The first thing he did, was to realize he didn't know what the heck it was. He stayed at his MSC desk, thinking about it until about nine in the evening, it was dark outside and his wife called him and asked what had happened. He said '*I'll be right home.*' Yet, he didn't leave for home until 3am, totally defeated, because he didn't know what Quality was. The next morning, he asked his students to write about Quality and this started his pilgrimage, and it really was a pilgrimage.

JE – I still don't really buy the idea that the reason he didn't ask Sarah for a definition of what she meant by Quality was because he knew it couldn't be defined. I don't really believe that. I think one of two things happened. I think, for all we know, he *may* have actually asked Sarah what she meant by Quality, and she may have come back and said something like 'Well, it can't be defined, Mr. Pirsig, you just know when it's there,' which would in fact be a pretty good answer, but Robert Pirsig may not have bothered to think that this answer was worth mentioning in his book, because what Sarah said may have seemed obvious to him, and in *ZMM* he clearly wanted to go beyond the obvious.

Alternatively, Pirsig may simply have felt that what Sarah had said was so momentous and awe-inspiring, and was having so much of massive impact on his life, that he didn't want to spoil that by going back and prosaically asking what would very likely have seemed to him a pretty banal question, namely, 'What do you mean by that?'

It would almost be like having one's first amazing kiss with a person one loves and then wanting to analyze it afterwards. One would feel, perhaps, that that was a pointless, and even impertinent thing to do, especially if one involved in the discussion the person one had kissed. Indeed, doing so might well make it unlikely that the person would readily want to be kissed again!

The most important point, perhaps, is that in *ZMM,* Robert Pirsig doesn't give the impression of being especially bothered about finding some definition of Quality. Instead, he becomes obsessed -- obsessed is not too strong a word to use -- with what the word Quality actually, at heart, means.

HG -- Whether or not, or why, Pirsig did ask Sarah directly about what Quality meant, my own theory is this => Originally Sarah's prodding wasn't momentous to him. After all, we have record of his saying upon three different occasion, ~ both Sarah and he were *tit-for-tat 'joking'*, and we can deduce from this, it was non momentous, and that he understood what she meant well enough. But at the time, the question finally trapped him into action. And as he 'tenaciously' dug deeper. He did finally see how momentous was (is) this word, and its implications were to him, and the true importance and meaning of Quality.

Although Pirsig's work at Montana State College was in the years 1959-61, even forty-five years later, Sarah's remembered responses (and in the above mentioned interviews and letter writings) were, still tremendously meaningful:

> *'Did the Greeks, the ancient Greeks, was that the Quality part of their thought?'* and her answer was, *'Yes, it was every part of their thought.'*

And as Pirsig gave this answer he was whispering ... for huge emphasis ... *'it was every part of their thought,'*

JE –I've got one final question and it's this. If you could meet Sarah and ask her one question, what would that question be?

HG – Let me try to think off the cuff, because sometimes that's better. ... Dynamic Quality you know. .... I would ask her what it was like in Greece, what it was she saw there when she travelled there twice. I would ask her to tell us the significance of the eight photographs, black and white glossies, she brought back, apparently from her European Trip, perhaps on her way to Istanbul. Why did she choose eight photographs (later given to me by Shirley Luhrsen), showing various Greek Orthodox churches from the Middle Ages? Why did she bring back just those eight photographs, and why no pictures of the Parthenon or other Classical Greek buildings from her trips over there?

JE –Wouldn't you use the opportunity to meet Sarah to ask her to elucidate about what she meant by Quality?

HG – If I had that question in mind, I would start watching her, watching everything she did. …. As she went about her daily life, I would study, how she would react, and do things, and watch her responses to other people. I would study her zest for life, willingness to understand and help, striving, even striving for excellence. I would try to confirm my current conclusions: That Sarah DID Quality, and Sarah mostly DID NOT talk about Quality. Then later, I would prod her to try to get her to talk about Quality, and try to get her to put it into words, and see if she refused, as I suspect she would. And I would ask whether she also knew, like Pirsig, that

Quality could not be defined just as God cannot be defined. Also, I would ask her if Professor M. S. Slaughter's infectious ways were the reason she chose Graduate School under him, and was he the reason she went to University of Wisconsin. Finally, I would ask her (how & why, as I conjecture) if her use of word Quality is her own (or someone else's) translation to English of the Ancient Greek word: *Arête.*

Conclusion:

Summing It All Up:

Sarah's Legacy

By Henry Gurr

'The Philosophy Of Lao Tsu [<u>& *Sarah Vinke*</u>] Is Simple:'

We serve whatever or whoever stands before us,

… without any thought for ourselves.

Te — which may be translated as 'virtue' or 'strength' —

… lies always In Tao, or 'natural law'.

In other words: Simply be.

In our biography, we have tried our level best to find all that is known of Sarah Jennings Vinke.
Having worked very hard at this and "scraped the bottom of the barrel", our sense is that there is little more to be found, or known. As much as practical, our findings have been written-into our *Sarah Vinke Biography*, OR in our *Sarah Vinke Biography Resource Page*, which Google will quickly find.

We have sought the threads of Sarah's life in the records about the Iowa farm and small town where she grew up. We have chronicled what her parents and grandparents were like, and various other formative experiences while growing up: Things like her physical environment, schooling, and other community influences, especially her education, elementary through PhD, in Greek & Roman Classics, and what all these were like. We have documented how her ancestors came to her Iowa farmstead, and how it changed hands to the persons who are now on her old farm. Most particularly, we have sought what were the circumstances that enabled Sarah to be able to raise her sights to a Doctor of Philosophy Degree, and just how her two Graduate Degrees happen to focus on two Ancient Roman Poets.

We have searched for and interviewed many living persons who remember Sarah. Unfortunately, ZMM Author Robert Pirsig's health had declined, and he had insufficient memory to answer our questions for this biography.

We have visited Sarah's home town and childhood farm, there consulting with knowledgeable persons about that area's history. We have accessed public records such as school and library archives, county courthouse documents, land records, government records, US Census Records, her hometown and state history books. Even consulted were historical maps, along with death and probate records, and grave information. Aiding us in our research were typical genealogical research resources such as State and Local Genealogical Societies, Local Library Archive, College, and University Library Archives, and "The Internet". With these we found A) Newspaper articles re Sarah, B) Her husband Louis Vinke, and C) Her Major Professor MS Slaughter. D) College and university yearbooks with photos of Sarah and her MSC colleagues. E) Ocean Passenger Ship Manifests with Sarah Vinke listed there, as well as F) Immigration port records of embarkation and port of entry data.

We have seen how Sarah's Grinnell College training was, of necessity, focused on Latin Language (and Ancient Rome), since Sarah's early career was to be four years teaching full time High School Latin. She continued, and built on her High School Latin experience by spending three years, with complete Latin focus in completing her two theses on two Ancient Roman Poets. And as we have emphasized: "It is clear that Sarah, in her thesis, was deeply interested in trying to communicate her fierce love of the effect of Catullus' Poetry! ... She was resounding for the love of the sound of Catullus', all in Latin!"

Despite Sarah Vinke's Academic Training and Early Career, Focused On Latin, Evidence Shows That There Must Have Been A Major Mid-Life Change Of Heart:

We have the following multiplied compounding evidence that Sarah must have changed, so her concerns are NO longer Latin and Ancient Romans! Her focus turned to the Ancient Greeks and Greece!

a) Her teaching after receiving her PhD, did NOT continue with Latin, but instead taught English at Montana State College (1923 to 1926), continued at Ft. Collins (1935 to 1945), and then at Montana State College (1945 to 1962), as English Department Chair, then Professor of English.

b) The change from teaching full time Latin to English, would certainly, involve, vastly different exposures, and life questions.

c) Perhaps for Quality, a lucky break! Because by ~1959-61, Sarah was a colleague of Robert Pirsig, and could say to him: . *'I'm a classics scholar. My field is Greek.'* And... *'Quality is every part of Greek thought.'*

d) Dennis Gary Also Tells Us:

"Dr. Vinke read to us short passages of Homer's *Iliad* aloud in Greek." "Sarah assigned to us the Richmond Lattimore translation of the *Iliad* which was new at the time and which she told us she felt came closest to capturing the flow of classical Greek." ... "She obviously had a remarkable knowledge of classical Greek and a great love of the subject. ... "Dr. Vinke, in fact, never made it to [discussing] the Romans. in our [Greek & Romans] Classics course, simply saying on the last day that the Romans were all a bunch of copycats and that all we had to do is substitute the Roman/Latin names for the Greek names and we would have it all."

e) Numerous newspaper articles about Sarah's foreign travels do NOT mention Italy or Rome, but, Sarah's examining war damage in post WWII, Greece.

f) And later travel NOT to Italy or Rome, but tourist traveling to Greece and Asia Minor, plus a half year teaching in Greece at Anatolia College.

g) There are NO corresponding newspaper mentions of Sarah going to Italy or Rome.

h) Sarah spoke to Dennis Gary and Robert Pirsig, about Quality, derived from the Ancient Greek Arête. She did NOT use some equivalent translation from Latin

This Leaves Us With The Question: What Caused Sarah Vinke's Evident Change, <u>AWAY</u> From Her Obvious Love of Latin And Ancient Roman Poets, <u>TO</u> Ancient Greek: Perhaps Her Change To The Teaching Of College English, Started The Process?

And with compounding maturing experiences (above and below, or because of travel to Greece), Sarah must have built upon her Classics training, and thus elevated her overall understanding of Arête in Ancient Greek life, key to her path to Quality. Thus we must ask: When and how did this discontinuity happen?

But for an answer, we as biographers really only have indirect circumstantial evidence. We may only observe (with our readers) that after receiving her PhD in 1923, Sarah became a teacher of English, NOT Latin. Was this her own chosen change of focus? Or was teaching English (and not Latin), the ONLY real higher educational position open to her? Was this a consequence of severely limited opportunity for a woman in the days when pretty much only men were favored?

And Then There Were The 22 Years Of Sarah's Maturing Experiences, Which In Addition To e) Thru f) Above, Include:

i) Sarah's already well demonstrated hatred of war.
j) Living through the horrors of WWII (added to that of WWI).
k) A very short marriage to Louis Vinke, and his death, as well as
l) Teaching English at MSC, then Fort Collins, then
m) English Department Chair back at MSC, plus
n) Disgrace and demoted by MSC Administration.
o) And returned to teaching English.

From this we may surmise, that the eye opener may have been, Sarah's actual physical (opposed to thesis intellectual) experience of repeated traveling (some a year in duration) to see the destruction in post WWII Greece and likely other parts of Europe. One trip was sponsored by the Economic Cooperative Administration for the very purpose of Sarah, with other experts, studying the destruction and relief distribution in Greece following WWII.

Added to this, as newspapers reported, is Sarah's actual direct experience in war deprived Greece, included teaching for half a year at Anatolia College, plus the fact that Sarah's friend Mary Ingle was Dean of Girls there.

Here we must remember Sarah had also had additional broadening experiences of post graduate study at Cornell University, the University of Chicago, and London University.

As evidence of her maturing: Sarah gave a speech to her National AAUW concerning the book *In the Cause of Peace* as well as repeated public speeches in support of the then new United Nations. This was a quite UN-popular stance to have in Montana at the time. And then there is the Bryn Mawr University connection: where Edith Hamilton and Richard Lattimore taught. (More research is needed, on these points.)

-o0oO0oo-

As we have illustrated multiple times, Robert Pirsig never forgot Sarah, vividly remembering =>

> *'That was the moment it all started. That was the seed crystal... The one sentence 'I hope you are teaching Quality to your students.'*

And readers who have loved and been deeply moved emotionally and intellectually by the eternally relevant ZMM are not likely to forget Sarah saying that, either.

The truth is that many millions of people have indeed had their thoughts radically stimulated and their lives changed, by *Zen and the Art of Motorcycle Maintenance*. Moreover, ZMM will, in the future, be stimulating, and changing, the lives of many millions of people still unborn. For how many years will its influence continue? Perhaps for as long as the life of the English language, and very likely well beyond that: ZMM has after all been translated extremely widely.

From All Above-Mentioned Investigations, We Have Seen That 1968 Was An Active Year For Robert Pirsig And Sarah Vinke:

June 1968 saw the first exchange of letters between Pirsig and Ken Landis, Editor at W R Morrow, Publishers. And a month later, Pirsig, Chris, and John and Sylvia Southerland, embarked upon their epic ZMM Route Trip, a journey written into the Travel Narrative of the 1975 *Zen and the Art of Motorcycle Maintenance.*

This year 1968 was also the year Sarah (with sister Catherine) traveled to their old home town of Dallas Center IA, to sell their interest in the old family farm. Subsequently (on same trip?), Sarah moved into a retirement community in Bradenton FL, to be near her sister. The same year arranged for the Manatee National Bank to handle her financial affairs to the end of her life.

During 1968, Sarah wrote her Last Will and Testament, in which she donated her body to science, and bequeathed her remaining finances at death, to the American Friends Service Committee (AFSC), a worldwide relief activity of The Religious Society of Friends (a Quaker and Anti-War Organization). The AFSC received $151,000 when she died in 1978. In 1968, Sarah was active donating money to charities such as the Mississippi Freedom Democratic Party, and wrote a long quite personally revealing letter back to Bozeman to her friend and fellow AAUW member, Stella Anacker.

Soon after Sarah's retirement (Spring of 1962), she was offered an honorary doctorate by Montana State University, but she declined this honour because she could not travel (from Florida) to attend the ceremony due to poor health. This is added solid evidence of the impact of Sarah, because an Honorary Doctorate, bestowed by a major university, means Sarah's stature was widely recognized, and appreciated! Like "Divine Sarah", not everyone gets one of these.

-o00O00o-

We truly hope that in reading this biography our readers see that Sarah Vinke is a VERY intelligent and VERY interesting woman! And that she had an extensive positive influence on many people. We hope readers have enjoyed the quest for the ultimate goal, of finding enough re Sarah Vinke, to say how she came to be aware of the Ancient Greek Arête. And from this, tease out why she introduced the corresponding concept of "Quality", to Robert Pirsig, author of book "*Zen and the Art of Motorcycle Maintenance*". In particular, we want readers to see *just why* Sarah asked Robert Pirsig, "*Are you teaching Quality?*" This was an especially intriguing question, because there was originally no clear pattern from Sarah's life as to why she would do this!

-o00O00o-

(NOTE: Our considerable Sarah Jennings Vinke research findings, which greatly exceed a biography book space, are available on a special supplementary Internet web page => *Sarah Vinke Biography Resource Page*" which Google will quickly find.)

-o00O00o-

From all this, we hope our readers will understand the extreme importance of the ZMM book itself, one of the most remarkable and most thought-provoking books ever written, and surely an immortal one. In the process of communicating our belief in the extreme importance of the *ZMM* itself, we hope we have established *the absolutely vital role Sarah Vinke played in it, and the key inspiration she gave its author Robert Pirsig to focus on Quality*. This was so our readers would fully understand how Sara Vinke and Montana State College were crucial to how and why ZMM came to be written.

We hope our readers have been stimulated by the vicarious feeling of, somehow, actually having met our heroine Sarah, and understand why her students would call her "The Divine Sarah!" We hope our readers have seen that it was Sarah's Classics training and most particularly her deep understanding of the Ancient Greek life practice of Arête (her Quality), that enabled and embolden her to be the outstanding person she became. There is no doubt, that it was the striking leadership abilities of her Major Professor M. S. Slaughter that pressed Sarah similarly into dynamic active leadership! And, further, if Sarah had not been at MSC when Pirsig was …. *Zen and the Art of Motorcycle Maintenance* never would have happened!

-o00O00o-

Thus: In writing our *Sarah Vinke Biography*, our investigative journey, we have answered many questions as to "The Mystery … The Mystique … The Enigma … of Sarah Vinke".

And without the wonderful anecdotes and information provided by those inspired from Sarah's enthusiasm, we would not be able to accomplish this biography of the inspiration behind Pirsig's legendary philosophic text, *Zen and the Art of Motorcycle Maintenance*. Her personality, intellect, and sense of purpose have thus inspired countless others to seek to live a life of Quality.

HOWEVER, In The Process We Have Documented A Major Discontinuity In Her Life, For Which We Confess There Seems To Be No Firm Answers!

And thus, there is a NEW Mystery, and a critical one, since this evidently turned Sarah's own path to the full realization, for all of us and especially Robert Pirsig, of the vital importance of the Ancient Greeks (not Ancient Romans). From this turn, Sarah must have become more fully aware, vitally aware, of the Ancient Greek living excellence, their highest aspirations, their Arête (Sarah's Quality!).

Hence Sarah's own journey ... in a change of heart .... There was a major turn .... as Robert Pirsig said, *"Following the track of Quality."* Thus, as a result of this major discontinuity in Sarah's life journey... Sarah in her own enigmatic way ... persisted and gave the third "Seed Crystal" to Robert Pirsig, in the midst of his despair and confusion: *"I'm so happy you're teaching Quality this quarter. Hardly anybody is these days.".*

-THE END-

And Thank You For Reading!
We invite you to share your thoughts & reactions

A few words would help others decide if the book is right for them.

Also what you say will help get the word out about Sarah Vinke, and her contribution to Quality: Her Influence in our lives: Her contribution to our awareness of The Ancient Greeks, and their Arête! (Sarah's Quality!)

If you are reading a Paperback, please type into Google … *Amazon + A Woman of Quality: Sarah Vinke Divine* ….

THEN in the results pick out & click what looks like https://www.amazon.com/dp/B07KDG7F59/

THEN scroll to near bottom of page and click on … Write a customer review … You may have to log on.

Please repeat similarly for *GoodReads* Or *FaceBook*.

-THANKS-!

www.ingramcontent.com/pod-product-compliance
Lightning Source LLC
Chambersburg PA
CBHW051747040426
42446CB00007B/254